POEM'S COUNTRY

OETIC PRACTICE

For Peggy,
We have a place in poetry!

THE POEM'S COUNTRY

PLACE & POETIC PRACTICE

With gratitude,

Shara Lessley

Edited by Shara Lessley and Bruce Snider

Bread Loaf
2019

ISBN: 978-0-9641454-8-1

Published by Pleiades Press

Department of English
University of Central Missouri
Warrensburg, Missouri 64093

Distributed by Small Press Distribution.

Interior design by Martin Rock and Paula Mirando.
Cover design by Noelani Piters.
Cover image "Geological Chart" by Levi W. Yaggy courtesy of
Barry Lawrence Ruderman Antique Maps, 7463 Girard Avenue,
La Jolla, CA 92037.

2 4 6 8 9 7 5 3 1
First Printing, 2017

Invaluable financial support for this project has been provided by
the Missouri Arts Council, a state agency. Our immense gratitude
to this organization.

CONTENTS

ACKNOWLEDGEMENTS

ACKNOWLEDGEMENTS

Several selections of this book first appeared in the following magazines and journals, to whose editors we offer continued thanks:

America: The Jesuit Review: "Homing In: The Place of Poetry in the Global Digital Age" by Philip Metres

Blackbird: "Tapping the Glass: On Poems, Aquariums, & Form" by Nicky Beer

Ecotone: "The Lyric City" by Wayne Miller

The Literary Review: "Place in Mind" by Peter Streckfus

New England Review (later reprinted at *LitHub*): "Trouble & Consolation: Writing the Gay Rural" by Bruce Snider

Ottawa Poetry Newsletter: "On Writing from the New Oceania" by Craig Santos Perez

The Poetry Foundation: "On Blackacre" by Monica Youn

Poetry Northwest: "A Poetics of Tectonic Scale: The Great Distance Poem" by Katy Didden

Poetry Society of America: "What's American about American Poetry?" by Kazim Ali

Poets & Writers: "Famous Mushroom" by Mark Wunderlich

The Southern Review: "One Cluster, Bright, Astringent" by Shara Lessley

The editors of this book are grateful to University of San Francisco and University of Central Missouri for their support of this project. For her encouragement and guidance, we extend our thanks to Eavan Boland. *The Poem's Country* owes much to Pleiades Press Editor, Kathryn Nuernberger, whose enthusiasm, keen attention, and thoughtfulness helped shape the anthology. We are indebted to interns Alan Chazaro, Paul Eaton, Tyler Hall, Priscilla Hoang, and Noe Piters, who provided additional research and editorial support. Special thanks to Noe Piters for her work on the cover design, to Lysley Tenorio for finding our cover image, and to Paula Mirando for her help with layout design. Finally, for their intelligence, generosity, and commitment, we offer sincere thanks to our contributors whose work continues to inspire us and deepen the conversation about contemporary American poetry.

FOREWORD

FOREWORD

THE POETS of the 19th century and the beginning of the 20th were comfortable with the concept of place. It was a starting point for memory, for location, for the nostalgia that could lead to elegy: all comfort zones for the canon. *Here /Should be my home, this valley be my world*, wrote Wordsworth in 1800 in "Home at Grasmere." For a long time the theme of turning a place into a world persisted. Then something happened.

This eloquent and energizing book of essays, arguments, viewpoints and perspectives addresses that something. The editors, Shara Lessley and Bruce Snider, have assembled a true adventure for the reader in terms of theme and have made wonderful choices in selecting the contributors. The subject is place and its intersection with poetry, but there is the widest possible range here: from meditation to assertion.

Elizabeth Bradfield asks "What is the ocean as a place?" and concludes that "it is horizon and connection and mystery." Katy Didden says, writing of Mount Rainier, "When it's invisible, you start to think it could be anywhere, and when it's out, it floats on air—you can feel it shift the cells of your body from single to double space." Sandra Lim echoes this braiding of place and poem: "Sometimes I think of lyric tone and sensibility in terms of a certain landscape that has quietly lost its mind in the words of the poem." And Peter Streckfus' thoughtful piece concludes with the sentence "The poem becomes finally our own place in mind."

Place in mind is important throughout a book that gathers very different outlooks towards one potential coherence. There are essays here on food, on the Internet, on childhood, on recent poetry, on more distant poets. There are the painful, valuable encounters with place as political fact: "On a bad day the border was a burden," writes Rigoberto González in his essay, and "On a good day it was a gateway." And then there is the encounter with the past. In his piece "Ghost Towns," Nick Lantz asks: "Why might particular places encourage poets to notice ghosts or seek them out?"

At first sight questions fly off these pieces, cascading in sparks all over the reader. Is the idea of place in poetry merely internal? If we extend it to the ocean, what happens to our definition of earth? Does one configuration of place—a border, for instance—overwhelm the poet's sense of any other? And if ghosts appear in a location, is that what place is—just another historical editor? And how do all these things affect the practice of writing an actual poem?

These are among the more visible questions here. But these searching essays elicit more challenging ones. Looked at more closely, there is a larger question, and a single darker argument. This is what makes the book intriguing, and at times both moving and compelling. The larger question is the easy part. It hovers over so many of the pieces here. Is it possible, some of these essays seem to ask, that place is just a fiction? Wayne Miller seems to acknowledge something of this as he writes about the glamour of the city after suburbia: "This was my early romanticized notion of the city—a space where I was unconstrained." Then again, fictions of place have traditionally offered consolations that are not to be discarded lightly. "I loved Lone Tree because it was just far enough away for me to forget how far away it was," writes Shane McCrae about his drive to a favorite destination. Spencer Reece, in a moving description of his visit to the Anglican Church in England, writes of another such discovery: "I had a place. I had a place."

Shara Lessley, in her eloquent, arresting meditation on Elizabeth Bishop, while not engaging this directly, emphasizes that extensions of the idea of place must still return to the disciplines and confinements of art. "The dancer's room is the studio; the poet's, the stanza" she writes, "Each has the task of perfecting the line." And Monica Youn in her essay "On Blackacre" refers to a pervasive "imaginary landscape," even if it's folded into a legal term.

But what is more intriguing here is not place as fiction. But something sharper, darker: a shadow that lurks in inferences, in the suggestions underlying many of these pieces. It goes like this—that place as it appeared on the poem's page was often shadowed by a history that poem might edit but not erase. What if place was a way for the poem to comply with power? What if—an even darker thought—the poet's relation to place was a code for compliance with empire, class, repression?

Inevitably as one century yielded to another, as modernism shelved into post-modernism, as the poetic self was suddenly up for revision, this version of place was dragged out and held up to the light. Scrutiny came in different forms. Often upheaval was itself a system of interrogation. The crypto-codes of a new sense of place demanded a new sense of self. In his provocative piece "The Cloud, the Desktop, & the Poetics of No-Place" Christopher Kempf—riffing on echoes of *Paradise Lost*—sketches a world in which the boundaries of place start to dissolve with the power systems that defined them. "The arrival of the Internet—for myself, for my generation, for our species—was a setting forth, I think from what Gaston Bachelard has called 'the consolation of the cave,'" he writes "a taking of our way, with wandering steps and slow, through an unknown, threatening, yet potentially liberating, possibly liberating global village." These themes suggested by Kempf are echoed in Philip Metres' query: "In our global digital age—with its information flood, its attenuation of attention, its transmogrification of subjectivity, its obscuring of our connectedness—what can poetry and the arts do?"

As I read these essays, resistance to the old power systems comes up again and again. And with it new, subversive questions, some of them necessarily harsh. "If the strength of American poetry is its hybrid qualities and leanings," writes Kazim Ali, "its weakness is also particularly American: its amnesia of history and language, but not a passive amnesia of forgetting, but a brutal and intentional act of erasure." And yet even within these doubts there can be also a sense of possibility, as Craig Santos Perez suggests, "I believe poetry can both enhance and disrupt our visual literacy." And even beyond that, perhaps, a moment where language and poetry can provide a remedy, as when Sabrina Orah Mark quotes Claudia Rankine at a poetry reading: "'I believe,' she said, 'in repair.'"

Inevitably, writers here reach not just for a new sense of place but a new sense of the poet. For instance Jehanne Dubrow's thoughtful piece on the military spouse-poet: "The soldier poet offers eyewitness accounts. But the poet who is married to a soldier, a sailor, an airman has a more complex task; her poems think across time zones, barriers of cultures and speech." On the other hand, Amaud Jamaul Johnson imagines that new poet almost brought to silence under the stress of an audience that might not hear him: "I don't know you. I don't know what assumptions you've made; what truly moves or motivates you. I'm not sure what makes you dance or weep, so I must admit I hesitate to say anything, especially about the complexities of place and history."

It seems important at this point to emphasize that despite its burdens of theme and query, so much in this book is also entertaining, inviting and readable. For instance Hayan Charara's enticing first sentence: "The past of my poems is usually called Detroit." Or Nicky Beer's opening gambit: "From childhood, I've been transfixed by poems and aquariums alike—I can't remember a time when I wasn't gazing deeply into one or the other." Or Keith Ekiss' engaging, erudite essay on food and poetry, with its way of winding back to the tradition, as when he argues that reading certain poem-songs "might help to point us in the direction of a useful attentiveness, to show how in another tradition food and the nature poem have always been naturally entwined."

But soon enough essential challenges re-appear. In our moment, place and poetic practice may have a dynamic relation, but as some writers insist here, also a troubled one. As Joan Naviyuk Kane puts it, "In poetics, and particularly newer iterations/packagings of ecopoetry, there persists a monopoly on depiction that presents the past and the human place in it as romantically as possible. This distracts us from more difficult truths."

Difficult truths. In so much of this book the concept of place slides inevitably into the idea of displacement, and may indeed never have left it. The contemporary poet surrounded by a dissolving wilderness, a limitation of memory, an uncertain future has to consider all over again how the poetic self can be shifted and re-stated inside displacement itself.

Emilia Phillips, in her essay on the body and poetic space, suggests a "poem about the body is a poem of place." That one sentence provides a fascinating perspective on the destination of so much poetic practice in a diminished world: The body. Its ordeals. Its survivals.

In his essay "Trouble & Consolation: Writing the Gay Rural," Bruce Snider follows the ideas of the body, place and displacement into memory and reflection. The invitation to entertainment seems at first to be there also: "I grew up in a small Indiana town famous for a 70-pound cantaloupe grown by a man named Verlie Tucker," he writes. But the small town, despite its domestic melon-marvel, signals exclusion. And so does, surprisingly, the gay poetry the young poet comes across in which neither he nor his world are named. In those poems "the rural, if it ever appears, is fleeting. It's the past, what's left behind, full of emptiness and regret, where love and beauty can never last, where a gay man can never belong."

Most importantly, inside Snider's narrative is the suggestion that place and poetic practice need to find each other in new ways: need to be open to a re-definition that will re-define more than the poem. If that happens, then even the intractable might change. "It is hard to live in a line break," observes James Allen Hall. But for change to happen that's where today's poets may have to live. As Snider writes in a powerful summary statement, "We're at a point where more gay writers have begun to complicate our myth of open farmland, heterosexual masculine knowhow, and pioneer spirit that stretches back to our country's origins."

This book will undoubtedly broaden and strengthen the discussion of contemporary poetry. Often enough, in the wider world, there is a suggestion that this old art has shifted to the margins of a society and even more, perhaps, to the edges of public consciousness. Maybe so. But these essays, with their bold arguments and combative perspectives, remind us of just how much that is free, exciting and unconstrained happens on those margins. So many truths can be told there, so many deceptions exposed, that would be censored or edited at the center. As a tribe of the margin, poets are telling some exciting truths in our time, within a powerful and valuable conversation. These writings join that conversation with grace and purpose.

In that sense, this is a book that will be re-read and cited for a long time. And for several reasons. This is primarily a book about place and poetic practice. But it is also a book about change. The sort of change that active and engaged poets can bring to ideas that seemed fixed and now are malleable. That only need powerful language and open minds to become the future of poetry.

Eavan Boland
Stanford/Dublin 2017

INTRODUCTION

The lyric offers the same radical illumination that chance affords us when we wander off the map. For poetry works where maps are useless: like a passport, the lyric allows us to enter the otherworld, but is neither road map nor field guide.

John Burnside

"WILL YOU COME TRAVEL WITH ME?" wrote Walt Whitman in "Song of the Open Road," the poet's invitation to explore late 19th-century America. Arguably our most iconic literary tour guide, Whitman traveled a road that, well over a century later, contemporary American poets still tread. In place of Whitman's famous walking stick and expansive optimism, however, today's writers carry GPS-capable mobile phones and a growing sense of a fragile and shrinking world. With increased Internet access and the exponential expansion of airline travel in the late 20th and 21st centuries, Americans have been confronted with an increasingly globalized perspective. Without leaving home, we need only go to Google Earth to "walk" the chestnut-lined streets of Paris. Cable television provides instant access to international events as they unfold. YouTube videos whisk us from the cloudy peaks of Annapurna to crystalline waters off the Florida Keys. With the click of a button, we can watch a jewel-bellied moth emerge from its chrysalis and complete its life cycle in less than a minute. The earth's vast beauty seems instantly within reach, yet our world appears equally—if not more—flawed and ecologically at risk than it has ever been. And for all of our virtual connection, our nation itself remains deeply divided by issues of race, class, religion, politics, and more. Negotiating such contradictions as they manifest on our home screens and in our home towns has become an essential subject for poets writing in the 21st century.

It's in this context that *The Poem's Country: Place & Poetic Practice*—an anthology that assembles work solicited from a diverse group of distinguished early to mid-career American poets—investigates how poetry is responding to the rapidly changing experience of place. How, for example, are American poets writing about politically charged landscapes such as Guantanamo Bay and the Mexico-U.S. border? How are they rendering rural Indiana or the sprawling lights of Los Angeles, or even the invented landscapes of their own minds? As our contributors show, contemporary poets have a lot to say on these subjects, and they say it in radically different ways. A lyric meditation on Guam's island geography as a model for poetic structure. A craft-driven analysis of poems set at sites like Ground Zero and the Ninth Ward where what is absent is somehow present. An impromptu visit to what was once The Virginia State Colony for Epileptics and Feebleminded, a facility whose fraught history ushers forth a "chorus of ghosts." Each entry in *The Poem's Country* explores questions about place as subject, metaphor, and formal strategy.

With only a few exceptions, the essays assembled here were composed specifically for this project. Within the limitations of our publishing schedule and financial constraints, we've aimed to create an inclusive and diverse collection that reflects multiple points of view. Ultimately, we solicited more poets than were able to contribute. We hope, however, that *The Poem's Country* expands the conversation about how verse merges or distinguishes the self and the world. While we know natural and manufactured places continue to exist on their own terms, we're also conscious of how cultural beliefs and attitudes shape perceptions of public and private spaces. Keeping these facts in mind, as editors we've worked to bring together a variety of voices. Does *The Poem's Country* accurately reflect the wealth of American poets' perspectives and aesthetics? Sadly, no. However, we believe that in its depictions of fields and factories, interstates and waterways, lands familiar and foreign, what the anthology offers is a snapshot of the beautiful and sometimes terrifying intersection where words and worlds collide.

As admirers of the featured authors, it's been an honor to travel from our home offices in Oxford, England, and San Francisco, respectively, to more places than we initially imagined. Throughout the three-year process of bringing *The Poem's Country* to print, as we corresponded with our contributors, coastal and continental boundaries dissolved. Via the page we visited places as varied as Cape Cod, Wyoming's Big Horn Mountains, Iraq, Afghanistan, Anchorage and King Island, Alaska. We entered aquariums in Spain and attended a horse necropsy in New Jersey. We toured the childhood home of the poet Elizabeth Bishop in Great Village, Nova Scotia. At times, the sentences ventured off the map as our essayists considered the human body as undocumented territory, faith as homestead, memory as a recovery site.

Yet it isn't just the destinations that have impressed us. Unlike Frost's guide, who "only has at heart your getting lost," the writers that populate *A Poem's Country* direct us with attention and insight. Their essays often recharge and renew places that once seemed familiar. In some cases, the more actively the essayists study their particular landscapes, the more those landscapes recede. In their alienation, in the very act of discovering through concentrated study the strangeness in the particular, we found echoes of the Romantics. As we pored over the drafts that filled our in-boxes, we often asked ourselves: does the poet define the place or the place the poet? After all, don't some of our most cherished writers become seemingly inseparable from the places they record? It's hard, for example, to imagine Gwendolyn Brooks without thinking of the kitchenette buildings and pool halls of Chicago, or James Wright without the dark barns of Ohio. Thanks to her Pulitzer Prize-winning collection, *Life on Mars*, we associate Tracy K. Smith with the celestial. We likewise link Vievee Francis with Detroit and Western North Carolina, Randall Mann with Florida and San Francisco. Recently, William Brewer's *I Know Your Kind* offered readers fresh insight on the opioid crisis in Appalachia, most especially West Virginia—a state that features heavily in verse by Steve Scafidi. Yet, it's also true that certain regions become somehow more essentially themselves through a poem's refining scope. "I see the blade, / Blood-stained, continue cutting weeds and shade," writes Jean Toomer in *Cane*, bringing Georgia's fields into a sharp and unsettling relief.

Some of our essays call attention to the duality that occurs when writing about place. As nature writer Barry Lopez has observed: one place resides outside the author, another simultaneously within. In the spirit of the verse Emily Dickinson compiled into fascicles in Amherst, poets like Wallace Stevens and John Ashbery mark a lyric tradition exploring the tension between interior and exterior. This strain of individualistic and sometimes hermetic work interests several of our contributors. Drawing on neuroscience, Peter Streckfus explains how poetry offers a kind of inhabitable space inaccessible outside the poem itself. Invoking the natural world as half dream, half reality, Sandra Lim considers how moments of time take root in the white space of the imagination before finally settling into their rightful place on the page. Lim's description of place as "a mercurial atmosphere of mind" seems to invoke Robert Duncan, who famously explained that the meadow to which one returns "is a scene made-up by the mind," an "everlasting omen of what is." Sabrina Orah Mark, on the other hand, reminds us of Flannery O'Conner's claim: "Art requires a delicate adjustment of the outer and inner worlds in such a way that, without changing their nature, they can be seen through each other."

Of course, these characterizations inevitably point toward another question: in what way is any engagement with place *limited* by a poet's subjectivity? As contributor Philip Metres explains in his essay on cosmopoetics and cognitive mapping, "I'm wary of broad claims about the representativity of my representations." And yet we find so many of the poets in these pages pushing back against the confinements of subjectivity, striving to render some "truth" of place while remaining skeptical about received notions of sight and knowing. "I want to advocate for the ocean as a muse," attests Elizabeth Bradfield. "But I also want to advocate for an oceanic muse that is not all about projection, but investigation." Drawing from her knowledge of America's indigenous diaspora and her own Inupiaq-Inuit heritage, Joan Naviyuk Kane adds, "I have a renewed skepticism of the American tendency to name, to know, and to master the land above all." And Katy Didden, who examines panoramic, cinematic, and documentary perspectives of Marianne Moore, Arthur Tulee, and Layli Long Soldier, takes things further. "[T]hat one way today's great distance poets assert vision is by calling us to take the long view not just across space, but also across *time*," argues Didden before positing "[M]aybe the new question…is one that calls us to re-trace the circle, asking: what am I not seeing? why can't I see?"

Indeed, what poets are seeing, or rather failing to see, in our current moment is of particular interest to our contributors. As he struggles to find poems that interrogate the Internet's profound impact on modern society, for example, Christopher Kempf questions the World Wide Web's deceptive sense of placelessness. Likewise, contributor Keith Ekiss observes that while field songs and harvest poems have a long history grown from the pastoral tradition, "we take both nature and the politics of food production for granted, or as outside the realm of lyric poetry." *The Poem's Country* charts not only these omissions, however, but also identifies exciting places where new voices are entering and widening contemporary poetics. Jehanne Dubrow, for instance, calls attention to an innovative kind of war poem written from the perspective of military spouses. Rather than a soldier's record of life in the conflict zone, this work reflects deployment's impact on those who are left stateside. Mark Wunderlich, on the other hand, describes a personal homecoming that, at least in part, represents the experience of an increasing number of gay writers who've begun to confront their complex relationships with their rural hometowns. What of ourselves do we recognize in the world? our contributors keep asking. And what does the world recognize in us? Taken as a whole, this world, as revealed by *The Poem's Country*, is simultaneously seen yet not seen, connected yet divided in places perhaps best considered through verse's paradox-friendly lens.

And yet what can poetry do in the face of today's profound cultural disruptions? "How useful are poems," asks Amaud Jamaul Johnson, who recounts his early years in Compton, California, "when there are bodies in the street?" For many of our contributors the answer is understandably complicated. Charting the journey from his childhood to college graduate to academic, Rigoberto González considers whether his professional achievements have "erased" his Mexican identity, and whether queerness itself is a physical territory—the body's borderland. As González recalls,

> my mother left Mexico to escape poverty and she lived in poverty in the United States. She died poor. She began to die on very fertile and wealthy soil. My task now is to mine the inherent contradictions of such possibility, to build (write) something that provides perspective, that accepts complexity. What I write is not indictment; it's response.

But can poems house under one roof the real and imagined, past and present, the living and the dead? As Craig Santos Perez suggests, "I imagine that poems are song maps of my own journey to find Guam across historical and diasporic distances." Several of our poets also echo Meena Alexander's elaboration of Shelley's "A Defense of Poetry." "Poetry's task is to reconcile us to the world—," observes Alexander, "not to accept it at face value or to assent to things that are wrong, but to reconcile one in a larger sense, to return us in love, the province of the imagination, to the scope of our mortal lives." As Johnson himself puts plainly, "[P]oetry has saved my life. I'm old enough and I've read enough to understand that this emptiness, this homelessness, this desire to reach back to something unknown shapes my identity."

In the end, several of our contributors argue for the poem as a place itself, echoing Polish poet Czesław Miłosz's claim that "Language is the only homeland." James Allen Hall extends this observation to include poetic form, a place as inhabitable as any set of coordinates on a map. "I want to live in a line break," Hall attests, arguing for in-between-ness, almost-ness, as well as the powers and permissions of transition. But what would such a home look like? If we can live even for a moment in a poem, how should we furnish its cramped rooms? Our writers seem to answer: in as many ways as there are poets.

Indeed, while compiling these essays, we often found ourselves thinking of "America, I Sing You Back," Allison Adelle Hedge Coke's homage to Whitman and Langston Hughes, of which she has said, "I wanted to represent the voice of a woman, and an indigenous person. We all see our country from different perspectives culturally." As Coke suggests, the more poems we encounter about a particular place, the richer and more nuanced that place seems to become. Paradoxically, rather than imposing private meaning onto specific locations, our authors' personal accounts of particular places seem to amplify their contemporaries' voices. For instance, reading Amaud Jamaul Johnson's memoir of Compton pre- and post-Rodney King made us think of Patricia Smith's poem, "Incendiary Art: Los Angeles, 1992." Likewise, the anthology's collective observations about the influence of technology on our experiences of place and language invited us to revisit Marcus Wicker's "Ode to Browsing the Web," Michael Morse's "Void & Compensation," Nate Marshall's "Oregon Trail," and Brian Spears' "Elegy: An Email."

This pattern continued throughout the editing process: essays arrived, prompting us to seek out poems by others, further widening and enriching our conversations about poetry and place. Inspired, we drew up the list of "Editors' Recommendations" included at the end of this text, the majority of which are available online. Ranging in form, our selections feature villanelles, sonnets, free verse, prose poems, persona poems, erasure, and so on, and also fall into several place-based categories such as region (north, south, east, west) and subject (ecopoetics, sexual identity, urban or rural locations, water bodies, history, love, technology, parenthood, illness, etc.). Coupled with our contributors' "Five Essential Poems of Place" by living writers, we hope that this catalog reflects well the contents of *The Poem's Country*, while also serving as a point of departure that will encourage readers to seek out additional places and perspectives beyond the anthology.

Despite the important role place has always played in American poetry, to our knowledge *The Poem's Country* is the first anthology of its kind to bring together a diverse group of American poets to discuss this essential subject in their own words. We're excited by the writers we've gathered here and honored to share their inspiring voices. "I dwell in Possibility—," wrote Emily Dickinson at the Homestead more than a century and a half ago, opening a door that our contributors step through again and again, exploring important dimensions of our moment's complex relationship to place. They invite us to interrogate the world around us, to inhabit it more completely. We are *here*, they seem to tell us. Where will we go next?

Shara Lessley & Bruce Snider
Oxford, England & San Francisco

SELECTED WRITINGS

FLUID STATES: OCEAN AS PLACE & POETIC

Elizabeth Bradfield

We'd rather have the iceberg than the ship,
although it meant the end of travel.
Although it stood stock-still like cloudy rock
and all the sea were moving marble.

Elizabeth Bishop, from "The Imaginary Iceberg"

I CARRY THIS POEM with me when I work on expedition ships as a naturalist. Every time I see ice, whether berg or glacier, I think of Bishop. "We'd rather have the iceberg than the ship," I whisper to myself. Sometimes, I say it aloud to a Zodiac of guests I'm driving around ice. We stare into the blue contours, listen to waves lap them away to dissolution. Bishop's words feel transgressive and true. Of course we would rather have the iceberg. It's so much better than diesel and cleats and bottom paint. It *is* the sea in a way a boat can't ever be. And yet, of course, we can't have both and still be us, still be alive to love the ice and water and the fluidity between them. One or the other.

We are traveling in dangerous waters. All waters are, really, dangerous. But the water. The water. The possibility and deep gladness of it.

I'm not talking about the water you see from shore. Not that edge-view, safe and turn-back-able. I'm talking about water as home. Ocean as home. Living upon (below decks, within) a medium that will drown you; loving it. Thinking about all that is hidden beneath its reflective surface—acres and miles and mountain ranges of salps and turtles and dinoflagellates and sharks and cephalopods and crabs. Catching glimpses of some of it. Missing most of the world you know is beneath you. Wondering. Drifting. Trying to keep a true course against the pull of tide, the push of wind.

———◦———

This morning, I went to the ocean before the August crowds arrived for their daily basking. I floated. I stared at the sky. The water was cool, a chill to it, but not uncomfortable. Terns flew overhead, their tails folded back into the tines of a strange fork, one for tuning or for turning meat on a grill. Above them, blue sky and a loose netting of clouds. The organs in my torso felt as if they were discovering their optimal shape and arrangement, and I felt buoyant, clear, as if the boundaries of my skin had eased. I was my body, but I was also something more fluid. Small swells rolled in. I floated just beyond the break, riding over the waves easily. Anything might swim below me: shark, striped bass, gray seal, sand lance.

I could talk about the specific planktonic tang in the air, the seasonal cycles of this shore, which I first came to when I was twenty-six. But I was drifting. Not scientific. This was Cape Cod, the ocean of Thoreau and of the cranky and yet celebratory Alan Dugan:

One thinks: I must
break out of this
horrible cycle, but
the ocean doesn't: it
continues through the thought.

—Alan Dugan, from "Note: The Sea Grinds Things Up"

What comfort Dugan's words were to me when I found them. The ocean continues through the thought. It doesn't stop. The imperative of the ocean is to carry on, no matter what. This is what I seek: continuing. Beyond moment, beyond self. This is the poetics of ocean: to be a bright and vulnerable concentrated heartbeat in the vast.

I remember being a child in Tacoma, standing at the top of the backyard stairs that took us down a steep, blackberry-covered bank to the rocky beach we lived beside. It was at least five hundred feet down in my mind. By the numbers, it was more like forty. In a big wind, herring gulls would hover in front of me and we'd eye each other. I remember trying to leave my body, to dissolve into Commencement Bay, into Puget Sound, into the ocean beyond that that I didn't yet know. I could feel my heart trying to leave my chest, to join all of that water. It was at once heartbreaking and joyful. It was the most pure sense of yearning I have ever experienced, and even now, thinking of it, I can feel a slight tingling in my pectoral muscles, as if they could open and disperse me. As if they'd love to do just that.

———— • ————

What is the ocean as a place? It connects disparate shores. It morphs. It is a mysterious source. It is a road, a barrier, a temptation, a trickster, a hazard. It is its own world, essential to our shore-biased selves and yet often overlooked and misinterpreted. I'm talking about those big basins, those seven seas, those horizons without the punctuation of land, disorienting but for the stars that still point their courses and the winds that blow across them in predictable paths, legible if you can read them.

Some poems, often the ones that move me most, feel in their unfolding like being carried by strange currents: "K was burn at the bend of the ear in the mouth of Remember. She was the fecund chill burn in her famish" (Harryette Mullen, from "Kirstenography"). And what strange eddies Emily Dickinson's poems swirl us through: "Done with the compass— / Done with the chart! // Rowing in Eden— / Ah, the sea! / Might I moor— Tonight— / In thee!" (from 249).

Ecology understands this transgressive mode better than poetry, perhaps. That is, a bluefin tuna understands this better than a poet. In the course of its life, it swims thousands upon thousands of miles, through the specific natural and legal dangers of each one. How can we know that kind of life? We plod along, gravity-bound. Cars and airplanes and boats open the world's pathways, but of course we know it's not the same as to glide through water, through a world mapped by the paths of currents and prey. And yet, isn't poetry like this? Slipping through all that seeks to fix us? Part of the worlds of syntax through which it travels, and yet operating by a different set of rules than daily speech, daily understanding?

Profound: "the vast depth of the ocean or the mind." We call things that move us in inexplicable ways "deep." Coming from a source beyond our perception. Aboard a ship, one takes soundings to figure out the contour and materials of the sea floor. We sound out words. The sounds of poems carry us into strange waters. A sound is an arm of the ocean forming a channel between and island and a mainland. To sound, if you're a whale, is to dive deep.

———————•———————

When I was twenty-one, I took a job as a deckhand on a boat in Southeast Alaska. It felt like a natural progression to follow the shore north from where I was born, from the waters my family traveled in the summer. Tacoma to the San Juan Islands to Desolation Sound. Dixon Entrance to Glacier Bay. Then south along the Pacific Coast to the Columbia River (crossing the terrifying bar at Astoria) to Mexico's Gulf of California. Suddenly, my view of the world was shifted. The demarcations that mattered were shore and inlet, weather fronts and gyres.

There is an academic framework for all this. "Oceanic Studies," which Hester Blum introduced me to, is a relatively new field of focus that feels inevitable, essential, and right. In her introduction to the field, Blum writes:

> the sea should become central to critical conversations about global movements, relations, and histories. And central not just as a theme or organizing metaphor with which to widen a landlocked critical prospect: in its geophysical, historical, and imaginative properties, the sea instead provides a new epistemology...If our perspectives have been repositioned in recent decades to consider history from the bottom up, or the colonizer as seen by the colonized—to gesture to just two critical reorientations—then what would happen if we take the oceans' nonhuman scale and depth as a first critical position and principle?

Thinking oceanically is to think generously. Oceanic thinking connects disparate cultures. It connects, as I feel is important, the facts of the world with our feelings about those facts, our use of those facts. It chuckles over their uneasy meeting. The boundaries of bodies of water are messy and turbulent and they are the most productive places in the sea. It's where the life is.

Terrance Hayes has a poem, "The Carpenter Ant," in his

collection, *How to be Drawn*, that feels oceanic to me. I was reading it this morning, so it is fresh in my mind. The poem drifts through language-play: "It was when or because she became two kinds / of mad, both a feral nail biting into a plank / and a deranged screw cranking into a wood beam." The aunt, the ant, the built house inevitably breaking apart. She "taught herself to carpenter and unhinged." Hayes has denied separateness, which is what poetry often does through metaphor and wild juxtaposition.

There are other poets who do this, who allow currents of understanding within their work to eddy and touch one another. It's possible that one could make the argument for most poems. But I hear the surge most clearly in work like the unspooling syntax of Ellen Bryant Voigt's *Headwaters* ("my mother my mother my mother she / could do anything so she did everything the world / was an unplowed field a dress to be hemmed a scraped knee") and W.S. Merwin's *The Folding Cliffs*, an epic poem about a 19th century Hawaiian family struggling with the introduction of leprosy to Kauai from European sailors:

> they talked faster and louder as the canoe came closer
> and they could see the black heads and blue skins of the strangers
> who were paddling backwards they were coming backwards
> they must be coming from afterwards or from somewhere
> that was already gone and people started to laugh

I hear it in Robert Hayden's "Middle Passage" and in Walt Whitman, who is everywhere and "out of the cradle, endlessly rocking."

Derek Walcott's *Omeros*, though, gets at this idea of oceanic orientation and understanding better than any poem I know. He charts an oceanic poetics and ocean itself is central to his epic. His Caribbean island *is* ocean, is connected by ocean to Africa, to England, to America, to history. All those places a comprehendible, if not easy, sail from St. Lucia. Through the ocean, through the drift of story and the recurring eddies of image, he brings his story into conversation with Homer's:

It was an epic where every line was erased

yet freshly written in sheets of exploding surf
in that blind violence with which one crest replaced
another with a trench and that heart-heaving sough

begun in Guinea to fountain exhaustion here,
however one read it, not as our defeat or
our victory; it drenched every survivor

with blessing. It never altered its metre
to suit the age, a wide page without metaphors.
Our last resort as much as yours, Omeros.

—Derek Walcott, from *Omeros*

A mountain or a city fixes us here. Ocean asserts we are also here, and here, and we could be there, too. We are less fixed and certain than one place and time. Emotion and memory flow as water, in non-linear paths, sometimes funneled into a quick current, sometimes so broad and unfocused they seem to be motionless.

———•———

I am a teenager, staying at a friend's cabin on Hood Canal, a narrow thread of an inlet at the western edge of Puget Sound. We are sleeping on her parents' speedboat, away from the closed woods of the shore, bobbing. It is warm and still. For some reason, we look over the side and see light in the dark water. Not reflected stars: phosphorus, as we called it. Bioluminescence.

Although I don't remember discussion, I know we got in the water. The air was soft and black, and our bodies were soft, black shapes within a confusion of light. No one knew we were in the water, and I know that I felt such a huge joy that it was also a little terrifying. And somehow that was tied up in the fact that it was my absence—or, not that precisely, but the non-glow of my body, its displacement of light and yet its triggering of light by my movements—and not my presence that was the source of beauty.

This is not the only time I've been in glowing water. There was Baja, sea lions zipping trails of light beneath me. British Columbia, each stroke of the oars dripping gleam. Cape Cod one cold winter, the shore-sand itself glowing under the pressure of my foot because of the ocean it still held. This is not unique or miraculous. This is miraculous and these are—there is no other way to say it—sacred moments. Moments of resonance that, themselves, become waypoints and markers on a life's map. Most of my sacred moments have involved the sea.

———◆———

But the ocean is not just muse or metaphor. It is not just a pathway humans have traveled with their fraught histories. It is an inhabited place, albeit not inhabited by humans. Not just a blank upon which the poet can write imaginings without any risk of betraying an actuality. We have so much work to do in order to understand even the hem of the ocean. How do we write the life of oceanic creatures in a way that honors the accuracy and the mystery of their lives? Poetry can do that. It can make vivid the impossible—there is something in the suspended state that a poem conjures that allows us to consider the strange, to allow the rich strangeness of non-land-based lives to come into focus and not lose their mystery:

> you would dare to be changed,
> as you are changing now,
> into the shape you dread
> beyond the merely human.
> A dry fire eats you.

Fat drips from your bones.
The flutes of your gills discolor

—Stanley Kunitz, from "King of the River"

What salt-rich analgesic allows
this self-division, as the disc parts
and tendril arms, each with a thousand
calcite eyes, sway into slender helixes?

—Linda Bierds, from "Questions of Replication: The
Brittle Star"

When poets and poems get specific about the ocean, when the writer has truly grappled with the science and found where it sings in verse…oh then. Then we are truly in both the drift and the detail. The Gulf Stream and the copepod nauplis and the memory of what it is to be more than singular.

I want to advocate for the ocean as a muse. But I also want to advocate for an oceanic muse that is not all about projection, but investigation. Feel free to imagine your kraken, your leviathan. They exist, after all. But it is also time for us to wake up and peer beyond the surface, to break through our own reflections and learn what goes on unseen. Those tales of bays so thick with fish that they could be traversed as bridge? Not so farfetched as they sound now, to our depletion-calibrated gaze. We are beginning to understand how deeply we will regret our assumption that the ocean is boundless, that it is big enough to carry on with its cycles despite us. It can't.

———— • ————

And what of the work of the sea? The lives of those who consider the sea a workplace? I suppose that's me, when I work as a naturalist—traveling by ship to explore coastlines, giving information to underpin our awe at bubble feeding humpback whales or a wandering albatross. But I'm talking about a longer tradition of work: fisheries.

The harvest of what can't be seen, of what can't be easily tracked or traced and crosses borders and boundaries throughout its life? That industry, too, needs poetry in much the same way that iconic poems about Detroit's factories and a doctor's surgery have found their place in letters:

> I cannot tell you
> How beautiful the scene is, and a little terrible, then,
> when the crowded fish
> Know they are caught, and wildly beat from one wall to
> the other of their closing destiny the phosphorescent
> Water to a pool of flame, each beautiful slender body
> sheeted with flame, like a live rocket

—Robinson Jeffers, from "The Purse Seine"

Beautiful, and a little terrible. Terrible now, because of what we know of poor fisheries management, of ocean acidification, of the consequences of certain aquacultures, of microplastics from not just our shore-lives of straws and shampoo bottles but also from the ropes and nets we put in the water to catch wild sea creatures.

I don't know that there is any line of work as tangled with myth and consequence as contemporary fisheries. Sometimes, when I'm working on local whale watch boats out of Provincetown and an old, rusty scalloper chugs by, gulls clouding the stern wake, I ask the captain if he misses fishing. Most of the whale watch captains used to fish commercially, or their fathers did, their grandfathers. Some of them still do on the side. But none of them has ever told me he would go back to it.

The thing is, they know the water more deeply and with more precision than anyone I have met. It's not just that they can read a swell or smell a patch of plankton. It's that they remember so clearly the details we can't see, the stuff beneath the surface that must be known. We steam along, looking for whales, and a captain, if he's feeling conversational, might say at a certain point that this is where he'd turn his dragger to avoid a patch of rocky bottom. I look up, trying to fix the location, and I know that by tomorrow I'll have forgotten what he's remembered for decades. It's not about having a good memory. It's about having a living relationship—a conversation—with the water.

Sometimes, young crew come on the boats to work in the galley or as mates. I can smell the romance of the sea on them. In the wheelhouse, they talk about fishing, about going out to George's Bank for tuna. They are all eager bluster, hopeful that the captain will acknowledge them as one of the tribe. But what the captain knows—we've talked about it—is that it's not the same as when he was out there, fishing. The fish are smaller. The numbers down. The sea is less than when he left it.

Ashore, gift shops sell pictures of fishing boats and calendars with images of fishermen hauling nets. Fences are hung with buoys from lobster pots. Fishing is scene and "attraction" as much as industry. And our love of that romanticized vision clouds us. Blinds us to bycatch, bioaccumulation of pollutants, the damage of ghost gear. This isn't the place, I know, to go on about such troubles. And yet it is. If not in poems, how else will we tell the story of the sea we once feared would erase us and now hope, despite all signs to the contrary, might absorb and disperse and dilute our presence so much that we become inconsequential to it? So much that it does not register the impact of us at all?

———— ◆ ————

I am standing on the bow of a boat traveling north along the coast of Mexico. The swells are widely spaced. No one else is up yet, other than the captain and crew working the four to eight. Deep blue light of pre-dawn. Coffee. Binoculars heavy on my neck. To my right, the rugged shore of Baja California Sur. Ahead, to port, astern: ocean.

At this moment, I am at once fully in my body and utterly separated from it. I am the horizon. It is almost sexual, the expansiveness. My lover is a few thousand miles away. We have been apart for a month. I have thought of her, felt her, every morning in this moment. The fluidity of time and space echoing something like love, or sex.

And although it's not a direct link, although I don't "think" of much of anything, I want in this essay to make sure I sing praise to the sea creatures that embody this fluidity. Squid and their flashing skin, their ability to sense and respond to color and light with something other than eyes. The way, too, that they move by pulsing water through themselves (and, not related, that they are supported by a pen). Parrotfish and wrasse and slipper limpets that change sex depending on time of life and the society around them. For a while, male; for a while, female. The sexuality of dolphins—wild and full of impulses other than procreation—or party-minded right whales.

The ocean reveals all the other possibilities of being this planet offers, including what can be defined as a "typical" sex or sex life or parenting strategy. From physical form to behavior. From life history to territoriality. What reassurance that there are so many ways to thrive. The ocean celebrates multiplicity.

———◆———

Seamus Heaney, in his essay "Feelings into Words," talks about finding his source and writing from that—for him it was from bogs and words of peat and spade. I write from scupper and splice, swell and trough. From the particular, superstitious cadence of supplication and curse that thrives aboard a ship. From the camaraderie of a crew that, ashore, would probably never form friendships. Crew from different countries and classes and politics who must work together to survive their work. And also from the path traced by shearwaters soaring over waves, the dappled shadow of a kelp forest, the thunderous glare of a calving tidewater glacier.

In looking back at all I have written and being honest with myself about the words that risk honesty and vulnerability about that most sacred thing, the deep and deeply personal origins of poetry, I can see that most are borne of ocean. Only once, though, have I tried to write directly and fully into this source.

It began with a conversation on a boat. I was on a ship heading into the Beagle Channel after spending two months approaching and then working in the Antarctic Peninsula, a place I'd been dreaming of and writing poems about for fifteen years. When Demet Taşpınar, the ship's doctor from Istanbul, shared her lyric films with me and suggested a collaboration, I said yes. Neither of us knew what would happen, and it wasn't until five months later that I could sit and drift with her images. My favorite of her films were just sparkles of light on water with, occasionally, a ripple or a chunk of ice passing through.

Watching the films and allowing them to serve as an incantation for poems, opening myself to their shifting, opened a channel. All I wanted was to be in that color, that drift, that unmoored state. And yet I also wanted to bring the mind to that deep emotion, to bring history and science and human story to water. The state those films engendered reminded me of that girl-self staring out toward a hopeful nothingness, of what all my life has most deeply resonated: the sea.

> Sifting atlas blue from yellow body   here again,
> gaveling the nail of the first ship   here again,
> crating star maps in corn husk   here again,
> unfurling a blank heaven over mapped earth   here again,
>
> —Sherwin Bitsui, from *Flood Song*

The truth is, I am most alive in my physical body and thus in the hum and thrum that drives me toward poems when I am on a boat on the ocean. In part, it's the monkishness of allowing myself to be removed from grocery stores and cell phones. In part, it is because weather is not just part of the environment, but something to be watched and speculated upon and planned around. But, more deeply, it's the unboundedness of horizon. That sense that shores touch one another through the medium of the water that touches them.

Did you know that there is a deep current of water that travels from the north pole to the southern ocean, and that, within it, small creatures like foraminiferans and certain plankton travel? It might take them 400 to 600 years for a one-way trip, 1,000 years for the full circle. During that long trip, they either travel suspended as larvae or eggs, or as live adults, reproducing over generations. The full trip is 9,500 kilometers.

What we hold as polar opposites, antipodes, are not so at all. They are connected by ocean.

What is ocean as place? It is not sand underfoot and breakers. It is horizon and connection and mystery. It is the vast volume beneath the surface we can scan and all that happens there: currents, creatures, topography, wrecks. It is the fact that we know so little, that the unknown thrums over the majority of the planet. And that the shores defined by nations and politics don't matter to all that water. And that, back and back and back in time, it was the source of all life on this planet, whether from the ancestral Choanoflagellates or from the huge turtle that islands sometimes. 50% of the oxygen we breathe (maybe even more) is produced by phytoplankton. We are, ourselves, salt. An ocean. And in that dark sea, what isn't possible?

THE CLOUD, THE DESKTOP, & THE POETICS OF NO-PLACE

Christopher Kempf

There is no weather
On the Internet.

Ariana Reines, from *Coeur de Lion*

I WAS TEN the year we got the Internet. I stood there terrified as the modem buzzed and snarled, its beeps and clicking and static sounding, I imagined, like some kind of demented animal was trapped inside it. On screen, my very first homepage shimmered to life, its tiny Netscape logo—an "N" with one foot perched intrepidly beyond the horizon—resolving pixel-by-pixel into focus. Because I knew only a single website those first months, that horizon was a close one, my browsing confined to the few links I could access from categories like "School Bell" and "Science & Nature" on Yahooligans. This, I understood, was the Internet—some facts about butterflies, a clickable barnyard. I sensed, though, like learning some strange new language, that somewhere, just beyond my ability to imagine it, the real excitement of the Internet lay hidden, that if only I stumbled onto the right combination of words and dots and slashes I might uncover at last that secret civilization behind the screen—chat rooms and search engines, something called "instant messaging" I'd been hearing about at school.

For a segment of the so-called Millennial generation born, as I was, in the middle of the 1980s, the arrival of the Internet serves as a kind of Genesis myth with which to fashion into collective form our widely disparate comings of age. Though online media venues like Buzzfeed and Gizmodo often curate nostalgic, ten-signs-you're-a-Millennial inventories of our shared childhood—Fresh Prince memes, pogs, Tamagotchis—perhaps our most important claim to collective identity is that ours is the last generation to remember a time before the Internet, a time, I mean, before those cultures of constant interconnectedness and of distraction that are, for us, indistinguishable from adulthood. For myself—as, I think, for others of my generation—the arrival of the Internet was simultaneous with the irruption into our lives of those great forces of history—of politics and sex and economics and technology—from which our homes, those first firewalls, had once protected us.

The Internet, when it came, was Bosnia and Desert Storm, Monica Lewinsky and Nancy Kerrigan. It was O. J. It was OKC. It was the World Trade Center erupting for the very first time into a cloud of smoke and dust. Like Milton's first humans, our generation stood shelterless and alone at the edge of the future, the cherubims' flaming swords wheeling overhead, that vast, magnificent garden receding behind. They looked back, Milton says, and beheld Paradise, "so late their happy seat":

> Some natural tears they dropped, but wiped them soon;
> The world was all before them, where to choose
> Their place of rest, and Providence their guide:
> They hand in hand with wand'ring steps and slow,
> Through Eden took their solitary way.

I've always been surprised by what seems to me the irrepressible joy of this passage, the last in *Paradise Lost*. Here, that greatest tragedy to befall the human species is merely the beginning of another more important story, the story of what came after. The arrival of the Internet—for myself, for my generation, for our species—was a setting forth, I think, from what Gaston Bachelard has called "the consolations of the cave," a taking of our way, with wandering steps and slow, through an unknown, threatening, yet potentially liberating, possibly revolutionary global village. We had swapped the shelter of our homes for the information superhighway, and where that highway might take us—to our neighbors' living rooms via AIM, to Dubai's palm-shaped islands on Google Earth—we had, and still have, no way of knowing. The world, as Milton says, was all before us.

It's this version of the myth, at least, that we love to perpetuate. That we have, in a kind of Promethean triumph over the old gods, transcended space for cyberspace. That we exist, now, not in a single place—some garden somewhere, some home—but in a placelessness that is every place, a web whose near-infinite interconnectedness streamlines the exchange of ideas and cultures across previously insurmountable barriers. "Electric circuitry," Marshall McLuhan tells us, "has overthrown the regime of 'time' and 'space,' and pours upon us instantly and continuously the concerns of all other men." Our old social and geographical formations, McLuhan says, are no longer viable in the new age of global data flows. "Nothing can be further from the spirit of the new technology than 'a place for everything and everything in its place.' You can't *go* home again."

Decades before it became standard Internet jargon, McLuhan lays out here, in 1967, the logic of what we would come to call the cloud, that every- and no-place in the ether from which we pull down, often with just a click, our photos and poems and mp3's. That cottony memory palace. That place where the angels lived. Whizzing and darting in the air around us, or enveloping us, perhaps, in its downy light, the cloud is the Internet as it would like to be, a bright, amniotic mist in which we're suspended together with our media, floating along, all of us, above the old, hard-wired world.

Popularized over the last decade by the tech companies behind Web 2.0, the cloud is the quintessential northern California dream-image, part new-age theology and part the kind of feel-good Silicon Valley marketing we've seen, perhaps most memorably, in the series of tear-jerker commercials produced by Google's in-house marketing team, commercials in which, for example, a father creates a baby scrapbook by Gmailing his newborn daughter, or in which we follow, in searches, a couple's relationship from "how to impress a French girl" to "how to assemble a crib." Like the cloud they depict in action, these commercials portray our interaction across hard drives and Wi-Fi networks as the most meaningful, indeed the most human, of relationships. Here, the alienating and distancing effects of technology—the Skype lag, the tinny sound of our loved ones in the iPhone's speaker—are re-characterized, via something like poetry I want to propose, into unparalleled forms of closeness and communion, into "personal" computing.

For the cloud, of course, is among other things an incredibly successful metaphor. Not quite, or not only, some rarefied distillation enveloping users in its buoyant embrace, "the cloud," at its most literal, is mile after mile of servers housed in the chilled, earthquake-resistant basements of Silicon Valley tech firms. Its placelessness—that everywhere and nowhere quality we demand from our media these days— is an epiphenomenal effect of its very rootedness *in* place, an effect, moreover, whose purpose is in part to mask the decidedly less feel-good hegemony of corporations like Google, each day exerting greater and more alarming control over an ostensibly liberated cyberspace.

Google, to be sure, is hardly first in making metaphor from clouds, historically, perhaps, our most "poetic" of images. Homer called Zeus the "cloud-gatherer." Shelley, just two years before his death, speaks as one who "wield[s] the flail of the lashing hail, / And whiten[s] the green plains under." Wordsworth too, most famously, "wandered lonely as a cloud," though less remarked upon is how that title image, "float[ing] on high o'er vales and hills," disappears entirely after the second line of the poem, replaced instead by the "host of golden daffodils [...] fluttering and dancing in the breeze" that is the poem's true subject. "I gazed— and gazed—but little thought," Wordsworth writes at the poem's conclusion, "what wealth the show to me had brought":

> For oft, when on my couch I lie
> In vacant or in pensive mood,
> They flash upon that inward eye
> Which is the bliss of solitude;
> And then my heart with pleasure fills,
> And dances with the daffodils.

While the cloud, as we know it today, is inherently social, that ether through which we share nearly every aspect of our lives— even our newborns, pasted across the Internet within minutes of their birth—for Wordsworth, to be cloud-like is to be alone, to experience one's media—daffodils "tossing their heads in sprightly dance"—in the blissful solitude of one's own thoughts. Remember those thoughts? It's no wonder, I think, the poem seems so maudlin to us now; its paean to the bliss of contemplative reflection is rooted in a conception of loneliness—or of aloneness—very different than we're used to. Here, rather, in the cloud to which we've fallen, we no longer measure "wealth" as the poem does, are no longer capable, perhaps, of the pleasure it speaks of.

Our own cloud, I've been suggesting, seems instead part of a broader effort by technology companies to paper over—and just think of these companies' obsessions with wallpaper—their more unappetizing corporate policies with positive associations cultivated through the skillful deployment of rhetoric. Despite, for example, Comcast's desperate rebranding of itself as something called "Xfinity," the company remains part of a fearsome oligopoly dedicated, among other worrying priorities, to eradicating net neutrality as we know it. Likewise, that myth, as powerful as Genesis, that the Internet is a kind of utopian "no-place" transcending national boundaries is belied by no less immediate a scandal than the 2014 PRISM affair, in which Google, Microsoft, and Yahoo admitted to providing proprietary user information to the United States government. And that government, of course, is at this very moment operating a massive data center in the Utah desert, caching phone calls and text messages, Gchats and Facebook posts by the billions to servers deep beneath the wind-carved rock and sand. Far from erasing place, the Internet and the cyber-technologies behind it perhaps more clearly delineate, then, those boundaries that continue to structure our stubbornly "placed"—national, but also gendered, and raced, and classed— forms of experience.

When users of the Microsoft-sponsored video game series *Call of Duty*—and sometimes, shamefully, I am one of them— log into their Xbox Live accounts, they're shown a Mercator projection of the globe with phosphorescent green pulses glowing and fading wherever users are most active. The eastern United States, in my experience, is typically the most brightly lit, followed, in turn, by the western U.S., Europe, and Japan, any Internet-connected citizen of which can play online in formats like "Team Deathmatch" and "Capture the Flag." In what I have always thought of as a damning exposé of tech's feel-good, ostensibly "new economy," Africa, long the so-called Dark Continent, shows not a single green pulse, its vast darkness a reminder, at the dead center of the map, that for all its claims to democracy, the Internet remains a mode of experience—of history and economics, of place and the people who live in those places—more repeating than rejecting those forms of western imperialism from which it rose. "There is no document of civilization," Benjamin says of these old imperialisms, "that is not at the same time a document of barbarism." There is no cloud, we might say now, that is not a storm.

———— • ————

I knew it was time to get out of the Bay. Like so many cash-strapped artists—and, more troublingly, like thousands of Asian and Latino residents who'd lived there for decades—I'd been priced out of San Francisco by the arrival of what everyone, including *The New Yorker*, was suddenly calling the "creative class," young, six-figured coders and programmers eager to surround themselves with the cultural cachet of neighborhoods like Haight-Ashbury, North Beach, and the Mission. Wherever they went, roving indiscriminately across the city's once diverse enclaves, the rents rose. Family-owned storefronts were replaced by sleek, industrial-looking bars. Michelin-starred restaurants popped up overnight. I'd managed, after weeks of searching, to find a comparatively cheap apartment in the Temescal area of Oakland, a dingy one-bedroom above an Ethiopian restaurant and something that billed itself as a "pagan metaphysical bookstore" called Ancient Ways. I was paying more than I'd hoped, $1100 a month for an apartment whose windows didn't close, but by scrimping on dinners out and drawing down an already meager savings account I was able to swing it.

Then the buses came. Long controversial in the Bay Area, the private, Wi-Fi equipped buses operated by Silicon Valley's largest tech companies whisk employees out of the city each day to their sprawling, carefully manicured campuses down the Peninsula. There's a direct correlation between these bus routes and a neighborhood's rents, and as first Google then Yahoo extended their coverage across the Bay Bridge into Oakland—and since they'd made my street their main thoroughfare through the west side—my own rent was slated to go up nearly 50% when my lease expired, an increase which, reduced as I'd been to a steady diet of Totino's pizza rolls, I was in no position to afford.

A throwback to the days of Roman senators lifted above the masses on cushioned divans, the buses have contributed not only to insupportable rents in San Francisco and Oakland but to the creation of a two-tiered transportation system throughout the Bay Area. Utilizing public bus stops and choking already crowded public byways, the buses visibly mark the distinction between northern California's "new" and "old" economies, between the haves and an unfortunate caste of have-nots relegated to increasingly under-funded public transportation. The buses are, I think, a local manifestation of tech's wider relationship to place. For tech's myth of placelessness, undergirded by blithe metaphors like the cloud and the global village, conceals often deleterious real-world effects on places as far flung as Hayes Valley and Shenzhen, China, where iPhones, designed, as we well know, "by Apple in California," are assembled at factories whose workers earn less than $2.50 an hour.

When the buses, like Yeats' rough beast, moved their slow thighs toward Oakland, long the site of a vibrant counterculture of artists and activists, I began to look for a way out, not necessarily, I should admit, for ethical, anti-gentrification reasons—I'd prefer to live in Temescal and Crown Heights and Royal Oak as much as the next person—but because enduring conversations about bandwidth capacity and the scalability of front-end HTML at the local coffeeshop seemed no longer justifiable at $1600 a month. Even, that is, with what seemed to me a ridiculously plush fellowship to write poems, I was easily priced out by an *arriviste* class of "creatives" trafficking in its own, far more lucrative, brand of metaphor. As our carpool of poets drove down the Peninsula every Wednesday for workshop, we passed, on the outskirts of Menlo Park, Facebook's palatial, Mediterranean Revival-style headquarters, a cheery, tree-lined campus resembling one of those outdoor shopping malls with names like Jefferson Pointe and Apple Glen. Somewhere inside, a team of engineers and public relations experts were debating, I imagined, the ethics of adding a "Dislike" button, or the metaphor of the news "feed," even while we, around our own workshop table, argued about Tony Hoagland and whether anthropomorphism was appropriative. There didn't, there in our northern California cloud, seem room for the both of us.

But tech's use of metaphor, despite my description of it as a recent phenomena, has always, even before the rise of the Internet, been its preferred modus operandi; what we overlook, in other words, acculturated as we are to utilitarian approaches to computing, is how our relationships with our machines are almost entirely structured by metaphor. As Alan Liu has argued, the concept of dragging "folders" across "windows" into a "Recycle Bin" with a "mouse" is simply the aestheticizing, in visual form, of that abstract flurry of code whirring behind our screens. "We see a graphically bitmapped main 'window,'" Liu writes, "whose menu bars and office-themed visual icons (file folders, trash cans, calendars, phones) construct a metaphorical 'desktop,' the great landscape of the cubicle." The function of such a desktop, according to Liu, "is to coordinate (and also subordinate) operations and modes," those habits of being that structure our relationship with computers and, increasingly, with each other.

As tech's wholesale uprooting of longtime minority residents in the Bay Area makes clear, these processes of subordination are sometimes all too literal in a real world which, made over in the image of cyber-technology, more and more resembles a kind of vast, manipulable desktop. We might note however—and with, perhaps, some discomfort—how tech's deft and thoroughgoing use of metaphor changes, or at least complicates, the way we conceive of the Internet and those who control it. At Stanford University, located in the heart of Silicon Valley and alma mater to some of its most important personalities, the most popular 100-level class is Introduction to Programming, with over a thousand students enrolled each quarter. At the University of Chicago, studying Python, Java, or C++ counts toward the foreign language requirement of Ph.D. students in the humanities. If our experiences of cyber-technology, indeed if our very desktops, are subtended by carefully structured, syntactically complicated code languages, languages whose purpose is not only to communicate but to elicit emotion, then perhaps the so-called creative class—despite its six-figure salaries—is more creative, more aesthetically invested than we, or I anyway, would care to admit. Perhaps there's something elegant, artistic even, in a well-designed app. Perhaps Facebook is the new Pollack.

Perhaps tech, in other words, is poetry.

———•———

If cyber-technology seems—with its use of metaphor and code, but also in the way it demands from us diverse forms of attention across the variously textured "languages" of cyberspace—to have incorporated poetic technique, poetry has itself absorbed in turn what we might think of as the Internet's fugitive, postmodern sensibility. Poetry in our new millennium, we know, has jettisoned the now antiquated narrative mode that dominated the second half of the 20th century, moving instead toward more "associative" representation of what Mark Doty has characterized as "temperament / subjectivity / thinking / in the moment." Tracking consciousness as it moves discontinuously across the surfaces of experience, associative poetry is, at least in part, an aesthetic response to the frenetic phenomenology of the information age, to forms of experience in which the human psyche, assaulted by cable news and News Feeds, Twitter and text messages, suffers from a kind of perpetual attention-deficit disorder, leaping about, as these poems do, from one perception to the next.

Yet while cyber-technology has profoundly affected the *form* of contemporary poetry, far less frequently does the Internet actually appear as a subject fit to be writing about, as content. In a cursory survey of an anthology of "American Poets of the

New Century," I found, in over 400 pages and 80 poets, barely a single reference to a computer, and this despite an overriding tendency, as in Juliana Spahr's excellent "December 1, 2002"— the nearest this anthology comes to direct treatment of cyber-technologies—toward what we might think of as a formal mimesis of contemporary browsing practices. "I speak of the forty-seven dead in Caracas," Spahr writes:

> And I speak of the four dead in Palestine.
> And of the three dead in Israel.
> I speak of those dead in other parts of the world that go
>   unreported.
> I speak of boundaries and connections, locals and
> globals, butterfly wings and hurricanes.

Spahr's work, both in its associative leaping and its elision of the technology that makes such balletics possible, is representative, I think, of our contemporary moment writ large. If my own poetic practice is typical, poets today are not only culling more and more information from the Internet but spending more time online even while writing. And while some poetry—Alex Dimitrov's Grindr poems, Gregory Shirl's *The Oregon Trail is the Oregon Trail*—does make mention of this, far more contemporary poetry simply ignores it. In eliding, however, those experiences and those machines that quite literally structure its relation to the world, contemporary poetry seems anachronistically wedded to a romantic notion of unmediated "poetic" reality, as if exposing the ugly, unpoetic technology that underwrites our associative flights of fancy would ruin the effect.

In Greek tragedy, an invisible machine—either a crane, known as a *mechane*, or a trapdoor—would bring actors playing gods to the stage in seemingly miraculous fashion. Likewise, Romantic poetry depended for its effect on the concealing of those material circumstances of composition that might detract from the sublimity such poetry sought to cultivate in its readers;

Wordsworth wrote his most famous poem not, as his title claims, a few miles above Tintern Abbey, but in a smoky room some twenty miles south in Bristol. Like these predecessors, contemporary poetry, with a few exceptions, prefers its *deus* without the *machina*, miming the forms of cyber-technology yet eschewing more substantive engagement with the social and political machinery that facilitates its theatrics.

Indeed, it's somewhat striking that the most important innovations of our lifetime should so dramatically resist poetic representation. While I'm interested more in diagnosing then critiquing this phenomenon, might it not, perhaps, be an abdication of responsibility that we so distort the nature of contemporary reality in the name of art? Where are the iPhones? Where's pornography and its influence on how we consider gender? Where, most recently, are the poems about how our experiences of race are often mediated by cyber-technologies in complex and sometimes contradictory ways? While much good, for example, has certainly come from hashtags like #BlackLivesMatter, might the technologies that facilitate this kind of consciousness-raising—and which typically charge for higher levels of visibility or "promotion"—also forestall more immediate action, venting political energy and bolstering the illusion that "sharing" our opinions via massive, multinational tech corporations constitutes a viable politics? "Liking," perhaps, is not enough. How, I hope my flurry of scare-quotes suggests, can poets be expected to understand—much less critique, or redeem, or beautify—contemporary forms of experience without accurately and honestly engaging with them and with the language in which they're structured? Poets, rather, seem to be practicing a kind of sympathetic magic with respect to the Internet and cyber-technology, behaving like prehistoric hunter-gatherers who, awed by a power they can't quite fathom, attempt to harness its magic simply by imitating it.

In the absence of widespread mainstream engagement with 21st century technologies, it has fallen to the avant garde to explore the relationship between these technologies and human subjectivity, first in Flarf and hypertext-based poetries and lately in what Kenneth Goldsmith has called in *The New Yorker* "post-Internet" poetry, poetry, that is, which takes for granted—rather than foregrounding the strangeness of or formally emulating—the influence of cyber-technologies on our lives. Though Goldsmith doesn't mention her, Ariana Reines is one of the most exciting poets writing in this mode. Her collection *Coeur de Lion*, self-published in 2007 and re-published in 2011 by FENCE, is an e-pistolary work organized around the speaker's re-reading of e-mails sent to and received from a lover whose Gmail she's hacked. The collection is thus, on one level, an account of that uncanny phenomenon with which we're all too familiar, namely the encountering of e-mails from what seems like another lifetime, a life which, however removed we feel from it, remains archived—and will remain so long after our deaths—in pristine condition on Google's underground servers. *Coeur de Lion* is also, in places, a document of the writer's process, revealing in its citation of websites like Wikipedia—and something called themiddleages.net (!)—the invisible online labor subtending poetic production, labor often occluded in contemporary poetry's effort toward romanticized, unmediated experience. Though the collection sometimes borders on sentimentality, Reines refuses, unlike Alt Lit for example, to ironize the relationships she depicts, exploring instead how cyber-technologies interface with human bodies, particularly sexed and sexual bodies, in a heady amalgam of YouTube, weed, de Manian deconstruction, sex, jealousy, American Apparel banner ads, famine in Africa, and ecological crisis. "I am trying to decide," Reines writes, "If the things humans emit / Between themselves / Have any reason."

Like Reines' treading of the confluence between human transmissions and emissions, Ander Monson similarly engages the often invisible machinery that structures those flows of data, language, image, and sound passing between us each day. Monson's 2010 collection, *The Available World*, uses the Internet as an extended metaphor for something like the Romantic sublime; behind our screens, that is, an entire, instantaneously available cosmos lies waiting, a cosmos in the face of which we are, as Kant suggested, simultaneously insignificant and—because we can fathom that cosmos, indeed because we built it—reaffirmed in the power of our humanity. Here's part of the poem "Loss":

> Let me say this now: it's impossible not to
>
> > > > > > eventual
>
> > & hemmorhage muchness
> > > > & the vast space of America & American
> conceptions of outer space as seen in 3 dimensions
> > > > on your growing screen of choice
> your choice of screens, your preferred streakers, tweakers,
> > > > > > hackers, phone phreakers,
> David Bakers and those wronged by David Bakers [...]

As I think this passage demonstrates, Monson's work is a playful, powerful meditation on how cyber-technologies intersect— sometimes profoundly, sometimes in the most banal of ways— with our day-to-day experiences, with theology and geography, phone phreaking and poetry. To be sure, experimental poetries' refraction of embodied experience can sometimes result in unfortunate misappropriations of that experience, as we've seen, for instance, in the response to some of Goldsmith's work. But if poetry's traditional purpose, as W. S. Di Piero puts it, is to quarrel with orders both human and divine, Monson, like Reines, shows how our own generation might honestly take up that quarrel now, in the globalized "no-place" that is not quite the utopia we were promised, how, in other words, we might revere, but also wrestle with and rebel against, these strange new gods.

———— • ————

Because it's not, after all, some desolate wasteland toward which Milton's first couple wanders off. I am writing this in the Plein Air Café on the campus of the University of Chicago, a cozy, Bauhaus-inspired little place whose name, "plein air," refers to the Impressionist habit of painting outdoors, where one could, as Monet did with his haystacks, reproduce actual conditions of light and of weather rather than painting toward the pre-determined look of the studio. This afternoon, thick beams of light are falling through the café's windows. It's summer. Vampire Weekend is playing. All around me students are typing away on their laptops, e-mails and essays, poems and stories flitting off through the ether. We stare transfixed into our screens, our headphones pumping their own tinny music, our computers purring. We're oblivious to each other. Only—as Forster put it—connected.

WHAT'S AMERICAN ABOUT AMERICAN POETRY?

Kazim Ali

O N THE TENTH ANNIVERSARY of their symposium "What's American about American Poetry?" I was invited by the Poetry Society of America, along with several other poets, to reflect on the question. It never occurred to me to write about anything other than writers from Indigenous American communities—their poetry and poetics seeming to me to be the closest literal answer to the question.

I wondered what was meant in the first place by the term "American." It neither really defines national origin, geographical placement ("America" outsourcing itself far beyond its own continental borders to islands across the world) nor linguistic or cultural unity. This country resists itself, has always resisted itself; what it claims to be chafes always against its reality. One of the reasons for this, of course, is that in its founding it delineated a set of defining values for itself that were false; those of different colored skin and different genders were excluded from the polity. More than two centuries in and we are still defined by gender and heterosexist based inequality enforced by executive, legislative, and judicial law. This disconnect between thought and deed is part of what must be thought of as "American."

"American" must also mean multiplicities as we are a nation of countless ethnicities, countless languages, and countless experiences, none of which have a greater or lesser claim to life in the "nation" than any other. And truth be told, in a place where any place has two names or more, we are not "one nation" after all, but many. When we think of a unified or singular American identity, we lose the chance to truly understand our selves and one another. As b: william bearhart writes:

> Biitan-akiing-enabijig is Ojibwe.
> I can't tell you what it means.
> > We sit on cuspis.
> > A horizon. A margin.
> > What makes us "not them."
> I only wish I could speak in tongue.

Bearhart makes an intentional and breathless grammatical mistake in the last line here, dreaming himself to a monolingual expression he knows he can never nor will ever have. A postmodern aesthetic shows us, on the other hand, the rich possibilities of living in the in-between zones, the horizons, the margins—our chance is to become a pluralistic society, diminishing old class, gender, race, national, and sexual lines that configured most historically hierarchical world societies, and then reconfigure a new "American" society that functions on collective enterprise, cultural and artistic growth, and individual human development and betterment.

The "American Dream" has always been not communitarian but individual, based on not only a desire but a need to "get ahead," despite any shortcomings. So, to cite only one example, Malcolm X once criticized our Civil Rights Movement for orienting itself around the individual right to vote or participate in unsegregated arenas of commerce (buses, businesses, restaurants), rather than building class-based solidarity within the United States with labor unions and movements and international solidarity with African nations who were at the same time struggling for independence against European and American powers who controlled mineral interests and thus the political and economic institutions of power on the continent. As Malcolm pointed out, without diamonds for industrial machines, all modern progress would (literally) grind to a halt. These were the types of connections between political theories and organizing communities that both he and, several years later, Martin Luther King, Jr. were beginning to build when each was killed.

Is another part of being "American" this self-orientation toward our own concerns and what happens within our own borders, while still requiring the labor, water, land and mineral resources of every other place in the world? In other words, our material comfort, cultural production, and individual human development and betterment does not rely on any reconfiguration of gender-, race-, class-, or nation-based hierarchies, but actually on an institution of them backed up by American military power (easy when more than 50 cents of every tax dollar goes to support that power), and global political and financial institutions.

We are a long way from the hoped for definition of "American" we aspire to and still aspire to somewhere in our minds, I believe. So as "American" poets, we do have both versions of America within us, since as citizens of the polity we still do (mostly) benefit from our luck and our willingness to go along, by continuing to elect and support leaders who subscribe to the "American Exceptionalism" doctrine and use U.S. financial and military power to support it.

But we have a chance also, with our language, with the form and focus of our art to begin delineating the truth of our lives as it is and to start imagining on paper and in space the differences we hope to enact.

In Sherwin Bitsui's *Flood Song*, he writes of a lost connection between language, locality and lived experience. In speaking of his grandfather, he writes:

Years before, he would have named this season

By flattening a field where grasshoppers jumped
into black smoke.

The season, in this case, like the American landscape itself, is not named for the explorer's imperialist ambitions—as Paul Virilio once claimed, the American imperial object is ever outward: once the Pacific was reached, the incursions continued into the ocean itself; once the hands of empire reached out and around the planet and met each other coming, the direction changed into outer space—or for a romantic idea of the self defined from or manipulated by "nature" but instead for the psychic and kinetic qualities of the land itself.

When the Poetry Society of America convened a number of poets—Sonia Sanchez, Michael Palmer, Louise Glück, Jorie Graham, Kimiko Hahn, and many others—to discuss the question "What's American about American Poetry?" a general consensus tentatively, if affably, emerged—a single lively panel kerfuffle between Thylias Moss and John Hollander aside—that the most "American" quality was the quality of constant undefinability. Was it a cop-out?

If the strength of American poetry is its hybrid qualities and leanings, its weakness is also particularly American: its amnesia of history and language, but not a passive amnesia of forgetting, but a brutal and intentional act of erasure: towns and neighborhoods named after plants, animals, and people who no longer exist there. There is a city in Florida called Miami and more than a thousand miles away in Ohio, there is a river called Miami. You have to draw a line that stretches the distance between those two places to spell out even the first letter of the word "America." And where are the Miami now? That's the start of the second letter.

In M. L. Smoker's poem "From the River's Edge," she writes about the fragmentation inherent in being separated from one's sources by a larger external narrative and the ability of poetry to bridge that divide: "Can a poet speak of a / second version of her mother?" She goes on to write:

> [...] The one who lives in a
> silent cave where she allows no visitors, gives no interviews.
> Her memoir is being written there by a shadow seven feet
> tall that can hold no pen or pencil, both hands missing.
> My living mother dreams of new waters that have no
> adequate translation.

So in this historical moment, the possibilities of the various American languages seem two-fold: to either homogenize and smooth out all difference (one American urge) or to continue to splinter, refract one another, create dozens of new and glorious forms of creative expression.

And about nations and languages that have disappeared or been suppressed: history isn't just something that happened. As Utah Phillips said, "The past didn't go anywhere." Native, indigenous, and aboriginal populations on the American continent and around the world struggle every day for political self-determination and ownership of their own local land and mineral resources; in other words liberation from imperialism, whether political, economic, or cultural.

So what we really need, every American poet, are forms and approaches and languages like Sherwin Bitsui's, M. L. Smoker's, Bearhart's—and, for additional example, Dawn Lundy Martin's, Gillian Conoley's, Mark Nowak's, Myung Mi Kim's, C.D. Wright's—forms that hold within them the voices of alterity, the parallels of experience, are lyric and narrative forms that embrace and present new possibilities of understanding America and American experiences.

At the end of his poem, "Ars Poetica," Orlando White writes beautifully of the real physical and erotic possibilities when language and experience twist around each other, when the form of the lyric is allowed to fracture and grow anew under the pressure of contemporary realities of alienation, distance and technology:

> I opened an envelope addressed to me. I pulled out a blank sheet of paper, unfolded it.
>
> In the letter: no message, no sender's name, just a white space.
>
> "I like that you exist," she said. Like the lowercase i, my body felt present on a page: fitted in a dark suit, white necktie, and inside the black dot, a smile.
>
> But it was the way her skin felt as she dressed into a black outfit. The way her body slipped into a long dark dress shaped like a shadow.
>
> He picked up a stone; held it to his ear. Shook it like a broken watch. He opened it, and inside were small gears, shaped like a clock.
>
> I am a skeleton, a sentence, too. Although like you, I am neither a meaning nor a structure, just silence in a complete thought.

Here language itself lives, changes through our actions. The stone has little gears inside and why would it: it is telling time. "In the Lakota language," Layli Long Soldier wrote to me, "the word for God or Creator, which is 'Tunkasila' which also means grandfather.) But the root of Tunkasila is 'Tunkan'—which means stone, a sacred stone or a stone of great power. What is the connection between a stone and God/grandfather?" In the case of White, who is Diné rather than Lakota, it seems not only the stones speak but also every component of conceptual and physical meaning-making.

Besides supporting art like this, art that confronts all dimensions of the "American" experience, we have to also acknowledge the real military, political, and economic empire as well as the cultural apparatus—what Nowak calls the "Neo-Liberal Language Industry" in his excellent short book *Workers of the Word, Unite and Fight!*—that supports that matrix of reality—a reality in which notions of "plurality" and "hybridity" and "alterity" are just three more convenient ways of organizing a population into compliant behavior and tokenizing a couple of voices of in order to avoid seeing or seeking out the rest of them.

After all, our present machine-driven sense of geographical placelessness isn't real. History and geography so still play a role in daily life in America. Jean Baudrillard in his book *America* painted a stark picture of our current landscape as a vacant series of sites of consumption (strip malls, some of which are even *designed* to imitate the small-town America main streets they brutally replaced), housing developments and parking lots linked by an interstate system, but it isn't really true. The urban spaces and wildlife, under duress and real political attack (especially by defunding public schools and university systems), still struggle to actualize their possible roles as instruments for a revitalization of real and substantial creative and cultural life.

Our multilingualism and cultural openness have made many spaces in poetry. Kimiko Hahn's writing between poetry and prose, Meena Alexander's innovations in the lyric between sense and sound (especially in her latest book *Quickly Changing River*), Agha Shahid Ali's transportation (literally) of the ghazal into English (or was it that he transported English-language poetry to the form of the ghazal?) are all examples that seem particularly American to me, as much the benefit of English as a meeting place.

Indian English, I can tell you, is a separate language, both spoken and written, from American English. It has different words, different intonations and pronunciations, different accepted sentence order, different syntax. In my book *Bright Felon* I tried as hard as I could to tell the story of my life the only way I knew how. I did not have the intention of writing "poetry" or "poems" or "memoir" while I was doing it, only sentences. The genre-queerness of that book, called both poetry and prose and prose-poetry, is specifically related to the idea that life-writing should follow the patterns of a "by-the-book" formula of both chapter, structure, sentence and paragraph, that a life can't fundamentally be "queer," impossible to tell in any other way. And besides, I'm not the first one to try it: Etel Adnan, Mahmoud Darwish, Alistair McCartney, Sarah Manguso, and so many others I am sure have written prose memoirs that dispense with all the usual expectations of what the form ought to do.

Writers like Myung Mi Kim or Sherwin Bitsui or Tracie Morris are actually making new spaces in American poetry, both in terms of what poetry is supposed to look and sound like and also in terms of what its social function as literature actually is. Lucille Clifton wrote, "i was born in babylon / both nonwhite and woman. / i had no models." At least in terms of poetry, for myself, I no longer feel this way: I feel there are so many models for me now.

We have a timeless tradition to draw from. At the original "What's American about American Poetry?" symposium in 1999 John Hollander caused a little bit of controversy when he criticized Thylias Moss for citing "the landscape" as her literary forebear. The two had a somewhat testy exchange about canonicity and lineages that ended when Moss leapt up onto her chair and declared to the room, "Some of us don't have people as literary forebears. For some of us whose ancestors lay in holds of slaveships, a crack of blue seen between the planes of wood was our literary forebear."

In dg nanouk okpik's poem cycle "For-the-spirits-who-have-rounded-the-bend," she confronts the tradition of the "identity" and "coming-of-age" poems in surprising and inventive ways that marry a concern with sound to the more traditional folk images. Rather than being a marrying of opposites, in okpik's work, it feels absolutely contemporary and unified:

> [...] Then as the ligature of Inuit light flux and flows
> like herds of walrus, passing along the coast, Yes then,
>   but maybe
> this is a seal hook of bear claws clipping me to the
>   northern tilt,
> pinning me to the cycle of night when the day slows, the
>   wind
> shifts to cloud, and the moon shadow grows to sun loops.

Since she is clipped to the "northern tilt" and pinned to movements of night and day, she is able to discover through the process of transformation she undergoes throughout the poem that nothing is lost, that she can live wholly and fully, connected to all her various human and animal sources. There is a danger in it, to be sure, but in the end it is the winged heart that speaks of hope and strength:

> [...] After the border of flesh and church, after the old
> book   is read,
> and ivory with scrimshaw is used with rib tools to create
>   Okvik
> not Christianity, when the bell tones across the sound,
>   until then,
> I will wash ashore in a dazed white-out, hide flesh to beach
> with my fore-claws hanging limply, my hooded golden
> eyes with concentric circles, lines on my chin,
> with a large backbone for my lungs, and a heart of spotted
>   wings.

I think of something Naomi Shihab Nye wrote, in 1999, in her response to the question "What's American about American Poetry?" Nye said, "When I was working overseas on various occasions, poets in other countries would remark that we American poets have a luxury they do not have: we are free to write about tiny 'insignificances' any time we want to...We write about personal lives, minor idiosyncrasies, familial details, tomatoes—not feeling burdened to explore larger collective issues all the time, which is something writers elsewhere often consider part of their endless responsibility."

There is a way in which all American life, American writing and poetry included, participates in the historical (and geographical!) amnesia inherent in the concept of "America." What is the responsibility of the writer? When you look one place, there is another place you are not looking. We will have to think for a long time to figure out where we are and who are and what we are doing in this place, thought to be ours from "sea to shining sea," ours by some form of "manifest destiny," some form of "American exceptionalism."

In her essay "Poetics of Generosity," Judith E. Johnson writes, "I am not Alterity: I will not play that role in your mind or in my own. I am not Shakespeare's sister Judith, whose existence Virginia Woolf divined in her prophetic sanity. I am Judith, and Shakespeare is this Judith's brother." She refuses to be defined by her "absence from the center of discourse." She goes on to suggest a new way of thinking about the American poetic landscape:

> Jane Austen, the Brontë sisters, and George Eliot define the 19th Century English novel; if that definition does not hold Dickens, Thackeray, and Meredith, they are the deviation from the norm, and their Alterity makes them contingent. Ethel Schwabacher defines Abstract Expressionism; Jackson Pollack is the deviation. Muriel Rukeyser defines the poetics of energy-transfer; Charles Olson is the deviation...you, our illustrious male colleagues and brothers, are the deviation. It will be healthy for you to see yourselves in the full brilliance of your own Alterity for a while, to study our practice as the human norm, and to wonder when and why you strayed from us.

American poets have so much to learn from each other; it has always been precisely those underseen or underheard texts that have provided the greatest influence on the literary landscape at large when they are revealed. Need we any more proof than Dickinson's poems, Nin's uncensored diaries, Melville's late stories? In the case of all three, gender and sexuality were at play in the suppression. Recent attention paid to a younger crop of indigenous writers—a recent weekend of events at Poets House, a feature on Native women writers that Long Soldier edited for *Drunken Boat*, Long Soldier herself being featured by the Academy of American Poets in their magazine, Orlando White being selected for Poetry Society of America's "New American Poets" festival (by me)—points to a long hoped for shift in attitudes toward Indigenous writing, not as "contingent" but as the real mainstream of "American literary tradition."

Natalie Diaz is one of the most exciting poets I have read recently. In her poem "Soirée Fantastique," she takes ancient European myth and weaves it together with contemporary American situations and idiom:

> Houdini arrived first, with Antigone on his arm.
> Someone should have told her it was rude
> to chase my brother in circles with such a shiny shovel.
> She only said, I'm building the man a funeral.
> But last I measured, my brother was still a boy.

As with most wild parties featuring the dead, things can only get crazier when Jesus shows up:

> There are violins playing. The violins are on fire—
> they are passed around until we're all smoking. Jesus coughs,
> climbs down from the cross of railroad ties above the table.
> He's a regular at these carrion revelries, and it's annoying
> how he turns the bread to fish, especially when we have
> sandwiches.

Neither the escape artist, nor the son of god, two men who specialized in fulfilling destinies are able to console Antigone and explain to her why she will not be permitted to bury the young brother. Only the speaker of the poem is left to explain it to her, taking away her spade, saying:

> We aren't here to eat, we are being eaten.
> Come, pretty girl. Let us devour our lives.

Part of our answer is to now start experiencing poetry not solely in the mind, nor solely visually, nor solely aurally but through all the senses at once. When I commented to Layli Long Soldier that I felt something of the influence of Gertrude Stein in her poems, she told me of her appreciation of Stein by both sight and sound, and of her various other influences including Cubist painters and the Canadian writer bpNichol. Referencing Stein, she told me of the traditional "jingle-dress" in many Native American cultures, a dress which would literally create a sonic experience as the wearer moved around in space. Here is the beginning of Long Soldier's prose poem "Edge":

> This drive along the road the bend the banks behind
> the wheel I am called Mommy. My name is Mommy
> on these drives the sand and brush the end of winter we
> pass. You in the rearview double buckled back center
> my love. Your mother's mouth has a roof your mother's
> mouth is a church. A hut in a field lone standing. The
> thatched roof has caught spark what flew from walls the
> spark apart from rock from stable meaning.

It's not enough to say as Americans we have to understand our history. We have to also understand the here and now, the voices we have not heard, couldn't or wouldn't, voices that help to construct and reveal new rooms in the houses of our understanding.

Stein said the wildest thing—I still love it—about America: "America is now the oldest country in the world because by the methods of the Civil War and the commercial conceptions that followed it America created the twentieth century." We can talk for a long time about what she meant, but the most interesting part for me is how America has gone—militarily, economically, culturally—global. The way I think about it, Mahmoud Darwish is a most "American" poet. He and his family fled his home in 1947, returning without papers, he lived in internal exile for most of his young life, and then as an expatriate in Moscow, Tripoli, Beirut, and Paris, before finally returning home in 1997. His poetry constantly engaged with the question of "exile," but it wasn't long before he realized that "exile" is a spiritual and metaphysical condition as well. How much more "American," or true to the American experience, both indigenous and immigrant, can you get?

He came to America only once, for an operation on his heart. Fady Joudah, the Palestinian-American poet who has been translating Darwish, writes a beautiful essay about his first and only meeting with Darwish—at a coffee shop in the local supermall. In that peculiarly American locale, poet and translator talk together for the first time, sharing stories, talking about poetry.

And that's the key, isn't it? In this life, supported by millions of gallons of oil, this strange life of buildings dropped on top of scoured land, this weird American landscape, this odd reality in which our primary responsibility as flesh and bone entities seems to be to consume, to receive and spend money, well where do you find the poetry, by which I mean any spiritual sustenance at all?

At any rate, I think the "American Century" is soon over. Within the next thirty or forty years, when the global food production and distribution system, utterly unsustainable, moves into crisis, when water availability and sustainability moves into a crisis point, as fossil fuels begin to evaporate and disappear, only societies who have been able to do more with less will be able to cope. Our society will necessarily be required to start making real and concrete steps in this direction, exploring free energy, free health care, and free primary, secondary and higher education for everyone within the borders.

Some time in the next century, we will have to learn, probably quickly and in an atmosphere of duress (whether external or internal or some combination of the two), how to live without many of the things we take very much for granted—to cite three varied examples: fresh vegetables in the winter, regularly scheduled air travel, and round-the-clock availability of electrical power and tap-water. Are we heading back to pioneer days? We will be pioneering in our own hearts the routes of connectedness between us and the earth, us and everyone around us.

Language, modes of communication, and availability to communication media will be critically important in the new world; they will save us, and by us I mean "all" of us: one of the things I think will need to happen is an end to Nationalism, not an end to nations, necessarily, but an end to the project of nation-building certainly. We will necessarily return to locally based economies and with it, naturally, we will probably return to locally based languages and forms of cultural expressions and a form of multilingualism quite common in the world and in marginal American populations but not yet in the mainstream.

As access to fresh water diminishes, silicon production must necessarily dwindle, so I wonder what the future of electronics will be. We'll find a way to stay in touch with each other, I'm sure of that, but I think a return to the most ancient sources of art, dance and poetry, seems also inevitable. I think poetry will move back to the oral, back to the musical and back to the mysterious and spiritual and difficult.

Long Soldier's poem "Edge" continues:

> Large car steady at the curve palest light driest day a field of rocks
> we are not poor sealed in windows. You hum in the back. I do not

> know what to say how far to go the winter near dead as we drive
> you do not understand word for word the word for you is little. But
> you hear how it feels always. The music plays you swing your feet.
> And I see it I Mommy the edge but do not point do not say look
> as we pass the heads gold and blowing these dry grasses eaten in
> fear by man and horses.

It draws both from her own personal experiences, landscape and physical environment, the sound textures of Stein, and a postmodern linguistic and theoretical sensibility. With visionary work like this, which looks backward and forward at once, which encompasses all of the magnificent differences and all the "Americas."

Maybe it is better for us to look at work like this—Bitsui, White, Long Soldier, Diaz, Bearhart, okpik—as the real American poetry and what we think of as the Anglo-American literary tradition as the tradition of alterity, of deviation, that this landscape, on this continent, this strange life, needs to be explained in terms of contemporary Native writers who have been able to fuse the Anglo-American literary tradition with Native languages, poetics and forms of expression.

As for me, let me wander anywhere and hope Darwish is waiting for me. True, he is buried in Palestine, but he died here, in a hospital in Texas, and perhaps something of his spirit also lingers here, haunting the place, reminding us, as he wrote in his great poem "Speech of the Red Indian":

> Oh white man, of all the dead who are still dying, both
> those who live and those who return to tell the tale

> Let's give the earth enough time to tell the whole truth
> about you and us.

> The whole truth about us.

> The whole truth about you.

MAKING SPACE: A NOTEBOOK

Sandra Lim

THIS MORNING I am in a little room in a little town in Wyoming, looking out my window at the Bighorn Mountains in the far distance. I am here to write poems. The silence of the morning is immense, it takes up space. Yet there is a feeling of roiling motion and process in the flaring blue sky; it's the biggest action painting I've ever seen. Hard-hearted Nature, I think. Not purely the mute, brute realism of the natural world or the teeming, man-made world of the metropolis, say. And not merely the regrettable sense of estrangement from these. Not really location and form given to inward speculation and emotion. What then, in fact, is the aura of place and its ground in a poem? Perhaps place is constituitive of a poem's thrilling sense of inevitability; even darkly so, as Franz Kafka writes, "There I sat, a faded being, under faded leaves." Being here in a new environment inspires me to consider how a landscape can take up residence in a poem. In trying to bring nature and artifice together in a lyric work, I am reminded of John Milton remarking: "The mind is its own place."

———— ◆ ————

Sometimes I think of lyric tone and sensibility in terms of a certain landscape that has quietly lost its mind in the words of the poem. Or, I picture place in a poem as a scene of consciousness depicted in nonpsychological terms. The yawning spaces this morning in Wyoming, for instance, with their long vistas and remote look, make me want to pare down my intuitions of spirit—make them fewer, stronger, sharper. But in this impulse I am asking space to still time, inner time, which is always so mercurial and restless and unpredictable. It is painful to harden one's heart, and it is painful not to harden one's heart.

———•———

"Time is the longest distance between two places," writes Tennessee Williams. Time is an idea about place, listing like a houseboat, raging like a forest blaze. "For the sake of a few lines," admonishes Rainer Maria Rilke, "one must see many cities, men, things...still it is not enough to have memories. One must be able to forget them when they are many, and one must have the patience to wait until they come again." My sense of life is of moments, and when I try to remember and write down those moments, shape and understand them, sometimes the white spaces in between turn out not to be so empty; omission can amplify the things one means to say. After this fashion, place in a poem can also be defined as a setting where things are not emblematic, decidedly and evocatively so. It might in some cases just lift away the tyranny of narrative linearity for a moment.

———•———

Yesterday afternoon, I walked around outside my cabin, restlessly and self-consciously: there was the fearsome productivity of the other writer in his studio; a porcupine on a tree nearby so slowly and languorously snacking, it seemed almost lewd; there was a coffee-brown mule deer that looked like a toy animal in the near-distance. The clouds overhead were studies in different shades of white and somehow unlovely. I thought meanderingly of the idea of the West and its senses of reticence or reserve. Then I returned to the vastness of the sky and the silence of the mountains and the trees, their utter indifference to life and death. It made me feel stupid and expansive at once: what can I say about the meaning of human experience? It made me want to go inside and read.

———•———

To arrive at any one place in a poem is like witnessing the poet come to his or her own senses: you see a vivid and reasonable hallucination before you. Lorine Niedecker's Blackhawk Island, James McMichael's California, Frank O'Hara's Manhattan: "First / down the sidewalk / where laborers feed their dirty / glistening torsos sandwiches / and Coca-Cola, with yellow helmets / on." There goes another fading being under fading names, places, and events, but the aura is bright and alive to risk and rapidity. Place in a poem is more like a mercurial atmosphere of mind, arrived at by intuition and with uncertainty, but once there I think, "This could be no other planet."

———•———

We are in the early days of September in Wyoming. The landscape, so storied that at first everything seems to emerge from Central Casting, as it were: the long swell and fall of the mountain ranges, the grassy plains, the persistent clumps of sagebrush and rabbit-brush, the gang of horses, mice, voles, deer, rabbits, cows, snakes, and magpies. And the sky! The sky gives one a distinct sensation of clarity, but it is never reducible. The sunsets here appear as a magisterial ambassador for the passions. We check the weather obsessively, even if there isn't much change in the days, because it is its character to be full of portent—it seems to underlie everything, impatient to break through. And a full moon here is so immense, it absorbs all our contradictions without conflict; it is a wonderful poem.

———◦———

With what do we choose to relinquish our days: space or time? In writing poems, I've primarily been interested in what time does to a person, and I'm still figuring out its deep complicity with space. In a poem, the temporalities of retrospection and anticipation constantly recondition spaces. In Robert Hass' "Heroic Simile," a woodsman and his uncle are standing "in midforest / on a floor of pine silt and spring mud," waiting for the poet "to do something." He says that "The path from here to that village / is not translated" and concludes, "There are limits to the imagination." But the sense of mind that comes through for me is that of a hovering, a drift of potential—it doesn't seem as if the poet is only enacting unsayableness. Rather the poet has made a new space from all the possibilities of language, a place of access after all.

———◦———

Place also strips down to nameless space in some poems. Arthur Rimbaud writes, "I have recovered it. / What? Eternity. / It is the sea / Matched with the sun." The poem's referent is the inwardness that the poem creates or enlarges in the reader. And there is something cool and slightly remote about this space, it speaks of a realism that does something other than represent reality.

———◦———

Still, looking at those mountains or the moon with no man-made lights around for miles makes me feel a sort of reversal of John Ruskin's pathetic fallacy in which he holds that artists attribute human emotions to nature. Maybe the impassiveness of nature around me will productively dwarf my own small and large depressions for a little while, my own human nature, and lend me some much-needed *sangfroid*. There is, in this, something about wanting to let go of my own grinding and unreliable will, and let form—and a new impression of space—arise of its own accord. You can call up emotions with shapes and sounds, no matter how abstract those shapes and sounds appear to be. I warm to the notion that this landscape could make some of my speculations clearer to me.

———— • ————

With a new place can come new instincts. Right now, in this becalmed space, in this state which feels like a large American theme of some sort, I ultimately feel humored by the world. Even knowing that time and the mountains will go on without me, it's becoming more and more interesting to become more and more earthly. This new setting inspires a spectral thrill of transience in me. It's neither happy nor sad. The day waxes denser, and it grows lighter and lighter in my room. Here I sit, a faded being, under faded leaves, trying to make poems. What I feel plainly now is the lonely accident of my being here to see those unsolvable mountains in the distance.

TROUBLE & CONSOLATION: WRITING THE GAY RURAL

Bruce Snider

There are…two great themes in rural writing: the theme of departure and the theme of return.

David R. Pichaske

THE FIRST GAY MAN I knew was the undertaker. Mr. Dorsey owned our town's one funeral home, a small red brick building to the right of the library and across from a beauty shop called *Dazzle*. From the library's circulation desk, you could catch a glimpse of a zip-bagged body unloaded from a white van or sometimes see Mr. Dorsey outside in his black suit, with his thin dark mustache and perfect white teeth, sweeping up cigarette butts after a service. Mr. Dorsey had grown up in my town, studied mortuary science at a nearby college. When his father retired from the family business, he inherited it. Which is to say: once you died, you went to the town queer.

———— ◆ ————

The first gay love poem I read was Frank O'Hara's "Having a Coke with You." I was a college freshman, and I came across it in a book of gay love poetry in the library's new arrivals section. I don't remember the title, but the cover showed two shirtless men leaning toward each other beside a vibrantly blue swimming pool. I hid the book under a stack of magazines and read it on the top floor in a tucked away corner behind some engineering journals. I remember the stab of excitement I felt from the ease of O'Hara's voice: "because of my love for you" and, as he says later, "the fact that you move so beautifully." How could one man be saying this to another, and with such manic excitement in a "warm New York 4 o'clock light"? There were references I didn't understand—"futurism," "the Frick," "Nude Descending a Staircase"—but reading O'Hara's language was like overhearing one side of a conversation that somehow, without even knowing, I'd always wanted to join.

Afraid to check out the book, I copied down the poem on a piece of torn notebook paper. Folded in my pocket, I carried it everywhere—to class, to the library, even back home where weekends I'd help cut wood for my grandparent's furnace. Sometimes alone in the grove at the back of their farm, I'd take it out and read it to myself, a poem in my handwriting but not by me, and feel for a moment that I *was* O'Hara: chatty, sophisticated, fearlessly reaching out to take another man's hand. I'd hear the roar of the chainsaw, see the red scatter of cardinals, smell sheep feed and crushed hickory leaves underfoot; but I could still picture his urbane world of New York art and art museums, of afternoon light I'd never seen cutting across concrete, steel skyscrapers, subway stops. It was the beginning of two impressions that would only deepen the more I read. The first was that if you were gay, you needed to live in the city. The second was that if you were gay and wanted to be a writer, you needed to *write* about the city.

———◆———

I grew up in a small Indiana town famous for a 70-pound cantaloupe grown by a man named Verlie Tucker. We had a roller rink, a KFC, a pair of rival grocery stores with a jail in between. In the summer we ate deep-fried Mars Bars at the annual 4-H Festival, where we watched swine-judging and poultry showmanship competitions. Afterwards we'd crowd at picnic tables outside the new Dairy Queen, blaring Hank Williams Jr. or The Oak Ridge Boys. All around us, all the time, were fields of corn, soybeans, wheat; and the population was booming, nearly 2000 at the start of '82.

Ten miles outside town, my family lived on a lake where we snagged bluegill and perch. On my grandparents' nearby farm, we shoveled manure, chopped wood, helped my grandmother churn butter, and some days I'd get to feed Napoleon, my grandfather's champion market goat. When chores were done, my brothers and I would play in the woods, where we built forts, played tree tag, war, hide and seek. I had my first kiss in those woods, from a neighbor boy who smelled like wood smoke and wore a T-shirt with a fading iron-on of Darth Vader. We were both thirteen, safe in the crisscross of shadows cast by the shagbark hickories surrounding us. We never talked about it, but we started sneaking away to meet there, keeping an eye out for his older sister or my little brothers. Leaning against a rusted-out wheelbarrow, we never thought about where we were, but if we'd closed our eyes, we'd have noticed the whir of mosquitoes above our heads and woodpeckers knocking the trees and the constant churning of my grandfather's tiller, far beyond us in the back acre.

———— ◆ ————

The earliest poems I wrote about gay love or desire were set in vague unnamed cities with subways and skyscrapers, club-going drag queens, strangers cruising in dark, cavernous bars. This was, I assumed, what gay life was about, so I decorated each poem with the set pieces I'd found in the work of gay writers I admired. In addition to O'Hara, I'd read Mark Doty's "63rd Street Y," ("The nude black man two windows over / is lying in bed [...]"). I'd read Tim Dlugos' "Summer, South Brooklyn," ("gusher in the street where bald men with cigars / watch as boys in gym shorts and no shirts / crack the hydrant") as well as James Schuyler's "This Dark Apartment" ("[...] I lived / on East 49th, first / with Frank and then with John, / we had a lovely view of / the UN building and the /Beekman Towers. They were / not my lovers, though").

Only years later would I read Mark Wunderlich's "Take Good Care of Yourself," but it captures much of what I imagined back then. The poem opens in The Roxy, Chelsea's legendary gay bar, where the drag queen onstage is "all black lacquer / and soprano laugh," where "the one bitter pill / of X-tasy dissolving on my tongue is the perfect / slender measure of the holy ghost." What's especially striking, however, is that, midway through the poem, the speaker suddenly imagines himself outside the club, outside the city entirely:

> There's no place like the unbearable ribbon
> of highway that cuts the Midwest into two unequal
> halves, a pale sun glowing like the fire
> of one last cigarette. It is the prairie
> I'm scared of, barreling off in all directions
>
> flat as its inhabitants' A's and O's. I left
> Wisconsin's well-tempered rooms
> and snow-fields white and vacant as a bed
> I wish I'd never slept in. Winters
> I stared out the bus window through frost
>
> at an icy template of what the world offered up—
> the moon's tin cup of romance and a beauty,
> that if held too long to the body
> would melt.

Here—as in so much of the gay writing I read back then—the rural, if it ever appears, is fleeting. It's the past, what's left behind, full of emptiness and regret, where love and beauty can never last, where a gay man can never belong as the speaker belongs, if only briefly, to the dance club, shirtless in "a sea of men all muscle, / white briefs and pearls" while "whole cities of sound" bear down on him.

———•———

A few miles from the funeral home past the fairgrounds, Mr. Dorsey lived with Mr. Metzger, a red-haired man from Ohio known for breeding Plymouth Rock chickens. Mr. Dorsey and Mr. Metzger never held hands in public or kissed each other, never came out publicly, but they were together, a fact understood by everyone, as certain as the corn fields and creeks, the feed trucks that zoomed past the farms up State Road 101. They were, as I'd heard people say, "Dorsey and that other queer who live off Bear Road." High school kids toilet papered their maple trees, soaped their car windows with *Fag* and *Up the Ass*. Even my math teacher, Mr. Miller, imitated Mr. Dorsey, his voice veering toward falsetto as his wrists went limp. His favorite punishment for boys: make them stand in front of the class and hold hands. *Shape up*, he'd say, *or I'll send you to that funeral home.*

When I entered sixth grade, Mr. Metzger became my geography teacher. Stocky and square-jawed, he'd stand at the black board, smoothing his red beard, a thumb-sized nugget of Skoal chewing tobacco in his lower lip. He opened each class with a new geography joke: *What did Dela-ware? A New Jersey.* Or, *Where do crayons go on vacation? Color-ado.* He loved maps and collected old ones of Scotland, England, and Ireland; he'd spread them out on the floor for us to walk around, reading out: *Cork, Waxford, Dublin*. Sometimes he'd tell us stories about the chickens he raised, how they stampeded the coop door, how he nursed the sick ones with an eyedropper.

He never mentioned Mr. Dorsey. But sometimes, in his wood-paneled, windowless classroom, I would try to imagine them at home, sitting across from each other at the kitchen table, side by side on the couch. What did they talk about? What did an average day look like, home from work, dishes drying in the dish rack? Did their coats hang one on top the other on pegs near the entry? I wondered if other towns nearby had their Mr. Dorseys and Mr. Metzgers. Could the gas station attendant in Merriam be harboring a secret? Was the check out boy in love with the bearded man who carried my Aunt's groceries?

Once, between classes, I saw Mr. Metzger give Kevin McEntire, an eighth grader with ripped jeans and heavy metal hair, detention for talking in class. As Kevin turned to leave the classroom, he said, *Fag*, under his breath. *What did you say?* Mr. Metzger asked. Kevin shrugged, said nothing, then Mr. Metzger grabbed him by the neck and threw him against the wall. *Say it again*, he said, *what did you say?* His hand trembled around Kevin's neck. Mrs. Hunt, the Home Ec teacher, leaned out of her classroom, looking into the hall. Kevin burst into tears and Mr. Metzger, finally, let him go. The bell rang, and I ran to class.

The next year, Mr. Metzger was gone. He quit teaching to open a plant nursery across from the pharmacy. Sometimes I'd see him out front in green overalls watering flats of tomato plants, carrying plastic bags of fertilizer. He grew flowers in a small greenhouse, a steady stream of carnations, white roses, lilies that each week he gave to Mr. Dorsey, who arranged them inside the funeral home, spring through winter, around the bodies of the newly dead.

———◆———

In her essay "The Gay Sublime," the poet and scholar Linda Gregerson identifies "an American canon" of poetry by gay writers that reconfigures and essentially queers the notion of the

Romantic sublime. Unlike the natural landscapes that spurred the recollections of Wordsworth and Coleridge, however, the landscape of this canon, she writes, "is urban; its characteristic vistas are the intricate fields of social nuance, material surface, manners, wit, and cultivated artifice." It's an observation that in some ways echoes "Late Victorians," Richard Rodriguez's essay about San Francisco architecture and AIDS. Since society has long rejected homosexuality as a sin against nature, Rodriguez speculates that historically "homosexuals have made a covenant against nature. Homosexual survival lay in artifice, in plumage, in lampshades, sonnets, musical comedy, couture, syntax, religious ceremony, opera, lacquer, irony [...]" For both Gregerson and Rodriguez, the emphasis is on a mastery of surfaces, on the cultivated and urbane.

To support her observations, Gregerson looks at, among other poems, Mark Doty's "Crepe De Chine," in which he writes, "That's what I want from the city: / to wear it." In one line, he fuses the urban and, as Gregerson describes it, "the aesthetics of drag." In fact, the conflation of homosexuality and the city undergirds much of Mark Doty's poetry. One of the most celebrated and influential gay writers of his generation, Doty used the names of cities as titles for three of his earliest collections, *Bethlehem in Broad Daylight*, *My Alexandria* and *Atlantis*. And the city as metaphor recurs throughout his work. His poem "Homo Will Not Inherit," for example, describes a man the speaker picks up in the gay baths, then turns outward:

> [...] This failing city's
> radiant as any we'll ever know
> paved with oily rainbow, charred gates
>
> jeweled with tags, swoops of letters,
> over letters, indecipherable as anything
> written by desire. I'm not ashamed

to love Babylon's scrawl. How could I be?
It's written on my face as much as on
these walls. This city's inescapable,

gorgeous, and on fire. I have my kingdom.

Here, Doty makes the city into the preeminent metaphor for queer desire. It's Babylon redeemed, "Paved with oily rainbow, charred gates / jeweled with tags," "gorgeous" even as it burns to ash.

————◆————

In my senior year at Indiana University, I took a class on the literature of rural America. Our main text was *Late Harvest: Rural American Writing*, edited by David R. Pichaske. In the introduction, Pichaske observes that Americans have from the beginning attached "a peculiar *moral* [his emphasis] glory to the countryside."

> [...] our national experience has something to do with America's impulse toward the rural. While most of the world's population lives rural lives, Americans especially have, until very recently, lived country, on farms, in villages, and even in the wilderness. For a long time we congratulated ourselves for being an agrarian people. Nineteenth-century Americans, weary of complacent Frenchmen and Brits proclaiming that an unhealthy climate and bad diet made Americans sickly and both physically and mentally underdeveloped, had formulated a contrary argument: urban (European) man, enfeebled by what William Blake called 'the mind-forg'd manacles' (of London, in Blake's case), would, transplanted in the American wilderness, grow healthy and robust— spiritually, mentally, and physically.

When I first read this passage, I was a twenty-one-year-old who had just come out to his father over Christmas break, so it seemed ironic that as we made our way through the anthology, I didn't encounter a single writer or character that I could've identified as gay.

Although I understood Pichaske was arguing for a rural literature defined in part by a generalized moral virtue that was itself rooted in American nationalism, I couldn't help but wonder if the omission of gay voices in his rural canon gestured toward a more pointed claim, that the "moral glory" of the American countryside somehow prevented, or at least denied, the existence of gay men and women. And yet I'd grown up in a world much like those described by the anthology's authors: Sherwood Anderson, Garrison Keillor, Gary Snyder, Bobbie Ann Mason, Thoreau, Wallace Stegner, and more. Like William Gass in "In the Heart of the Heart of the Country," I'd seen trucks weighed on grain scales, the wind "blowing the smell of cattle into town." I'd even watched, behind my own childhood home, a "tremulous ripple thrill the water" as a muskrat kit emerged "paddling from its den" (Annie Dillard, "Seeing"). I could imagine these worlds vividly, but the anthology seemed incapable of imagining people like Mr. Dorsey and Mr. Metzger, people like me. Despite this, of course, I knew that gay people lived in rural America, and as I was beginning to understand, always had.

A year later, I came out to my grandparents. *You're not the first in our family*, my grandfather said. He told me about his Aunt Charlotte and her best friend Bonnie, who'd lived together in a small house five miles from the family farm. They were avid poker players, famously good cooks, and staunch Democrats who once refused to shop at a bait store with a picture of then President Eisenhower on the wall. When my grandfather took them fishing, as he did each summer, Bonnie often fell asleep with her head on Aunt Charlotte's lap. *Nobody ever said it*, he told me. *Didn't need to.*

———— ◆ ————

In *Object Lessons* the poet Eavan Boland writes that "what we call place is really only that detail of which we understand to be ourselves." If that's true, I can say that my early years as a writer were spent uncertain how to claim the details of myself in the small area of northern Indiana where I'd grown up. How could a gay poet claim his sexuality in a so-called "natural" landscape if, as Rodriguez has argued, what we consider to be the aesthetic of contemporary homosexuality is urban, predicated on a resistance to the natural? How could he render his first same-sex kiss if it happened near the buckshot-dented water barrels at the back barn? Coming of age as I did in the shadows of poets like Frank O'Hara and Mark Doty, it was difficult not to internalize the growing tension between what I perceived as the language of "legitimate" gay culture and the language of the place where I was born. As another gay writer once said to me, "Nobody wants to read about some queer milking a cow."

In the end, my literary coming of age involved a search for works that challenged these assumptions, a kind of shadow canon that hadn't been included in what I'd been taught. I discovered Don Schueler's memoir, *A Handmade Wilderness*, about a gay, interracial couple in 1968 who bought eighty backwoods acres in southern Mississippi. I read Jim Grimsley's gay-themed rural novels, *Winter Birds* and *Dream Boy* as well as, long before it became an award-winning movie, Annie Proulx's "Brokeback Mountain." Though I'd been taught Whitman as a poet of 19th century New York City, I found passages that celebrate love between men in a natural world: "To cotton-field drudge or cleaner of privies I lean, / On his right cheek I put the family kiss." I discovered James Wright's poem, "Sappho," about a rural woman's love for a married woman, as well as Adrienne Rich's, "For Julia in Nebraska," which contains the lines: "for Willa Cather, lesbian, / whose letters were burnt in shame." These works, I learned, existed, but weren't widely anthologized, weren't part of how I'd been encouraged to imagine what it meant to be rural or gay.

One essential discovery was the poet James L. White, also born and reared in Indiana, and the author of a single volume of poetry, *The Salt Ecstasies*, originally published in 1983 and out of print for decades until it was reissued by Graywolf press in 2010. Many gay poets—Mark Doty among them—have hailed White as a pioneer of contemporary gay poetry because of his early and frank depiction of love and desire between men. What particularly struck me when I first read his work, however, was that this frank expression of sexuality was located in a landscape that I knew well. Although the poems aren't entirely rural, erotic longing is paired with glimpses of the agrarian Midwest: "I leave you first in sleep," writes White, "[...] then take the early bus to Laurel / away from the raw and nameless // Some farm kid presses against my leg. / I look at the long backs of men in the fields / and doze to dream you're going through me / like winter bone [...]" ("The Salt Ecstasies"). Throughout the poems, his lovers aren't gym-sculpted Adonis-es from gay bath houses; they're working class men—a "guy who hauled parts for a living" ("The First Time"), or a man who fills "the room with gasoline smell from [his] overalls" ("Making Love to Myself"). White's was not the urban gay world modeled by poets I admired deeply, but couldn't fully enter. It was a world I knew first hand, had grown up in, and finally, it seemed, might be able to reclaim for myself.

———◆———

It's taken a couple decades but more gay writers are beginning to claim their rural Americas. Michael Walsh, one such young poet, won the 2011 Lambda Literary Award for his first book, *The Dirt Riddles*, which includes "Haying the Fields," "Morning Milkings," and "Barn Clothes." Among these renderings of Midwest farm life, there's, "Wish," which opens:

> When I kiss him, weed sour
> and tomato green

after hours in this garden,
I taste the darkness
suspended between bone and skin,
the loam and manure
we eat through bright leaves.

In Walsh's hands, the language of the farm—"weed," "tomato,"
"loam," "manure"—becomes the language of queer desire, an
embodiment of Salman Rushdie's claim that "description is itself
a political act," that "redescribing a world is the necessary first
step towards changing it."

I've long wondered if given the chance, what particular rural
America would men like Mr. Dorsey and Mr. Metzger have
described? We're at a point where more gay writers have begun
to complicate our myth of open farmland, heterosexual masculine
knowhow, and pioneer spirit that stretches back to our country's
origins, and which has gone on to be recorded and revised by
generations of American writers. As queer icon Dorothy Gale
from the *Wizard of Oz* shows us, a journey to the Emerald City
only returns you to Kansas. All roads lead back home.

———————•———————

Visiting Indiana almost a year ago, I went one night for a drive
and found myself by chance on Bear Road, passing wheat fields,
crumbling barns, until I reached the house where Mr. Dorsey and
Mr. Metzger lived. I hadn't seen them for almost twenty years.
I'd heard that Mr. Metzger retired, but could still be seen some
days helping Mr. Dorsey at the funeral home. I stopped for a
moment in front of their driveway. A small chicken coop lay to
the right beside an old unpainted barn hunkered in shadow. The
porch bulb lit up a red windsock hanging slack near the front
door. Their curtains were drawn, but I saw shapes pass behind the
lit windows. I sat in my car wondering if the two of them could
ever know how much they once consoled and troubled me. Their

presence had assured me I wasn't alone, yet I feared my fate was to become them—subject of smirks and eye rolls, the town joke. What I couldn't imagine then was what it was to *be* them, what they endured, what pleasures and duties kept them there. What would've happened if I'd had the courage to ask? What would they have said to me, a boy they might have barely noticed, a boy so hungry to understand his world through the books he read?

After college, I returned home for short visits to see my family. I moved to Austin, Texas; briefly New York, then Washington DC, San Francisco, always looking for that city I'd imagined as a young man. But all the while I carried with me my memory of the aluminum fish shed beside the cattail-lined lake, the vinegar stink of sheep manure mixed with tractor fumes, even Mr. Dorsey and Mr. Metzger feeding chickens, staking their claims on the vast distance between official history and the more complicated past. I'd like to believe that one day they'll be buried together in the cemetery off Route 9, but all I know is that eventually they'll vanish from the landscape sharing the voice of Percival Sharp, one of the talking dead from Edgar Lee Masters' *Spoon River Anthology*: "I stirred certain vibrations in Spoon River / Which are my true epitaph, more lasting than stone."

Note: names and some details have been changed to protect the privacy of people in this essay.

GHOST TOWNS

Nick Lantz

The Battlefield

THE YEAR I SPENT in Gettysburg, Pennsylvania, was a year surrounded by battlefields—expansive, rolling meadows peppered with statues and stone monuments commemorating the fighting that took place there July 1-3, 1863. By the time I arrived, the National Park Service had already expended a great deal of effort and money to restore these sites to their period state, buying up land and clearing away modern buildings and crops. It was not unusual, when running errands in town, to cross paths with a reenactor, dressed in Union blue or Confederate gray, on his way to some historical society event. The town's penchant for historicity meant that many older buildings, even those not directly involved in the battle, were kept as "authentic" as possible, and when walking through the town, I often had the sense of being pulled back and forth through time. Seeing a man dressed as Lincoln eating a burrito at one of the local Mexican restaurants was a jarring experience, but fascinating too. My wife and I availed ourselves to frequent tours of the battlefields—by car, by bus, even by Segway—and in November attended the

Remembrance Day parade, in which hundreds of volunteers form regiments and march through town in full costume. As a poet, it was impossible not to feel the various dissonances the battlefield evoked, and it got me thinking about a poetics that begins in ghostliness.

A Poetics of Ghostliness

Quickly, a few premises on haunting: ghosts are, by their nature, self-contradictory. They occupy a space that ignores our accustomed dichotomies of the material and the immaterial, of life and death, of imagination and reality. To see a ghost would be to confront the insufficiency of such dualities. We feel a ghost as a presence that we cannot explain or define or categorize but that we nonetheless cannot deny ("I might not this believe," says Horatio, "without the sensible and true avouch of mine own eyes"). Ghosts are the unreal made real. They represent the infiltration of the unknown (and unknowable), the chaotic and the mystical, into mundane life. It is precisely this cognitive and emotional dissonance that makes ghosts so alarming, so uncanny. Their existence, even hypothetically, compromises our understanding of what it means to exist. And though we cannot account for them, we must. Ghosts come in many shapes and forms, but if they have rules, one seems to be that they are confined to their particular places: houses, roads, cemeteries. A haunt after all, is a place. No surprise, then, that poets seeking to invoke the dead, to write poems that haunt us, often begin with a location.

A poetics of ghostliness is one that draws on the self-contained contradictions of the subject, eliciting an irreconcilable unease. What is absent but somehow present, visible but occluded, past but present. And because *place* possesses an inherent stability that can act as a foil to various forms of loss and change, it figures prominently in many poems one might describe as haunted. Place endures. Its features may be altered or destroyed, but our connection to it transcends such effacements. A childhood home, a neighborhood, a city, a whole civilization may be wiped away, but its coordinates remain. In Jesse Lee Kercheval's poem "The Hotel Where My Family Used to Stay," the hotel is razed by fire, but it is precisely the building's absence from its proper place that triggers the poem's cascading imagery of haunting loss: "our cat, closing its mad gold eyes, / my family, father, mother, sister, lost army marching into the sea." It is thus often what is missing from a place—the juxtaposition of endurance and loss—that makes it ghostly.

Haunted Houses

Why might particular places encourage poets to notice ghosts, or seek them out? The intimacy of domestic spaces charges those sites with a human imprint, transforming them into an index of former inhabitants' lives: layers of wallpaper under wallpaper, scratches on a door jamb recording a child's changing height, the painted-over holes where family pictures hung, patterns worn into the carpet. When my wife and I moved into our turn-of-the-century row house in Gettysburg, I found an older woman's robe hanging on the back of the bathroom door, some balled-up Kleenex still in the pockets. Simply touching the garment felt improper, as if I were violating this woman's privacy.

Kate Northrop's "The First House" demonstrates the unease evoked by this sort of ghostliness. In the poem, the detritus of a home's former inhabitants "keeps surfacing." The speaker rattles off nuisances that might plague anyone living in an old building, including a yard whose soil is full of "mirror shards, bits of brick," and—abruptly plunging the poem into ghostliness—"a ring engraved *Cherise*." The annoying garbage suddenly has a name, which is not an insignificant fact. In Northrop's book (*Things Are Disappearing Here*, her second collection), the living are not named, and in this poem, we already know more about a dead girl than we do about the current inhabitant of the house, the speaker of the poem. The inclusion of "First" in the poem's title suggests that, at best, the speaker's life in the house is secondary to the lives of its first inhabitants, lives that continually reassert themselves. Here, the living are not just overrun by the artifacts of the dead; they are overshadowed by an image of the dead conjured by those artifacts. And as the poem progresses, that image deepens and grows more alarming. The speaker's neighbor asks,

> [...] do we know
>
> about the girl? the alley? Do we know
>   what people find in outhouses
>
> like ours, out back? She drops her voice. So *sad*,
>   those limbs, those infants
>   *pitched in*

When we hear "the girl," we ought of course to think of that ring, of Cherise, though it's just as likely the two have nothing to do with one another, historically speaking. But that one identifying, humanizing detail has primed us to read the remainder of the poem in a particular way. Without it, the image of infants "pitched in" the outhouse pit might come off as merely grotesque, gratuitous. But instead, a narrative coalesces around the artifact of the engraved ring, found buried gravelike in soil behind the house, and the image of a discarded infant becomes more particular, and therefore more vivid, more deeply suggestive. The presence of the dead in this poem has become, well, larger than life. That presence makes its final incursion in the last lines of the poem, when the neighbor warns the speaker of an underground creek beneath the property: if rains flood the cellar, they'll have "scattering / in the kitchen—silverfish for days." The image of subterranean water occurs elsewhere in the book: in "The Visitor" ("I am waiting, // at the sink / with my hands under the spigot, under the water drawn / from darkness / into the order of the house") and in "Her

Apology, and Lament" ("A knock at the door. / It's the water rising in the basement. / It's your mother, Regina."). Such water is an infiltration of chaos into the world of order, and in "The First House," that chaos is the echo of the dead, which refuses to fade. Just as the image of the ring primes a reading of the discarded infants, so too do those infants prime us to read the infestation of silverfish not merely as an unfortunate accident of nature but as the dead reasserting their claim on the world of the living. One can scarcely imagine a more fitting envoy of the underworld than a silverfish—of perhaps any insect, they are the most unsettling to encounter. They are otherworldly. Spooky. Ghostly.

In Cynthia Marie Hoffman's "In Dresden, a Wall Without a House," the house in question is no longer occupied, but the poem begins by describing similar domestic ephemera (a rug, a piano, dresses on their hangers in the closet), etching them in images even as they subside back into smoke, ash, memory. From the 21st century, the speaker imagines a carriage pulling up to the house as if it were still 1945, and "In the windows, / three stories high, six white ghosts stand at attention." The poem pulls us back and forth between the sedate present, where "No one is screaming," and the firebombing that destroyed the house decades earlier. When a passing child looks the speaker in the eye, she wonders, "What can I say to her?" This disturbance, this need to explain the ghostliness of this place, drives the poem. The nearby clock tower may have "a new golden face," but there is still "a chill in the air." The ruined domestic setting of the poem makes the losses feel humanly personal, but the connection to World War II connects us to a broader sense of public disaster.

From Ground Zero to Ninth Ward

As a site charged by absence and tragedy, it's certainly no surprise that Ground Zero would become a locus of poetic elegy and ghostliness, though poets have handled this hauntedness in different ways. Molly Peacock's "The Land of the Shi" transposes a mythical world over Manhattan, one in which everyday details are hypervivid ("All green is Green"; the rain is "silkier"). Here, ghostliness is palliative, "running water" that the "detritus" of ash and suffering can "vanish beneath." Kimiko Hahn's Boerum Hill tankas show New Yorkers struggling in a liminal space between normality and fear: "Once an afternoon for groceries, it is still an afternoon for groceries—and a fear once called the bridge, the stray suitcase, the rental truck parked too long on the corner." Here, the ghostliness is terrifying. But both poems trade on the doubleness of New York after 9/11.

Yusef Komunyakaa's "The Towers" begins by asserting that those who died in the 9/11 attacks are "dead, but not gone," a familiar formulation of ghostliness in self-contained contradiction. He goes on to show us the dead in life through a montage of their former actions: eating melon, looking up through a skylight, handing some coins to a homeless vet. These images are undercut by our knowledge that their subjects are lost to us, many of them literally disintegrated, accessible only through memory and imagination. Komunyakaa arranges the poem in two narrow columns—twin towers—of text, one of assent and one of denial (they begin with "Yes" and "No," respectively), physically embodying both the literal site of the World Trade Center and the opposing features that constitute the poem's ghostliness (affirmation and denial, acceptance and refusal, living and dying). Many elegies struggle to reconcile themselves to the reality of death, but poems about death on a massive, sudden, public scale tend to be particularly defined by bewilderment. If ghostliness of place is the disorienting sense of irreversible change encountered within a fixed moment in space and time, then destruction on a massive scale only heightens this sensation. It can be jarring, after all, to return to a familiar neighborhood years later and see new shops gone up, old buildings repainted. Even such small changes may provoke existential pangs. To witness structures as prominent as the towers (and the lives contained therein) so swiftly and violently erased—there, then gone, and yet somehow still there—eludes comprehension. "Nothing," Komunyakaa writes, "held together anymore":

> [...] few now believed
> their own feet touched the ground.
> Signed deeds and promissory notes
> floated over the tangled streets.
> [...]
> The cash registers stopped on
> decimal points, in a cloud bank
> of dead cell phones and dross.

Our fundamental sense of physical orientation and alignment comes unglued. The legal framework dependent on a predictable future is turned to meaningless chaff. The gridded streets indicative of our civil order become a tangle leading nowhere. Our sense of precision and communication breaks down into a fog, a mound of rubbish.

Nicole Cooley's "Four Studies of the Afterlife" evinces a similar bewilderment in the aftermath of Hurricane Katrina. The ghostliness of the New Orleans landscape after the storm unnerves her:

> You and your mother drive and drive and she shows you
> this Familiar, overturned. This Reversed.
>
> This Inside Out. This Unfixed. After water
> she explains, there is no water.

Because place endures continuously, both pre- and post-Katrina New Orleans coexist for the speaker. She can't disentangle what was from what is, and the result is a haunting paradox: water everywhere, but no water. Throughout the poem, she tries to find (or make) sense of what has happened. Looking at a rack of pants in a ruined clothing store, she exclaims, "How you want it to tell a fortune!" A massive pile of tree limbs becomes "a brain, / sliced and / scanned and ready / for dissection," but before we can learn its secrets, it becomes a tangle of hair from a brush. Similarly, a shower stall in a flooded home is likened to a body a surgeon might open, explore, repair—this too, though, is revealed to be a fantasy, as when in childhood she "tried / to climb inside the books my mother read to me." If it wasn't already clear, the line break on *tried* underscores the impossibility of such attempts of comprehension. While place can provide a connection to what we've lost, it can't heal that rift. Rather, it exacerbates it. The fixedness of place gives us the illusion that the features of a place are similarly fixed. The realization that this isn't so—that the natural and human contents of a site can be rubbled and swept away—is what makes the dissonance of ghostliness so haunting. It troubles our sense of balance, order, and justice.

Spirits of America

If one trope of ghosts is that they are connected or limited to particular places, another is that they are often aggrieved victims of wrongdoing. Such ghosts are spirits of conscience, the rattling reminder of injustices that the living fail to reconcile or even acknowledge. If a ghost has a purpose, that is often it. They seek witness for their grievances—grievances we may be implicated in. So we remain silent. But it is in the absence of justice that ghosts appear: they howl from our silence.

Lucille Clifton's poem "at the cemetery, walnut grove plantation, south carolina, 1989" enacts this sort of invocation, as she calls to the dead slaves buried there:

> among the rocks
> at walnut grove
> your silence drumming
> in my bones,
> tell me your names.

It is not simply that these people are dead that makes them ghostly—rather, they contain contradictory qualities (*silent*, yet *drumming*), and that dissonance alarms the speaker, haunts her. She repeatedly begs the dead to speak, though of course they cannot. The poem's tension hangs on the contrast between what is left unsaid versus what is known: "nobody mentioned slaves," Clifton writes, "and yet the curious tools / shine with your fingerprints." This place quietly insists on a truth in the face of silence. The identities of the slaves have been omitted, and the speaker wryly points out that "the inventory lists ten slaves / but only men were recognized"—further omissions, further erasures, have obscured not just the names of the male slaves but the very existence of the women. The poem culminates in a repetition:

> here lies
> here lies
> here lies
> here lies
> hear

Clifton extends the poem's ghostliness in this moment by playing on opposing double meanings. The phrase "here lies" locates the deception of the slaves' erasure but at the same time reasserts their presence. Clifton dispenses with the more diplomatic "nobody mentioned" in favor of the more blunt "lies." The omission of the slaves' identities is not an unfortunate historical oversight but part of a larger, deliberate, ongoing machinery of racial erasure. The human identity of the slaves was an inconvenient fact not only for the antebellum plantation owners but continues to be so for contemporary whites who would prefer to declare such ugliness over and done with.

In 1994, Susan Smith murdered her two young sons by rolling her car into a lake with the boys trapped in the backseat. She told police that a black man had stolen the car and driven off with the children, a fiction that persisted until her confession nine days later. Cornelius Eady's *Brutal Imagination* posits a speaker who is "the young black man / Susan Smith claimed / kidnapped her children," a speaker whose very existence is defined by white imagination and fear, an existence that encompasses mutually exclusive and constantly shifting features—a ghost. In "Composite," he warns us:

> I am here, and here I am not.
> I am a door that opens, and out walks
> No-one-can-help-you.
> [...]
> I might tumbleweed onto a pant leg.
> You can stare, and stare, but I can't be found.

And, in "What I'm Made Of":

> Nothing fits upon my back.
> Nothing actually catches my eye,
> I am hidden and found,
> I am North, South, East, West,
> My dark skin porous and in-between.

The speaker's ghostliness is entangled with his race. Like the unnamed slaves in Clifton's cemetery, Eady's speaker also represents a form of racial erasure, though this might seem counterintuitive. After all, as he says, "Susan has loosed me on the neighbors." She *has* asserted his existence, but that existence is defined by an anonymity that effaces and subsumes all black men at the whim of white imagination. In "Next of Kin," the police arrest a man "They thought looked like me," and Smith has "lent me / His cheekbones, / His gait." There is no detail about the speaker that can't be adapted for the convenience of Smith's account.

Amid all this contrived ambiguity, however, are a few fixed points. Like any ghost, Eady's speaker is tethered to a place: John D. Long Lake, where Smith's car and dead children lie submerged. References to the lake nag at the edges of the story. "I rustle like wind upon / the surface of a lake," the speaker says in "What The Sheriff Suspects." The lake is a stable reality, held temporarily at a distance by a collective fiction:

> Looking for Michael and Alex means
> That the bushes have not whispered,
> That the trees hold only shade
> That the lake still insists on being a lake.

The entire sequence of poems trades on this tension: we *know* the boys are dead, that the speaker doesn't exist, even as he describes the real-life witnesses who claim to have encountered him at hotels and gas stations. But the dissonance between reality and fantasy is unsustainable, and so, fittingly, the sequence's final poem, "Birthing," returns to the irremediable fact of the lake at the moment of the speaker's creation:

> I'm not me, yet.
> [...]
> My muscles aren't her muscles,
> Burned from pushing.
> The lake has no appetite,
> But it takes the car slowly,
> Swallow by swallow, like a snake.
> [...]
> Susan stares at the taillights
> As they slide from here
> To hidden.
> [...]

> She only has me,
> After she removes our hands
> from our ears.

Excerpts from Smith's confession are interspersed throughout this poem as well, but it's worth reiterating that the poem ends not with the speaker's evaporation but with his creation, the moment when Susan's hands become "our hands." The speaker is a particular ghost, connected to a particular criminal case in a specific place and time, but the resolution of that case does not resolve his ghostliness, because he is emblematic of an ongoing process of racial erasure not limited to Susan Smith or South Carolina or the twentieth century. What's so damning about these poems is the ease with which Smith's fiction works. It's a fiction that depends on the preexisting and pervasive racial fears of white imagination. And just as Clifton doubles the meaning of "here lies" to both assert the identities of the dead and implicate those who have erased them, so too can we read the closing lines of Eady's poem in two senses. First, that Smith has blocked out the cries of her drowning children and in so doing has displaced her guilt onto her created ghost. "[O]ur," in this sense, refers only to the speaker and Smith. But an alternative reading is that the first-person plural—that slippery pronoun—includes and implicates Eady's readers, or Americans more broadly, or white Americans in particular. In this sense, "we" have been deliberately insensate to the ongoing injustices of racism, but the enactment of Smith's racist fantasy has opened "our" ears, if even briefly.

The "Walls"

Today, I live in Huntsville, Texas, a city famous as the resting place of Sam Houston (senator, governor, and president of Texas), but also as the site of the busiest death chamber in the United

States. Since 1982, more than 500 prisoners have been executed at the "Walls" Unit, an imposing red brick building in the middle of town. At the local Prison Museum just up the highway, one can view "Old Sparky," the electric chair that was, in an ugly twist, built by prisoners, and used from 1924 to 1964 in over 300 executions. The pauper's cemetery where the unclaimed bodies of inmates are still buried is known as Peckerwood Hill. Not surprisingly, Huntsville chooses to focus its historical boosterism on Sam Houston, though this is not without its own macabre moments: at the Sam Houston homestead, across the street from my campus, visitors can look in on the bedroom (and bed) in which Houston died. When I was interviewing for my job, I was given a tour of campus that ended with the performing arts center, where my guide and I looked in on a dance class on the top floor. A handful of men and women flexed and moved with an astonishing lightness. And though my guide did not point it out, through the high glass windows behind the dancers, I saw the death chamber, just three blocks away. Did the dancers consider this juxtaposition of their vitality with the machinery of death, I wondered as I watched them. Did they, in their own poetry, feel haunted?

UNPEOPLED EDENS

Rigoberto González

WITH EACH OF MY BOOKS I have become more interested in absence and silence, the painful evidence of loss. *Unpeopled Eden* explored this world through its ghosts. But I'd argue that their stories and therefore their lives continue to inhabit the spaces their bodies once occupied. I subscribe to the notion that land carries memory, so people are never truly gone, not with so many prints and impressions left behind. Our actions, positive and negative, become absorbed by the land. This is how we simultaneously nurture and poison the ground beneath our feet.

The ground that interests me particularly is of the Americas, and more specifically of the U.S.-Mexico border. The Chicana theorist Gloria Anzaldúa said it best in the opening chapter of *Borderlands / La Frontera*:

> The U.S.-Mexican border es una herida abierta where the Third World grates against the first and bleeds. And before a scab forms it hemorrhages again, the lifeblood of two worlds merging to form a third country—a border culture. Borders are set up to define the places that are

safe and unsafe, to distinguish *us* from *them*. A border is a dividing line, a narrow strip along a steep edge. A borderland is a vague and undetermined place created by the emotional residue of an unnatural boundary. It is in a constant state of transition. The prohibited and forbidden are its inhabitants. Los atravesados live here: the squint-eyed, the perverse, the queer, the troublesome, the mongrel, the mulato, the half-breed, the half-dead; in short, those who cross over, pass over, or go through the confines of the 'normal.'

By the time I came across this passage in college, I had experienced life on the border firsthand but had never thought to articulate it or thought that it merited language. Or rather, I didn't understand the border to be so complex because I could explain it to myself so simply. The border kept my people out and divided my family. Some of us had permission to cross it, others crossed it without permission. On a bad day the border was a burden. On a good one it was a gateway. But on any day it was an inconvenience, a stretch of suspicion, danger, and thirst. I had to uphold my family's negative view of the border out of loyalty and out of guilt because I was one of the lucky ones who had been born in the United States, who could cross without the fear of reprisals from the gatekeepers. My mother never shook the constant threat of deportation because she was an undocumented alien. My father never overcame the anxiety of losing his wife in one of those immigration sweeps that descended on the packinghouse workers only when they went on strike.

I recall those evenings at the small kitchen table with three chairs—the fourth was used to prop shut the broken refrigerator door. My father would come home drunk and my mother would cry and their grievances were expressed so openly that it embarrassed me. I'd close my eyes and question my mother's decision to cross the border when she was pregnant with me.

Maybe I *should* have been born in Mexico, not in California, and maybe that would have forced my father to quit drinking and stay home. Maybe there was a happiness we might have known, had my parents stayed in Michoacán that spring of 1970 instead of heading north. What did we have here in the promised land but money troubles and heartaches?

Those moments of sadness and the private sorrows of my parents followed me to the page when I began to imagine the landscape of the poems that would eventually compose *So Often the Pitcher Goes to Water until It Breaks*. I wasn't compelled to write biographical poems about my parents—I wouldn't be ready to write about their journeys until I began to write nonfiction many years later—but I did want to give my homesickness, my nostalgia, my memories different shapes and voices, so I created people who shared paths with my family and who, like my family, lived in that "third country" that Anzaldúa spoke of, a country defined by hard labor.

The border is a place where people work. And what created a demand for Mexican bodies in California was the agricultural business—the fruit and vegetable fields, the orchards, the groves, the packinghouses—they called upon the hands of Mexicans and blistered them, bloodied them, wore them down to scar tissue. I remember those hands on my father, on my grandmother, and that might have been the fate of mine had I not been fortunate enough to find my way to college. I owed my escape, my luck, to generations of damaged hands. My responsibility was to honor their stories with paper and ink—the only tools I knew.

The people in my poems work. They till the soil and harvest the land, but they also fix refrigerators, change bedsheets, pump gas, and sell trinkets on the streets. They're the working class, very much aware of what they have and what they don't. It is a class of hunger, desire, and want, and yet somehow there's also room for life and light. Anzaldúa calls this survival, perseverance, and hope. That's the ugly beauty of the border: it keeps promising and we keep believing; it keeps calling and we keep answering.

I declared *So Often the Pitcher Goes to Water until It Breaks* my love letter to Mexico and the border. I never worried about becoming sentimental in my verse because I witnessed too many teary scenes to name my experience happiness, let alone bliss. My family worked the gardens of Eden every day, and every day broke into a sweat to prove it. Where did the body end, and where did the land begin? The demarcation—the border—between the worker and the field was indistinguishable. This was a symbiotic relationship because one could not exist without the other and, therefore, one could not be imagined without the other. But there was nothing romantic about that bond since in the consciousness of the typical American both the agricultural fields and its laborers were invisible—a narrative that took place offstage. I became determined to bring that narrative back to the center so that my people could exercise their roles as protagonists.

By the time I began to write *Unpeopled Eden*, most of my family was already dead. My mother had died. So had my father. So had my grandparents. The border was still there but it had changed, certainly. It is in a constant state of transition. New stories were unfolding over the old ones. The living walked into ghosts. I felt a sense of urgency to look back once more and take a panoramic view of the border. I took in its expansive landmass but also its timelines, its history, its identity as home: *the prohibited and forbidden are its inhabitants.*

This time I did engage biographical material, since I consider *Unpeopled Eden* an elegy to my father. My father left Mexico to escape poverty, and he lived in poverty in the United States. He died poor. But I don't consider his dream unfulfilled because I'm his namesake, his firstborn, and the heir to his journey. It is because of what he did and did not do that I became the person I am. And so I returned to the border to unpack my birthright as a bordercrosser, an outsider, a dreamer, a laborer, a dead man who left much evidence behind of having lived and loved.

Writing those poems while living in New York City, I had to travel back twenty-eight hundred miles and twenty years. Once I arrived at the border I took another quantum leap back to 1948, to Los Gatos Canyon, the plane crash site that claimed the lives of twenty-eight deportees. I morphed into a Gila monster and spat out my haughty monologue. I kept a pillow book as I crossed the desert with a man I was secretly in love with. I visited the village of missing fathers and its terrible companion the village of missing sons. I took my place among ghosts and felt oddly at home. *Los atravesados live here: the squint-eyed, the perverse, the queer, the troublesome, the mongrel, the mulato, the half-breed, the half-dead; in short, those who cross over, pass over, or go through the confines of the "normal."*

It was that word—*queer*—that welcomed me. I was a U.S. citizen, a college graduate, an academic—I had pursued the typical middle-class American journey so successfully that I had forfeited my place in my working-class community. Except that in other ways I remained an outsider. As an artist. As a gay man. *Queer.* And none of my professional achievements had erased my Mexican identity, and certainly not the memories of poverty and struggle. I continued to be emotionally connected to the border. The visceral experience was still so palpable. I too had picked grapes, and onions, and green beans. The heat had burned right through my bones, and I imagined them charred inside my body. I not only remembered sand, I could still taste it. The smell of sulfur was unforgettable. I had taken myself out of the border, but the border had not taken itself out of me. All I had to do to access the landscape was to listen to my own body—the desert in my breath, the heat in my blood. And then there were the ghosts.

Ghosts are stubborn. They are the stories that want to be told again and again. They refuse to be ignored or overlooked, and so they latch on to the physical world—to our clothing, to our kitchens, to our streets—everything that becomes part of a narrative. *A borderland is a vague and undetermined place created by the emotional residue of an unnatural boundary.* In Mexican culture, ghosts are evidence of the incomplete or the unresolved. Perhaps a task was left unfinished, a message was left unspoken, and so the yearning for closure outlasts the life and defies silence, absence, and death. They are another manifestation of the bordercrossers, the soldier of Mictlán (the opening poem in *Unpeopled Eden*)— the restless fugitives from the Valley of the Dead.

I continue to be intrigued by this Otherworldly borderland, the place that houses, on the same plane, the living and the dead, the past and the present, the real and the imagined. Binaries are broken here, or rather, they meld together into a single stone. But what kind of emotional energy is being preserved there? As I look back at the portrait my poems have painted of the border, I am slightly mortified by how I favored the deeper, darker hues on the palette. I offer no excuses, only more context: my mother left Mexico to escape poverty and she lived in poverty in the United States. She died poor. She began to die on very fertile and wealthy soil. My task now is to mine the inherent contradictions of such possibility, to build (write) something that provides perspective, that accepts complexity. What I write is not indictment; it's response.

In the last few years I have felt haunted by the three wounds of social injustice on the Americas: Ferguson, Iguala, and Ludlow. These troubled communities illustrate the volatile nature of racial and class borders—how the disenfranchised are subject to institutional oppression. Ferguson is a city in the state of Missouri, but its dynamic exists in many other American cities. Iguala, in which forty-three student protestors were kidnapped and killed, is a town in southern Mexico, but its tragedy is a familiar headline across the nation. And Ludlow, Colorado, in 1914 was the site of the infamous slaughter of innocent women and children—the families of striking coal miners—perpetrated by the National Guard. The year 2014 was the centennial of the Ludlow Massacre. And 2014 was the year Ferguson and Iguala bled on the map. In each of these places, an abusive and corrupt power descended on the land to victimize its people. *Borders are set up to define the places that are safe and unsafe, to distinguish us from them.* The Catholic in me imagines that the ground opened up and an evil ascended from all the toxicity that had been collecting there over the centuries. America is, let's not forget, a continent of genocides.

Currently, I'm envisioning my next book to be one poem about one land—the Americas. What comes after the singular unpeopled Eden is the plural—unpeopled Edens. I'm listening to the testimonies of the land, an expansive territory whose unpeopling happens again and again, whose inhabitants leave (or get pushed out), die (or get killed), and disappear (or are vanished), but whose energies, whose stories—whose ghosts— remain inextricably planted in the soil.

Land is the most politicized of spaces—it is taken, it is stolen, it is dissected and eviscerated, it is bought and sold. It is always the casualty of the tug-and-pull between communities, religious and competing interests. It is the seed of many wars. When Anzaldúa gave language to the dynamics and intricacies of the border, she brought with her a lifetime of personal experience and lifetimes of memory, much of it from the land itself. The land spoke to her in the indigenous tongues, in English, in Spanish, in the coalition of all three. I suspect that my next project will also manifest itself that way. Just as one setting is not enough to express a continental narrative, one language is not enough to communicate that narrative. Besides Anzaldúa, I'm also seeking direction from Eduardo Galeano and Claudia Rankine, whose multivalent narratives (*Open Veins in Latin America* and *Citizen: An American Lyric*, respectively) piece together a shattered (and shattering) story, not exactly as an act of healing (though the books are quite sobering) but as an act of revealing. Revelation is akin to revolution—it dethrones silence, particularly the kind whose power is amplified when it remains unnamed, unchallenged, and undisturbed.

I return now to my parents, to that fateful evening when they decided to cross the border so that I could be born on U.S. soil. Once, as we were driving back from a summer visit to my cousins in Mexicali, my father pointed out the little green house he had rented as a newlywed. The house seemed too small to be the site of such a life-changing decision. It was made smaller by the presence of a dwarf palm tree squatting next to a miniature window. I imagined my five-foot-two-inch father and my five-foot mother—an adolescent still—dreaming large inside their tiny temporary home. I regret never having asked how that conversation unfolded. Who proposed it? And how? My father, always a comic, might have offered it up as a joke. And when my mother took that suggestion in her hands, she shaped it into a viable option. Or maybe it had been my mother, frustrated with my father's slow way of doing things, who gave breath to the idea, who convinced my father to go through this outrageous notion. Now that they are both dead, there is no one left to ask, but the story continues to live inside that little green house, which still stands, last time I checked. I trust that over the years the occupants of that little green house have heard it, or sensed it, that youthful courage. No, my parents are not the ghosts in that little green house, their energy is. Once, as my brother and I were driving back from Mexicali, I asked him to pull over so that we could see the little green house close up. Music was playing from a radio inside, and a feminine voice sang along off-key.

"Are you going to knock?" my brother asked, incredulously.

I resisted the urge. Instead I simply placed my hand against the wooden door as if to verify the sanctity of this mythic place. But I felt nothing. I don't know what I was expecting—an electric shock? A spiritual vision? Disappointed, I climbed back into the car and said to my brother, casually, "That's my first home." But even the truth in that statement didn't take hold until I saw the little green house begin to shrink in the side-view mirror. I had left something of my own energy there as well that many years ago as I moved inside my mother's belly. Ask the little green house, which despite its apparent indifference, had acknowledged my touch. This was a certainty on the border, place of long memory, collection plate of story. A person might come through here and remain anonymous or invisible, but only to other humans. The land itself, it kept a perfect record, heralding each welcome and each goodbye. I had passed that little green house so many times it didn't need to feel me to recognize who I was and who my parents had been and what the circumstances of our many crossings were. When the car hit a pothole on the neglected road, the entire vehicle shook, and the little green house in the mirror gave me a knowing wink.

THE BROKEN LINE

Joan Naviyuk Kane

Taimana issuminaiqpaliarut kiuagun. Qanukiaq nunaminun kizian utiumik, utaalaliumik qaamitun. These people of one village all lived as close relatives; that's how they used to be. They probably can never be the same again. If somehow they could return to a village of their own, I wonder if they might go back to the way they lived long ago.

Mary Muktoyuk

I remembered
like an islander   my island

Jean Valentine

I AM CALLED FOR NAVIYUK. My first born son, John, carries three Inupiaq names: Suu, Utkiduaq, and Qasulaa. These names are from King Island (Uguivaik), Shishmaref (Qiiqtaq), and Little Diomede (Ialiq). My younger son carries one Inupiaq name: Kizik. He and I are named for King Islanders. Kizik's older brother can find relatives on three islands (if one is able to find Shishmaref in years to come—it is a community on a Chukchi Sea barrier island and may well be underwater by the time this essay is published). Utkiduaq has found his relatives, and his relatives will be able to locate him.

One of the most important Inupiaq conventions that I was raised with, and raise my children with, is the idea of our continuous relationship to each other through our names, through language. This belief is embodied by the way in which we are named and name each other for relatives or community members who have passed away in order to commemorate them, to contextualize our survival and our death. We are said to carry some of the characteristics of our ancestors' *inua* (life force, for lack of a more or less precise term), but very practically, too, their kin and social relationships. On a figurative level, it reminds us that we belong to the world beyond our nuclear family and the communities in which we reside: we belong to history, we presuppose a life beyond the one we construct and inherit. We also belong to language and to our namesakes and relatives that come after us.

I was born and raised in Anchorage, 1,049 miles from Nome; 1,049 miles between the cities as measured by the Iditarod dog mushing trail—the original route of which was brought to celebrity through the efforts of big city doctors as they labored to get serum to Nome in the face of the 1925 diphtheria epidemic. I was brought up yet more distant from King Island, my mother's own childhood home, by an additional 72.52 nautical miles. Until 1959, King Island had been the home of our family for untold generations before us. As a young child in Nome, I asked my mother why all the buildings there were painted gray. Had I been able to take my children to King Island when I went for the first time in the summer of 2014, they may have asked the same thing about the few remaining village site houses. Not painted gray, I'd tell them, but weather-beaten by the gale force winds squalling across the Bering Sea through the Bering Straits. I don't know what—or even if—they'll ask about the decaying plywood of the long-neglected homes spilling down the island's steep slopes, or the thin layer of soil surrounding them that is falling endlessly into the Bering Sea. Or, the way formerly-farmed foxes—now feral—have overtaken the isolated, granitic outcrop through seasonal feasting on the thousands of seabirds that still nest there (until the entire complex is thrown into greater havoc by the continuing shifts in the ecosystem's finer features).

———◆———

Language connects us to the world we inhabit and the one(s) we imagine we inhabit. I write about Uguivak because I want to think about and remember it, though my first visit to my mother's home on the island was brief and improbable. Through language, it continues to be a place, not an abstraction. We teach our children to say *Ugiuvamiugurua* ("I am from King Island") because doing so suggests our identification with our culture, history, language, and other contemporary King Islanders because of the relationships our ancestors shared with a particular place that makes our survival possible. Language, then—and poetry in particular—confers imaginative and literal access to the site of King Island in the Bering Sea and delineates my relationship to it in ways that are encoded in the Inupiaq language and in ways that I inscribe upon English, through poems. The Inuit language, across the thousands of miles in the circumpolar north where our dialects have permitted us to survive for thousands of years, is agglutinative. Words become precise through the words around them. Poetry, too, is a practice of precision. And such a practice is necessary to ensure that the line, broken or intact, persists.

I am not interested in perpetuating notions of indigenous people as endangered or imperiled or extinct. I suppose that I look to language, and the role of the lyric—the (unidentified) fragment—as a place of refuge and possibility, a generative space. Not a space of loss, but contingence. Some of this, I remain convinced, is encoded at the core of my very being. As a real person (*Inu* means "person", *-piaq* means "real"), and a mother of young children. As a poet whose concerns are not so much about performativity or portrayal, but about the problem of place and the emphatically American preoccupation with it. That is to say, for me, poetry is outside of and necessarily informed by history—my family's personal history and the significance of place in that history—and the imagination, as I imagine poems exempt from history in a way that still acknowledges its debt to it and understands its place and function in relation to it.

I write some of my poems from the (imagined) perspective of my immediate namesake (Naviyuk). I also write with consideration to the generations of Naviyuks that lived with and in relation to others in the arctic and subarctic. I write out of due gratitude and reverence for their memories and the lives they made, and for a real connection to the past and my place in this land, in language. My mother recalls how generations preceding hers taught younger people formal and eloquent Inupiaq terms about the places and stories they would need to know about in order to survive.

Nunamiłu, sikumiłu inuunialaniq ("land, and survival on land and sea") figure, then, in my conception of the world. *Resettlement, assimilation, displacement*: these practical and policy matters shape not only my life, but my poems. I write not to claim ground, but to understand my place on the periphery. The lyric accommodates this because it works outside of the narrative structure, outside of stories with plots, beyond and before them. As an indigenous poet, I am necessarily concerned with the periphery. There is little in my poems that claims to be at the center. They progress, I hope, through elision, image, escape. Survival.

———◆———

My mother, born in 1949, was not born an American. She was born a King Islander, the child of an orphan from the mainland (my grandmother survived the 1918 flu pandemic, and lived at the Catholic orphanage at Pilgrim Hot Springs until the priests married her and two of her sisters off to King Island men) and a subsistence hunter born and raised on King Island (Uguivak) who spoke the elaborate and nuanced King Island dialect of Inupiaq and never learned English. They lived on King Island until 1959, when Alaskan statehood arrived, and the Federal Bureau of Indian Affairs shut the school on the island down. Most King Islanders relocated to Nome, far from King Island on the mainland. Others chose Anchorage, Fairbanks, Seattle, Los Angeles, or any number of places that may have had a ton of things going for them but all shared one distinguishing characteristic: they were not King Island.

They were not places, in other words, that were perfectly situated to nourish lives through subsistence hunting of marine mammals. Not places that sustained people for countless generations without American schools or stores or supply ships. Not places that gave rise to highly specific dialects, stories, dances, and songs that passed down knowledge that is absolutely necessary for survival of the body and the intellect. They were places that made a whole culture's worth of knowledge and imagination irrelevant because these new and different places disregarded and discounted all the place-specific knowledge and imaginative capacities that my family needed in order to survive and flourish for thousands of years.

———◆———

In Inupiaq, the word for the ocean, the sea, is *imaaruk*. Land is *nuna*. We are taught always to identity ourselves by the place names where our ancestors lived: therefore, *Ugiuvamiugurua suli Qawiaramiugurua* ("I'm from King Island and Mary's Igloo"). I don't say *Americamiugurua*, even when I am outside of America. Part of that is because I have a renewed skepticism of the American tendency to name, to know, and to master the land above all. My poems may be overly critical of the kind of self-invention that often accompanies a reductive and romantic relationship to place. I come from a dispossessed people. I can never restore King Island through language. I cannot even adequately catalog all that is lost, or has been lost, or what we are losing still. Certainly, I cannot pretend that repatriation is easy, or possible.

My mother told me, and tells my children, what it was like to grow up in a shack in Nome distant from her real home on King Island by an entire day's journey in an open skin boat across the Bering Sea. She retells my sons stories of how she listened to her father sit with his drum as he sang sad songs about King Island: what he missed, what he was meant to do and see there. Which was to provide for his family by hunting on the moving sea ice, harvesting birds and eggs from the perpendicular cliffs that comprise almost every surface of the roughly one square mile of granitic rock that thrust the island vertically out of the sea, building boats from walrus hides and drift wood. How his songs, composed in the moment but related to the entire tradition of Inupiaq musical expression, did not only function to lament, but also asserted something essential about himself. Something that could only be communicated through lyric: recitative, patterned language.

The songs, as composed, were not for public consumption. Unlike songs in the men's houses on King Island, he did not make them and give voice to them in order to explicitly instruct his wife or his children or his brother's children, or to otherwise discursively connect with them or coerce them. As my mother recalls, they were unconcerned with audience. They were pure lyric. She remembers their artistry and emotion, and perhaps they are fixed in mind not because they spoke directly to the trauma and conflict that arose simultaneously with displacement, but because they were not the usual speech or way of speaking around the facts at hand.

I have long tried to find sense and make order, through poems, of the continuing Inupiat diaspora, of the modern (and particularly American) myth of upward mobility. Like my mother, and perhaps already like my children, in my life I have grappled with homesickness, heightened by language and through it, distance from a complete identity that seems to further confound me with each passing second. I claim the periphery of these identities through poetry because poetry has allowed me to dwell on the emotional resonance of place, and is a kind of utterly sentimental cognitive and psychological exercise. One that can be redeemed or justified, at least to my mind, through the right word, image, or rhythm.

———————————————

In June of 2014, three other women brought me to King Island after more than a year of planning. Imagine, if you will, the trust and goodwill it took our families—all of us mothers, our two elders grandmothers—to support the undertaking of an arctic expedition organized by a poet. It takes someone like me more than 26 hours aboard a 42-foot aluminum-hulled boat to travel back and forth to King Island from Nome's small boat harbor, across potentially volatile weather on the Bering Sea, one of the world's most dangerous bodies of water. Then, several more hours in a small inflatable zodiac dinghy, two at a time, between the boat anchored offshore and the island itself, navigating at turns by oar and sputtering outboard motor toward one of the three possible landing sites on the island's vertical and boulder-strewn periphery.

Here, perhaps, some might wish for me to narrate the island physically. To describe what it was like to hear the millions of birds that nest there when the boat captain cut this engines and told us to sleep before we attempted to make the hazardous transfer to shore. How the light, at 3:00 a.m., struck the granitic spires at strange pink angles below a cap of fog and beneath the low arctic sun distant on the southwestern horizon somewhere over Siberia. How it felt to finally make landing on a huge weather-worn granite boulder. The island is, in many ways, received by others' recollections of it. I arrive there as I arrive in my poems. The private and devastating moments of arrival and departure will make their way into my poems and inscribe themselves within each word I manage to commit to the page for the rest of my life.

One of my original impulses in wanting to go to King Island was to bring my mother and as many of her surviving siblings back home as I could. As if I could make up for the way their lives changed in 1959. As if I could understand the difficulty of leaving a place. As if, by going to that place, with them, I could address or comprehend the trajectories our lives take. Now, I understand how little I know, can know, and how much I need the guidance and direction of the King Islanders and Kawerak people that comprise my community. Poetry is a way for me to navigate this terrain. Surely I flatter myself when I think my poems have any connection beyond the wished-for-ones to my grandfather and family, to the greater reserve of Inuit lyric, but at least now I know that I can locate part of myself in place, on and from King Island.

The relationship to King Island that we carry within us and pass on to our children is exponential. For me, and in these poems, it is concerned with the exponentiation of the self through language. In The Bering Straits I become aware, anew, of the momentariness of human life, the tenuous and uncountable associations that hang between phenomenon and perception. And I am grateful. There is no certainty I will see King Island firsthand again. The poetic imagination that is concerned with loss and reclamation, the poems I make and pass along may or may not find their place in the memories of my children. Perhaps my phrases and lines will be remembered by no one. But at least I have participated in and have made at least one pilgrimage. And how essential the journey, both in actuality on that aluminum-hulled boat, and metaphorically, through poems, has been to my survival. And too, I hazard, to my family's survival. And one return to my family's homeland is far more than I ever imagined

I could make. My poems relating to this place, a place that will continue to thrum with life and memory, look up and out, away from the self.

———◆———

In a country like America with a post-contact past that is so lucrative and exploitative, the true and the hyperreal are not a commodity. In poetics, and particularly newer iterations/packagings of ecopoetry, there persists a monopoly on depiction that presents the past and the human place in it as romantically as possible. This distracts us from more difficult truths. Our literary establishment in the Americas doesn't want to betray its greedy, silencing and bloody origins. A poetry of the self, rather than of the self as it is informed by place, may perpetuate this tendency. And this is troubling.

Not just as an indigenous poet, but as a mother. As the child of a woman who watched millennia of tradition reduce and reconstruct itself, through chance and persistence. Through my mother's work of listening, observation, reflection and recounting, I was able to see the self that she is, but also glimpse my grandfather. And his grandfather before him. And the women named Naviyuk who lived along with them. And so, through poetry, through poems on the verge of self and site, I find the periphery not just another separation or expression of power and trauma, but a place where the words I make might meet the world I know of and know.

THE LYRIC CITY

Wayne Miller

I GREW UP ten miles north of Cincinnati, Ohio, in a quiet suburb that once had been a small village in its own right until it was engulfed by the city's suburban expansion. It remains, today, a collection of tree-lined streets, strong schools, and well-maintained Victorians inhabited mostly by the families of Procter & Gamble's engineering staff and middle management. My hometown's symbol—which shows up on everything from the neighborhood newsletter to the town's governmental website—is a flower basket situated beneath a street sign: a little nest of curated nature juxtaposed with a publicly named street—an agreed-upon word, an essential tool of urbanization.

Suburbs are inherently uncommitted. They exist doubly bordered, such that when suburbanites want to travel someplace that's not their familiar environment, they're faced with a choice: to turn toward the country or toward the city. From the time I could drive and, thus, my world was "freed for movement," as poet Craig Raine has put it, I found myself steering primarily away from Ohio's back roads and farmland and toward the urban core of Cincinnati.

Sometimes I would go to Arnold's Bar and Grill, in business since 1861—the oldest bar downtown—which in the early 1990s was frequented almost entirely by people my parents' age. The servers would look at my baby face and pitiful fake ID, then laugh as though we were improvising a little joke together. Then they would serve me a beer.

The music was usually bluegrass performed from a ragged stage in the corner of a brick-walled, almost chimneylike courtyard. I would sit in my wrought-iron chair and picture the bar's collective noise rising toward the narrow pool of sky above the string lights. I would try to imagine how many other spaces in the city were giving off this same sort of sonic smoke. There was always *someplace else* in the city—another street- or room-in-motion hovering just beyond the periphery of wherever I was. I wondered at the people seated around me hearing the same notes in that very same moment in time. I imagined the history of the bar, the building, the men who placed the bricks; I considered the invented instruments, the time it took to learn them—all those threads converged in this one slender moment as if it were no big deal to come together in such a way.

This was my early romanticized notion of the city—a space where I was unconstrained by the rules and narratives of my hometown; where, rather, I felt joined both to the sweep of history and to the focus of the present. Often not a lot of people were there in that courtyard—or, beyond the walls, perhaps even knew it existed—and yet a bar like Arnold's in a fading city such as Cincinnati offered a small hive of light, a tiny moment of intimacy and correspondence inside "the vast empire of human society."

Around that time, I'd learned in school that, according to the transcendentalists, the main purpose of venturing into nature is to focus entirely on whatever's before our faces—to throw off social entanglements and become "a transparent eyeball" so the "Universal Being" can move through us. I'd also been given a copy of Michael Collier's *The Wesleyan Tradition: Four Decades of*

American Poetry, and so was beginning to read (and even write) poetry without prompting from the classroom. I was fascinated by Emerson and Thoreau, but I was more fascinated by the city, where I felt I was entering the heart and history of our societal activities and ambitions, choices and accidents, actions and reactions. Even today, walking around a city, I can't help but feel myself surrounded by the collective imagination of our human past.

———◆———

When I was five, my family lived for one year in Rome. Many of my early memories occur in that ancient, layered city I've never returned to. I learned to ride a bicycle in the Villa Borghese, I spent Saturdays with my dad at the Castel Sant'Angelo, and, in one memory that particularly and mysteriously persists, I watched a man shape boat after boat from tin foil and float them on the Trevi Fountain. Rome hovers dreamlike beneath all the cities I've lived in, which perhaps is why as an adult I've never wanted to return.

In addition to Cincinnati and Rome, cities I've spent significant time in include Anchorage, New York, Houston, Madrid, Kansas City, Belfast, and Denver. Sometimes I find myself rounding a corner or cresting a hill that feels suddenly familiar, and for just an instant I lose track of what city I'm in. It's the briefest feeling of vertigo, as if the distances between my cities have momentarily collapsed.

Each time I move to a new city I find myself describing it in relation to the cities I previously inhabited. When I moved to the Montrose neighborhood in Houston, I would explain it to Cincinnatians as Houston's Clifton. Malasaña in Madrid was the East Village of Madrid. Later in Belfast, I was surprised to discover how similar the city's sectarian divide felt to the racial divide in Kansas City. Now that I live in Denver, the Cherry Creek neighborhood—an upscale, pedestrian-friendly shopping district just a few miles from downtown—has become for me the Plaza of Denver. (My own neighborhood, North Park Hill—socioeconomically and racially mixed, close to downtown but suburban in feel—is perhaps Denver's version of Kansas City's 49-63 neighborhood.)

Drawing such equivalencies assumes that cities are, by their nature, templates. Nearly all cities contain business, education, and entertainment centers; museum districts; parks and cemeteries; markets and shopping centers; arts districts and bohemian enclaves; various socioeconomic classes of neighborhoods; new and old immigrant communities; uncomfortable flash points between opposed or segregated groups; government centers and court districts; warehouses and transportation hubs; hospitals and red-light districts. The overall composition of a city is a representation of who we are as humans, both collectively and individually. (The hubris shared by the twentieth century's totalitarianisms was an attempt to eradicate one or more aspects of the social fabric—to raze whole neighborhoods of the city.)

On a trip to New York a few years ago, I had drinks with a group that included an orange-tanned news anchor who kept bragging about all the fancy places he'd traveled: the Seventh Arrondissement in Paris, Kensington in London, Orchard Road in Singapore, Salamanca in Madrid. As he rattled off his list of opulent locales, I kept thinking, "But those are all the same neighborhood—you've only ever been to the same place." At a certain point he leaned toward me and said, quite pointedly, that he would *never* visit a city like Kansas City or Houston because he was afraid of the people there. As if every city isn't filled, basically, with the same people—though in different proportions and, as would be important to him, different levels of prestige.

———◆———

In "Crossing Brooklyn Ferry"—probably the best-known American "city poem"—Walt Whitman presents the world of the ferry as an urban microcosm in which the human activities of past, present, and future become mirrored in Whitman as he stands paused amid the vastness of the city-in-motion. In Frank O'Hara's numerous I-do-this-I-do-that poems, O'Hara remains in motion, picking up small details as he moves among the city's diversity of people and activities. Here are two primary lyrical approaches to the city: (1) a depiction of a stilled space inside the city's movement—often from which the speaker contemplates or observes something large about the city—and (2) an attempt to capture or articulate the city's motion through a deluge of apprehended details. Sometimes these approaches combine, as in William Carlos Williams' poem "The Great Figure," where from the passing blur of a fire truck, the speaker is able to catch and hold static in his mind "the figure 5 / in gold."

In Rick Barot's poem "Reading Plato," which I've admired since it came out in his first book, *The Darker Fall*, nearly fifteen years ago, the speaker recalls sitting on a bus or in a taxi—simultaneously still and in motion. To further complicate things, the motion Barot describes is both external (he's sliding through the city) and internal (he's becoming, however slowly, his adult self, capable of love, sexual desire, and intellectual engagement). Around him, we repeatedly encounter other individuals similarly in motion, "figures earnest with / destination" who ultimately leave "hearts penknifed on the windows / of the bus." Formally, the poem is one sentence broken across thirty-three lines, which propels the reader steadily down the page—and yet the lines are gathered in regular three-line stanzas, which offers a sense of balance and containment. What "Reading Plato" manages to capture so brilliantly in its thinking, image-making, and formal construction is that complex and paradoxical simultaneity—stillness and motion, interior and exterior—that's at the heart of the city's lyricism.

In Brenda Shaughnessy's "Panopticon"—another city poem I've kept returning to for more than a decade—the speaker finds herself able to peer into her own apartment from the observation deck of the (pre-9/11) World Trade Center—where she discovers her roommate "experimenting with [the speaker's] vibrator." The speaker feels connected to what she's witnessing not just because the vibrator is hers, but also because, despite the roommate's obliviousness, the act feels charged by her observation. She's sure the roommate "can feel it, my seeing, even through a trance of fog. / I've lit her with it."

What does it mean to be "lit" by being seen? It means that one's actions, once observed, reflect the largeness of the human matrix—that observation is a kind of acceptance into the party of human action. It's of course very possible—even likely—that the roommate would prefer not to be observed in that moment, and yet the city's vastness and proximity require us to acknowledge that we all can't help but basically do the same things. The city offers proof!

Shaughnessy, here, echoes Whitman's sense that he feels thrilled by seeing what others have seen, standing exactly where others have stood, which ultimately offers a kind of embrace: "Just as you stand and lean on the rail, yet hurry with the swift current, I stood yet was hurried…These and all else were to me the same as they are to you…" But Shaughnessy also compresses that idea to the present moment, implying that simultaneously seeing and being seen—even unconsciously—offers value and meaning. The poem closes with the image of the speaker "in the dark, watching whoever is / watching me, watch me."

Since the beginning of recorded history, people have been leaving the provinces for the city. Folks who are artistic, queer, ambitious, talented, or simply feel they don't belong where they're from imagine in the city a more sympathetic world. What cities offer, metaphysically speaking, is not just escape or excitement or transgression, but also—and more importantly—the paradoxical combination of anonymity and a perpetual audience—the potential to light one's interior life with a vast audience for one's unscrutinized self. Barot's and Shaughnessy's entanglements of observation, anonymity, stillness, and motion capture within the city an electric kind of stasis—the stillness of a spinning top.

———◆———

In college I took a class with the Frederick Law Olmsted scholar Geoffrey Blodgett, who one day showed us Olmsted's sketch of the way he imagined a particular section of Central Park would look decades after he'd planted it. Professor Blodgett then showed us a photograph of that space from roughly the time Olmsted was imagining; Olmsted's vision, miraculously, was almost perfect. We could go there now and walk right through it—still alive and moving at its own slow pace along the trajectory he'd imagined.

What Olmsted made there looks like a simple country field left untouched by the colossal city that rose around it. In fact, the city is older than the field.

———◆———

In early 2003, I was living in the town of Warrensburg, Missouri (population 16,000)—from which stealth bomber sorties to Baghdad were, at that time, being regularly flown. After a few months in a one-bedroom apartment around the corner from the dingy student bars on Pine Street, it became clear to me there were two urban outposts in that otherwise provincial county seat: the public university where I taught, and the air force base. Most people in town saw these institutions—both of which regularly drew outsiders to the otherwise culturally isolated Warrensburg—as opposed. (Never mind the many students who were enlisted and/or worked on the base, such as a brilliant poetry student I taught who obsessively read Charles Simic when he wasn't fixing airplane engines.)

It's easy, particularly in today's politically polarized environment, to envision cities as declaring *¡No pasaran!* (as leftist Loyalists did during the Siege of Madrid) in opposition to American conservatism, which has, over the past few decades, largely consolidated in exurbia. Despite the strange and irrational fears of that news anchor I met in New York, even Salt Lake City and Dallas voted for Obama during the 2008 election.

But let's not kid ourselves. The rents in New York are outrageous because Wall Street—not the art world—sets the prices. And no modern war has been fought in the interests of rural or small-town people. As centers of power—political, economic, cultural—cities serve as primary engines of colonialism and violence. Even the history of pastoral poetry is that of the city colonizing the countryside.

When so many small-town and rural men and women set off to fight in Iraq and Afghanistan, they did so mostly to defend the security and interests of people living in the very cities many of them likely distrusted or even despised. When they returned, whatever spoils came from those wars flowed mostly into those same cities. Meanwhile, many of their friends and classmates had already been swallowed by cities, returning home only on the occasional holiday. From the vantage of the provinces, the city is a mouth.

————◆————

Cleanth Brooks asserts in *The Well-Wrought Urn*—his 1947 book of New Critical close reading—that "the language of poetry is the language of paradox." Kenneth Burke argues in *A Rhetoric of Motives*, published in 1950, that the same human hierarchizing impulse that gives us the very pinnacles of artistic achievement also gives us, paradoxically, the Holocaust.

When I first became fascinated by cities as a high school student, I was drawn to those paradoxes that were most abstract and lyrical: stasis and motion, anonymity and audience, the palpability of history in the city's present.

But as I've grown older, I've found myself equally compelled by the city's sociopolitical paradoxes. On the one hand, cities contain enough openness and multiplicity to offer to the creative and marginalized a full and sympathetic world—which draws political liberals from suburbia and beyond in significant numbers.

At the same time, those same cities contain enough economy of scale to assert their political and hegemonic power far beyond their geographic borders—and, thus, to generate violence far more significant than the minor muggings and gang violence exurbia tends to fear. As William Matthews explains about cities in his often-anthologized poem "107th and Amsterdam," there's *"room for us all if we be alert."* Yet, as Katie Ford asserts in her post-Katrina New Orleans poem titled "Earth,"

> If you respect the dead
> and recall where they died
> by this time tomorrow
> there will be nowhere to walk.

———◆———

In April 2001, Timothy Thomas, an unarmed Black teenager, was shot by Cincinnati police after they attempted to arrest him for several misdemeanor warrants, nearly all of which were traffic violations. Police had also killed three other Black men and a Black twelve-year-old boy in the previous seven months, and Thomas was the fifteenth Black male to be killed by Cincinnati police since 1995. Just weeks prior to Thomas' death, the ACLU had filed a complaint accusing Cincinnati police of three decades of discriminatory practices.

What then occurred from April 9-13 in Cincinnati has played out at various moments in cities around the world. After a peaceful protest at City Hall was largely ignored by the city council then in session, the poor, mostly Black Over-the-Rhine neighborhood just north of downtown erupted into rioting and looting—at the time, the most destructive urban violence in America since the 1992 Los Angeles riots. The chaos continued until Mayor Charlie Luken instituted an all-city curfew and, equally important to the ensuing de-escalation, several evenings of rain set in.

Whenever widespread violence occurs in a ghettoized area, a chorus of voices from beyond its boundaries asks the same question: "Why do *they* destroy their own neighborhoods?"

But the question—however racist, or classist, or simply callously unimaginative—fails to recognize the complexities of the city. This same Cincinnati neighborhood that was a beacon to poor Blacks escaping the South (and, to a lesser extent, poor whites escaping Appalachia) throughout the first half of the twentieth century has also managed to seal many of them in, like a finger trap. Without exploring the historical and economic factors that have decimated neighborhoods like Over-the-Rhine, there's the simple fact that a neighborhood or even a city becomes—especially for the urban poor—a limit. When people push hard against limits they reveal the paradoxes that lie beneath them. And faced with fear, loss, and violence, people need comfort and hope far more than some arcane consideration of paradoxes. In such moments of exposure, people tend to respond in kind—with eruptions of paradoxical activity.

Perhaps the clearest, most honest presentation of who we are as human beings is a neighborhood simultaneously looting and defending itself.

———◆———

In the 2007 documentary *The Rape of Europa*—which catalogues Nazi Germany's stealing of art and the extraordinary measures cities like Paris took to protect it—there's a sequence of archival footage in which Hitler travels with his entourage through a silent, newly conquered Paris. He'd always wanted to visit that glorious city—the cultural capital of Europe—and now, thanks to his massive military mobilization and conquest, he gets to do so.

A shot of Hitler with a cadre of uniformed underlings standing in front of the Eiffel Tower. A shot of Hitler being chauffeured through Paris' empty streets, all the windows shuttered against his occupation. How happy he looks!

Our slim revenge from the future (if such revenge is possible or meaningful, I should hasten to say) is our certainty that Hitler died having never seen Paris at all.

———•———

Sometimes I wonder how many pictures and videos exist in which I'm somewhere in the background—just passing through, oblivious to the camera's moment of capture. It must be thousands. Tens of thousands.

When I'm traveling I occasionally meet a person who's from a city I've lived in—at which point the same conversation inevitably occurs: What neighborhood? Do you know this person? Have you been to this restaurant? Do you go to that park?

There's no good reason for this sort of talk. We're unlikely to become friends, since our time together is brief and we already have our own well-constructed lives back home. We've probably at some point already passed each other in a store or on the street.

But here—elsewhere—there's a charge to the person across from me. It's as if we've each carried to this unfamiliar location a suitcase, then opened them both to discover they're full of the exact same belongings. How strange that we've never met, yet these same things have been carried here by both of us.

In a picture somewhere on a sill in Italy—or it could be anywhere, really—a towheaded boy is chasing pigeons through the Piazza Navona. He's in the distance beyond a couple posing on a trip together, a family gathered on their last day in town, a little girl chasing her own pigeons in the foreground.

I was nothing to you, and yet I've been a quiet presence in this corner of your world for more than thirty years. And all the people I've carried with me, and the people they've carried, and the people they've carried—. I can imagine a meshwork of threads stretching between us, so thickly woven it makes a kind of surface. We build cities on it. We inhabit those cities as they—however messy or rapacious—inhabit us.

BROAD DAYLIGHT

Amaud Jamaul Johnson

*...and blackness ahead and when shall I reach that somewhere
morning and keep on going and never turn back and keep on
going*

Robert Hayden, from "Runagate Runagate"

ESCAPE isn't the right word. Neither is exile. When Claudia
Rankine writes that "the condition of black life is one of
mourning," she points to a state of anxiety and vulnerability that
transcends place. Compton didn't hurt me into poetry, and I don't
believe I'm writing out of some form of survivor's guilt. As one
might imagine, I have lost close friends to gang violence, police
brutality and the prison system, to substance abuse, depression and
suicide. Given the horrors of this particular political moment, how
we have traveled from "Post-Blackness" to reposting the murdered
Black body on our Twitter and Facebook feeds, my childhood seems
both a precursor and metaphor to a poetics of outrage and fear.

As Compton changes, and my family continues to negotiate
the hardships of the city, the double-edged pleasure and pain
implicit in shaping most Black communities, our story unravels.
Have I "survived"? What constitutes "escape"? I realize that most

of what I've written—poems on race riots, meditations on Black folks in blackface—extend from an effort to reconcile my past. The personal is historical, and the historical is rooted in place. Our bodies are in conversation with the dead, with what came before us, with time. Our work reflects what we honor, what we choose to critique and what we attempt to transform. History isn't a burden, but it tests our psychological and emotional strength. We carry these stories, these names, and even as our individuality takes shape, that sense of responsibility hovers in the consciousness. In my poem, "Names We Sing in Sleep & Anger," the speaker wrestles with accountability in the final stanzas:

> When I came home from college proud, my educated
> mouth agape, a tackle box of words, slick and glossy
> and I saw the names of my friends, the young men
> I fought with, learned to drink with, and left behind
>
> *Lil' Rocc, Pumpkin, Ulysses, Junebug, Aghoster*
> names spray-painted throughout our neighborhood
> in memoriam, I couldn't understand how a god
> could make one life possible and strip the world
> clean of so many, or how, like high-watermarks
> the dead remind the living of the coming of storms.

From Civil Rights activist Ida B. Wells in 1897 to my grandparents in 1987, "Lift as We Climb" has been the mantra of Black middle-class political awareness. But where are we going? Who do we take with us? As Robert Hayden writes in his re-imagined spiritual, "Runagate Runagate," there's only "blackness ahead." It's as if that darkness contains our past, present, and future. Poetry, if nothing else, has provided a platform for me to address this continuum. What we characterize as literary tradition, or specifically, a Black vernacular tradition, like the Black body, exists in limbo. Place, home, family, memory, tradition: Compton is my private conundrum, where I've felt the most loved, the most alive and the greatest danger.

When I say I'm from Compton, that I was born and raised in Compton, maybe you've already made up your mind. Maybe you listen to "Gangsta Rap." Perhaps you've heard Compton joked about so often over the last 30 years that the name has become shorthand for something else. You hear "Compton" and think "ghetto" or "bottom," or Big Black Africa, Crip, crack, or Blood. Maybe you think, poor baby. Maybe you picture a black box, a mouth void of teeth, or bottle glass. Maybe, the barrel of a gun.

As a poet, I make certain assumptions about audience, about my imagined reader. Poetry makes sport of silences, assumptions, and inconsistencies. Thinking about Compton, writing about home, my challenge is negotiating an exterior narrative while confronting intimacies. We had a house. A nice front and backyard. One massive palm tree. We strung lights from the rooftop and through the trees each Christmas. We had a gardener. We could out barbeque anyone on our block. And occasionally people were murdered. They were murdered near us, or in front of us.

As a native son of Compton, I realize I own real estate in American Popular Culture, but I'm not interested in statements of "authenticity." I don't want to feed the voyeurism of trauma or boil down my identity into a commodity. I don't want to use my personal narrative to validate someone's "mix-tape." People respond, when I say I'm from Compton, just as they respond when I say I'm a poet: "That must be so difficult." We weren't "gangsters." We didn't sell drugs. No one in my family has ever been in a fight. But maybe I'm leaping too quickly to conclusions. I don't know you. I don't know what assumptions you've made; what truly moves or motivates you. I'm not sure what makes you dance or weep, so I must admit I hesitate to say anything, especially about the complexities of place and history.

Texans were the last to free the slaves, and Black Texans were the last to flee the South. Juneteeth (June 19th) is my family's holiday, marking the moment the 13th Amendment was enforced in Texas, six months after Congress passed it. Poverty, racial violence, and hard weather made Texas life difficult, but people in Texas took pride in outlasting hardships. It can't be taken lightly, what it means to walk away from land, loved ones and tradition. Two generations removed from slavery, my grandparents hoped for a better life, hoped that their children would grow up in a stable home without fear of violence. With thousands of other Southern Blacks seeking opportunities West, my grandparents left shortly after WWII. In "Junior Goes Home," I write about this final leg of The Great Migration, when over six million African Americans turned to city life, shaking the rural dust from their heels:

> When Junior returned to Texas
> The sky caravanned down behind
> Him, narrow as the fishing creeks
> He often described in his stories.
>
> He spoke of those who wouldn't leave,
> Women who thought California
> Was too far, that we'd be sliced
> And swallowed whole by the ocean.
>
> He spoke of men who couldn't trade
> Cotton and cattle for steel; couldn't
> Leave home, this family, this history.

My grandfather, "Junior," came from a well-established, highly educated family: both of his parents had graduate degrees. His mother was a teacher. His father, a Morehouse Man, became the superintendent of a "Colored" school district in Texas. He was also a gifted orator, and one of the early members of Melvin

Tolson's "Great Debaters" at Wiley College. My grandfather served in the Air Force, which helped him land a position at the VA hospital in Los Angeles. After completing his Master's in Chemistry, he became the first African American in the state of California to own and operate a clinical laboratory. He was a part of a small cluster of Black physicians, dentists, and lab technicians who served the health care needs of Black L.A. We weren't wealthy, but I can't overstate what these accomplishments suggested about his determination, or how his example shaped my relationship to education.

———◆———

I wasn't exposed to poetry at any point I can remember as a child. Excluding a Bible and a random copy of *Ivanhoe* by Sir Walter Scott, I didn't grow up around books, and we rarely talked about college. My parents were teenagers when I was born, and my grandparents took me in after I started getting into trouble in elementary school. I started running away and hanging out past midnight at the park or in front of liquor stores. It seemed a matter of time before something bad happened. I'm certain I wouldn't have finished high school if it weren't for my grandparents. At eleven-years-old, I was barely literate. Because we didn't have anything that looked like a library, my grandmother would sit me on the floor of her bedroom and force me to read aloud vocabulary lists from *The World Book*. In our encyclopedia set, Kennedy was still President, and there were no citations for Martin Luther King, Jr. or Neil Armstrong.

It was difficult and often embarrassing, stumbling over those words. My grandmother would just listen and encourage me to push myself. "Don't get bogged down," she used say when depression set in. The world outside that room didn't matter; gunshots, sirens, helicopters, none of that madness touched us. I learned to listen, to hold on to the sounds of words. I believe what Yusef Komunyakaa says, "the ear is the first editor."

As a poet, I still read everything aloud. I feel as though I don't know a poem, I don't trust it, unless I experience its vibrations in my chest, unless I hold the word in my mouth. Form is breath. The beat of a line reflects a personal relationship to each syllable. Coleridge's definition of poetry always made the most sense, that it's comprised of "the best words in the best order." Before I knew anything theoretical about a Black vernacular tradition, I fell in love with the music of language. I still wish I could sing. Music represents a kind of control or mastery over sound. Of course, poetry is a mastery of language, and the most I could hope for is a lifelong apprenticeship.

———— • ————

In the 1950s, my grandparents were part of a small group of middle-class African American families looking to integrate Compton's west side. The city (almost completely white working-class) had a thriving downtown shopping district, a solid school system, and beautifully manicured stucco single-family homes. Compton was nicknamed "The Hub City" because it's centrally located between three major freeways, (the 91, the 110, and the 710) and one could get anywhere (Disneyland, downtown L.A. or the beach) in twenty minutes.

Compton was the kind of place former President George H.W. Bush and First Lady Barbara Bush felt comfortable raising their children in the late 1940s. There were no "White Only" signs, but like most American suburbs at the time, restrictive covenants held the quiet line of racial segregation. As more middle-class Blacks moved in, however, developers couldn't cut down the orange groves in Anaheim fast enough. In an effort to frighten white homeowners into selling, it's rumored that predatory real estate agents hired Black actors to push baby carriages down streets or knock on doors, asking if a home was for sale. By the time I was born in 1972, people started short selling property for a dollar. Here's a stanza from my poem "Tar Baby":

And who among us even remembers
Our white past, Fruit town and the Farms
Before the wig shops and gutted lots,
Miss Compton's tinseled scepter, her bob,
A motorcade of Impalas peeling the corner
Of Cocoa and South Oleander.

Compton became a Chocolate City, and what emerged with this new identity was a groundswell of race pride. My earliest childhood memories consist of Afros, beads and incense, butterfly collars, wig shops, neighborhood burger and taco stands, family cookouts at local parks, church barbecues, and watching movies at the Compton Drive-In. We had Black mayors, Black congressmen, Black police officers and firefighters. Our teachers and principles were Black. It was a kind of utopia. It was the Dream incarnate. Compton was so Black, as a child I thought middle-class Mexicans were white. We didn't have the Jazz-age lore of Harlem or the Civil Rights pedigree of Atlanta, and Compton wasn't Motown, but it was ours, The Hub City, a city so Black, Compton High's mascot was a Tar Babe, a Tar Baby, a snaggletooth baby Tartar, and no one blinked, no one dared to joke.

---·---

"We begin with history," Nikki Finney states in her 2011 National Book Award acceptance speech:

> The ones who longed to read and write, but were forbidden, who lost hands and feet, were killed, by laws written by men who believed they owned other men. Their words devoted to quelling freedom and insurgency, imagination, all hope; what about the possibility of one day making a poem? If my name is ever called out, I promised…so too would I call out theirs.

This sense of race pride and solidarity shapes the politics behind my poetry. If it was ever illegal for a people to read or write, if it was a question whether a people possessed the spirit or intellect necessary to produce poetry; then yes, my writing is political. I can't find a better resource to synthesize my interests in history, rhetoric, colloquial speech, images and emotion. Like Finney, and poets like Rita Dove, Robert Hayden, and Etheridge Knight, I feel accountable to the past. I don't see any separation between the personal voice and a voice that represents the larger community. How can I speak without considering my family and, by extension, my city? I know I'm not obligated to write about history. But I don't feel my individuality is at odds with a historical identity. I think we are connected, and I want a poetics that demonstrates that bridge. I've often joked that I'm too moral to be a politician and not moral enough to be a preacher, so poetry seems somewhere in-between.

———◆———

Watching Compton transform in the late 1980s must have been one of the saddest moments for my grandparents. Small businesses failed. Banks closed. Chain stores started leaving shortly after the Watts Riots in 1965. Watts was just over the city boundary and served as a harbinger for Compton's collapse. I have fond memories of buying Garanimals, Underoos, and bell bottoms at the Sears on Long Beach Boulevard. While in elementary school, I remember having clothes on "lay-away" there. It was the economic anchor for downtown. It couldn't have happened this quickly, but when it closed, overnight, Compton seemed to become a city of burger stands, donut shops, churches, and liquor stores. The Sears building was converted into the now infamous Compton Swap Meet. If we shopped for groceries, went to the movies, or wanted a nice dinner, we had to drive elsewhere. It was a depressed state. Yes, we had limitations, but I never used the term "ghetto." My grandmother, my sister, my aunts, uncles, and cousins don't live in a "ghetto." We didn't attempt to integrate a "ghetto."

Crack cocaine was an atomic bomb. I don't think there was a family in our neighborhood that wasn't touched by substance abuse. In junior high school I used to breakdance with a boy named Tony, who lived a few doors down from us. He'd taped a sheet of linoleum to his garage floor, which was perfect for backspins and head spinning. We had matching Puma windbreakers. We wore the same color fatlaces in our shell toe Adidas. We weren't great, but we were pretty serious, and battled the other neighborhood crews at Skateland or the local mall. Tony, BJ, James, and me: we called ourselves The Twilight Def MCs. This identity shielded us from the surrounding gang activity. It was easier to say that we didn't "gang bang" because we danced. We beatboxed and rapped. We were different. I can trace my identity as an artist back to this period. I wasn't writing poetry, but I began to experiment with self-expression and style. We ended up at different high schools and grew apart. I didn't see Tony in the neighborhood as much. By the time we were sixteen, his parents had kicked him out. And the last time we ran into each other Tony's eyes were different. It seemed as if something had shattered inside him. He came to my house one night and asked for deodorant. He tried to sell me his shoes. The crackheads always seemed older than us. I never saw Tony smoke, and he never offered me anything. It's not that I just felt bad for him. I was afraid that whatever happened to him could happen to me. The whole decade was a slow drum roll. There was heartbreak all around. More addiction and murder. I was always waiting for the other shoe to drop, for bad luck, or a bad decision to change the course of my life. This feeling stayed with me. But poetry has given me some tools to process my anxiety. Of course, writing challenges us to make broader connections between the personal, the historical, and the political. Compton's story isn't isolated. I think I started writing because I wanted to understand the nature of my condition. I wanted to hold someone responsible, but I didn't know whom to blame. I explore this in "L.A. Police Chief Daryl Gates Dead at 83":

> So the parents blamed the children,
> and the children marched barefoot
> through the alleys, spray-painting
> their age. And the preacher introduced
> the word lascivious and accused
> the congregation of not tiding
> when the daughter died.
> And the deacon board smoked.
> And the economists saluted Reagan.
> And the police called it an economy of dust.

In Compton's 1980s, you might find violence at any turn: a drive-by shooting outside a skating rink, or a stray bullet through a child's backyard birthday party. If I stood outside, I watched every car pass, looking to see if the windows were rolled down and who might be inside. How I dressed, how I spoke, whether I made eye contact, were all matters of life or death. And I felt sandwiched between the gangs and the police. In "L.A. Police Chief Daryl Gates Dead at 83," I use repetition to mirror the weight and monotony of fear. There were weekend murder counts, clean sweeps, and wild drug busts. Our neighborhoods were so heavily policed, the first person to place a gun to my head was a sheriff. There was danger in all directions. Yet, as bad as things were, I didn't want to leave. I cared about the city. My friends used to joke that I'd grow up and run for mayor. Compton had a small town feel. People knew each other. When discussing my past, I still have trouble saying I'm from L.A. Los Angeles was what people saw in the movies. That world didn't have anything to do with my world. Southern California is made of pockets and islands. It's a segregated place. Before my 18th birthday I'd been to Hollywood once on a kindergarten field trip to see *Snow White* at Mann's Chinese Theatre.

Regardless of this disconnect, and even now after 25 years living away from home, I can hear my father's voice saying, "Who would want to leave sunny Southern California?"

The worst things happen on the prettiest days. The afternoon of the Rodney King verdict was ordinary. For Los Angeles, ordinary is beautiful: warm and windless, the sky was a cloudless blue. Earthquake weather. Even now, a quarter century later, I struggle to express what it means to watch a neighborhood burn. My grandfather had lost a meat market in the Watts Riots, and the sting of that memory never dimmed. Places I'd shopped, places connected to some of my earliest childhood memories just disappeared in a matter of hours. I don't recall any fire trucks, water hoses, or even hand buckets. We watched whole blocks vanish.

With everyone else, I was out in the street. I wasn't holding a brick and I didn't carry matches, but the whole thing felt like a protest march, one without songs or signs, just bodies shuffling in all directions. The strangest thing is that I felt so safe during the riots. For the first time I experienced city-wide racial solidarity during those three days. Because I was born after the Civil Rights Movement, those images of Selma and Greensboro always seemed like ancient history. What was the point of marches or sit-ins? MLK's assassination could have been Lincoln's. I was born into something; I was the product of something I didn't completely understand. April 29, 1992 changed my world. When such a cold rush of anger runs through your body, you never forget it. I didn't feel a call to poetry, but I knew I'd experienced something I would forever struggle to articulate.

How useful are poems when there are bodies in the street? Living through that riot changed me. It was the intimacy of violence. Maybe it's possible to live and write in a vacuum, if you believe your personal tragedies will inspire outrage. If you have some Helen of Troy syndrome, you think the world will respond to your personal needs. You believe in justice. If Black lives don't matter, what use are Black voices? How could someone living in constant danger shape an aesthetic of recklessness? I was trying to find control. I wanted order. I wanted a poetics of self-defense and power. I didn't understand at the time how our personal histories linked us to these larger questions.

When I was in my twenties, all my role models were martyrs. I wanted to scream. I wanted to write poems that broke windows and set off alarms. But a poetics of recklessness reeks of privilege. Some people speed because they know they can make bail, or at minimum, they believe they can sweet-talk their way out of a speeding ticket. Initially, I was drawn to the work of the Black Arts Movement because it was an artistic call to arms. As Amiri Baraka writes in "Black Art,"

> Poems are bullshit unless they are
> teeth or trees or lemons piled
> on a step. Or black ladies dying
> of men leaving nickel hearts
> beating them down. Fuck poems
> and they are useful...

I wouldn't dare write a poem like this. Baraka, naming Imagism, the pastoral and romance as hallmarks of bourgeois artistic practice, attempts to shape of vocabulary of revolution. His voice is wedged between rage and love. The year of the L.A. Riots I was a part-time student at El Camino Community College while working as a cashier at Target. I was taking a Communication Arts course, "Oral Interpretation of Literature," and we were assigned short pieces of prose and poetry to read expressively. It hadn't occurred to me to read a poem before that class. Baraka, Etheridge Knight, and Audre Lorde transformed how I understood the limits of language. Their words formed a door. That semester I also read a poem by Reginald Lockett, who was a former member of the Black Panther Party in Oakland. Ten years later I was in a poetry workshop with Reggie at Cave Canem.

No one plans to become a poet. That's like planning to become a jewel thief or taking up professional archery; it's a strange balance of hidden gifts, passion, and pure insanity. I was on a six-year track to receive a two-year degree, so on a whim I applied to one school—Howard University. Howard was my academic advisor's alma mater, and she encouraged me to take a chance. Her name was Elaine Moore, and she put the application in my hand. There wasn't anything in my transcripts to suggest that I wouldn't flunk out after my first semester, but I'd fallen in love with history, poetry, and the romance of Black Nationalism. I couldn't think of anything more glamorous than walking in the footsteps of Zora Neale Hurston, Sterling Brown, Lucille Clifton, and Toni Morrison.

The night I came home from work to find that acceptance letter (which my grandmother had already opened) still outshines everything I've experienced since. It was more important than Cornell or Stanford or any poetry prize. She was resting in her bedroom. She smiled, placed her palms on both sides of my face and kissed my eyes. I knew my life was changing. I'd only taken an airplane once before I left for college. Looking back, I always thought I'd return. She knew better.

———◆———

Today, video evidence of a Black person being beaten or killed by the police sadly seems commonplace. But in 1992, during the infancy of the camcorder, the image of Rodney King being mobbed by the "authorities" was so shocking and such an undeniably grotesque example of excessive force, people in my neighborhood hoped real change was possible. Such beatings often took place in back alleys. Reports of racial profiling and abuse were dismissed or met with threats. Black people were often accused of being paranoid. King was unarmed. He was clubbed 56 times, kicked, stepped on, and tasered. He received a fractured skull, a broken leg, and organ damage. While the devil is usually in the details, without watching the video, one can't digest the degree of malice those officers held for King. I can't tell you how many times I've been stopped, handcuffed, and then let go without explanation. I was never in a gang, and I've never committed any crime, but that didn't stop anyone from treating me like a felon. Without understanding it then, everything I'd experienced led to that moment, to those three days. It was real unity; the only time I didn't worry about police brutality or gang violence. And I felt free. I spent the next few months working at our church's food drive and clean-up projects. Compton didn't recover. And by the end of that summer, I was gone.

————◆————

I started Howard knowing little about Modernism or Greek mythology, so Ulysses still reminds me of a stubby, mean, sweet-faced boy with a sandy-brown natural. I assumed the purpose of education was to help us process our past and hopefully redirect our future. I debated whether to major in History or English. I lied to my family, telling them I was pre-law. I didn't know what I wanted. I still don't. I took one poetry workshop my senior year, and I fell completely for the mysteries of poetry, its strange and quiet music, its hidden intensities. I'd read Jean Toomer's "Georgia Dusk," a beautiful and horrific meditation on a lynching, published in his 1923 book, *Cane*. He seduces his reader into participating in the violence. He pulls at the senses. The music here lulls the reader into a false sense of security:

> The sky, lazily disdaining to pursue
>> The setting sun, too indolent to hold
>> A lengthened tournament for flashing gold,
> Passively darkens for night's barbecue,
>
> A feast of moon and men and barking hounds,
>> An orgy for some genius of the South
>> With blood-hot eyes and cane-lipped scented mouth,
> Surprised in making folk-songs from soul sounds.

I think I learned from Toomer how to navigate contradictions. He bounced between poetry, prose, and drama; shifted between North and South, rural and urban landscapes. Struggling through my first reading of *Cane*, I shaped new fantasies about a life of poetry. This wasn't Baraka. Like many young writers, my early poems were overwritten and painfully sentimental, but I knew instantly I'd found something that would carry me through my life. Poetry is the only thing I can name that feels natural, as if my mind, how I hear language and connect images, is just wired for it. It's my bridge between the physical, intellectual and spiritual, my past and present. I had new experiences, new thoughts, I was changing, but I lacked the vocabulary to articulate what was happening to me.

———◆———

It's been 25 years. I've lived in Washington, D.C., Ithaca, NY, Atlanta, and Madison, WI, but I'm still a Californian. I miss the arid mountainous landscape, the sunlight, and the effect the smog has on the sunlight. I miss the ocean. I never thought I'd be gone this long. Yet, the longer I'm away from Compton, the more I understand myself, the more I miss its odd seasons: June gloom, the Santa Ana winds, El Niño, the tart Christmas berries in our patio, the smell of pecan wood smothering in the barbeque pit. Even how fear forced people to notice each other; Californians look at each other. They aren't afraid to make eye contact. I miss what made that world bittersweet. I've worked hard, and I've suffered profound setbacks; however, a series of public and private victories have shaped my life. I'm still in awe and sometimes embarrassed by my success. There are people I wish I could talk to, people I need to talk to: old friends, the dead, family, the teachers who saw something in me.

When I'm trying to make sense of this journey, how poetry carved my strange path from El Camino Community College to Howard, Cornell, Stanford and now the University of Wisconsin-Madison, I often turn to Cornelius Eady's "Gratitude":

> Everyone reminds me
>   what an amazing
>   Odyssey
> I'm undertaking
>   as well they should.

The first words I spoke to my wife and even the names of our children, Hayden and August, were born of poetry. I know it sounds evangelical, but poetry has saved my life. I'm old enough and I've read enough to understand that this emptiness, this homelessness, this desire to reach back to something unknown shapes my identity. Compton and Texas, the shadows of slavery, and West Africa. This longing directed my parents, grandparents and great-grandparents, and its echo will follow my children. What will they say about Wisconsin? I don't know what I owe Compton, and I'm not sure if Compton has anything left to give. I know I'm tired of running, but I struggle calling this place home. As Robert Hayden asks, "[…] and when shall I reach that somewhere / morning." Hope is dangerous. It's the plaything of loan sharks and politicians. I'm not sure what this world has in store. Returning to Eady:

> And I know
>   the blessing
>   of a
>   narrow escape.
> And I claim
>   this rooster-pull-down-morning glee
>   on behalf of anyone
>   who saw me coming.

HERRICK TO HARJO: LOOKING FOR FOOD IN THE NATURE POEM

Keith Ekiss

Herrick's Dirty Nails

IT'S JULY in Northern California and there's no rain in sight. This, blessedly, is normal. San Francisco gets most of its yearly 20 inches between October and April. By the time you read this, an El Niño year widely forecast for the winter of 2015 and 2016 may have swept through the state, likely causing mudslides due to hardened soil and only partially restoring the water loss of the past few years. The throat of our state is parched. Everyone needs the rain.

To understand the cultural dialogue around drought, you need to dig through multiple layers: there's the economic impact, the short-term worry about jobs; there's the wholly-justified fear that we've irreparably harmed the earth and its weather and that the rain might never return to its usual patterns, even patterns that include regular, if not predictable, periods of drought. But underneath these concerns lies a perhaps more fundamental and less-often voiced fear: that California's drought, and droughts in other parts of the United States and the world, might mean a forthcoming and ongoing crisis, a significant lack of food, higher prices, and at its worst, starvation and mass migration toward food-producing regions. As a friend of mine likes to say, "Our society is three hot meals away from complete chaos."

The poem of harvest, the song of tilling the earth, is largely (though not entirely) absent in the canonical English-language nature poem; a poem that, while present in various forms in the writing of John Clare, Larry Levis, Gary Soto, and others, finds itself marginalized in the official histories of poetry. Traditionally, poets turned to nature to exercise their wit, support rhetorical arguments, find God or beauty or a refuge from society, but they rarely wrote about whether they would find enough food on the table. In part, this history reflects the poem's author and the formation of literary canons, rather than the point-of-view of the yeoman farmer. But this absence touches a fear that's so fundamental, not just of personal mortality (death in the abstract), but of one particular means, starvation, that it might seem taboo, a subject beyond the decorous taste of verse.

As a younger reader of poetry, I remember my first disappointment with the pastoral. I went to the genre looking for translations of Bion and Moschus, the ancient Greek bucolic poets, in search of the way the earliest poets absorbed and transformed their encounters with nature. At the time, I was writing my own book of poetry about growing up in the harsh Sonoran Desert of Arizona and, naturally enough, looking for examples and histories. I didn't find what I thought I'd discover: a clear-eyed account of the non-human world. I hadn't yet read any historical criticism of the pastoral, and I didn't understand its role as a medium of veiled argumentation and verbal play. I had expected from the pastoral a poem informed by natural history, a world where the poet names the species in her watershed and documents the habitat of the fish in her river. Only later would I learn that I never should've expected to find dirt under the pastoral's nails.

Although the nature poem, as opposed to the pastoral, took a long time to absorb elements of the naturalist's field guide (the tradition of the georgic exists as an important, though rarely practiced exception), you still can find much nature poetry that won't teach you anything about flora and fauna from a scientific perspective. To no one's surprise, there is no pure poem of nature; we're always bringing our cultural backpacks into the woods, trekking out more or less what we expected or hoped to find. Even in the writing of Theodore Roethke, a poet I deeply admire, you'll find a poetry less concerned with the naturalist's objective observation and more with a seething intuition of primal energies.

> This urge, wrestle, resurrection of dry sticks,
> Cut stems struggling to put down feet,
> What saint strained so much,
> Rose on such lopped limbs to a new life?
>
> I can hear, underground, that sucking and sobbing,
> In my veins, in my bones I feel it,—
>
>   "Cuttings (*later*)"

Courtly pastoral verse, the typical argument goes, begins to give way to the modern nature poem during the Romantic era around the time Wordsworth returned to Tintern Abbey. However, I'm interested in exceptions to this timeline, instances where the poet figures nature as a source of food. One exception from the mid-Seventeenth Century stands out, Robert Herrick's "The Hock-Cart, or Harvest Home: To the Right Honourable Mildmay, Earl of Westmorland":

> Come, sons of summer, by whose toil
> We arc the lords of wine and oil;
> By whose tough labours and rough hands
> We rip up first, then reap our lands.
> Crowned with the ears of corn, now come,
> And to the pipe sing harvest home.

The verbal counterpart to the genre of landscape painting, "The Hock-Cart" tracks the arrival of the laborers (the "sons of summer") who bring the fruits of harvest to "the lords of wine and oil," the Earl of Westmorland and, by association, Herrick himself. At last, the pastoral gets physical, with ripping and reaping. Herrick's delight in the sensual overflows in music: the end rhymes, especially in those first two couplets, suggest a natural affinity between work and language as "oil," the product of labor, is already contained within "toil." "Hands" by acoustic association seem meant for "lands."

The poem continues with its earthy language to catalog the procession of the harvest.

> Pressing before, some coming after:
> Those with a shout, and these with laughter.
> Some bless the cart; some kiss the sheaves;
> Some prank them up with oaken leaves;
> Some cross the fill-horse; some with great
> Devotion stroke the home-borne wheat;
> While other rustics, less attent
> To prayers than to merriment,
> Run after with their breeches rent.

There's much to admire in this jubilance, "some with great / Devotion stroke the home-borne wheat." After all the work, the farmer treats the fruits of the harvest with celebration and care. There's also much to question in this passage—for example, how much of this poem would've been observable, capturing life as it was more-or-less lived, and how much constitutes a recasting of pre-digested themes and images (the "rustics" with their "breeches rent") designed to entertain the Lord of the manor?

> And, you must know, your lord's word's true:
> Feed him you must, whose food fills you.
> And that this pleasure is like rain,
> Not sent ye for to drown your pain
> But for to make it spring again.

Whatever one might say about it, "The Hock-Cart" doesn't fit within the pastoral tradition of courtly love and it's not a Romantic register of the sublime; Herrick's subject is the social world as it relates to food production and class difference. The poem reads at once as a token of appreciation to the Earl of Westmorland and as a warning to those rustics: "Feed him you must, whose food fills you." In other words, although the farmers have shouldered the burden of the work, the poem warns them that they serve at the pleasure of Westmorland. In its political honesty, the poem is, despite its wonderful music and imagery, loaded with threat and contention. It's also a rare acknowledgement in English poetry of the political reality of food production, which is to say, human survival.

Which brings me to the contemporary Creek poet, Joy Harjo.

Setting the Table

We need a criticism based on how poets get their food.

Joy Harjo

Years ago, as an undergraduate at the University of Arizona, I heard Joy Harjo make this statement at a poetry reading. At its root, Harjo's words acknowledge the typically great distance between a poet's emotional and formal means versus their actual way of life. Hers was an odd, off-hand remark, but I was struck by its argument—the way we physically *live* our lives and the content and form of our poetry seem utterly disconnected. This is almost always the case in contemporary American poetry and, as I've discussed, in the canonical history (the poems that get taught and anthologized) of the tradition in English. In contrast, Harjo makes the centrality of food the subject in her prose poem "Perhaps the World Ends Here," which starts:

> The world begins at a kitchen table. No matter what, we
> must eat to live.
>
> The gifts of earth are brought and prepared, set on the
> table. So it has been since creation, and it will go on.

And ends:

> Perhaps the world will end at the kitchen table, while we
> are laughing and crying, eating of the last sweet bite.

Other notable exceptions, where food comes foremost, exist outside the dominant tradition of the nature poem, including numerous translations—by John Dryden and C. Day Lewis to more contemporary renderings—of Virgil's manual of farming and beekeeping the *Georgics*. Larry Levis's "Picking Grapes in an Abandoned Vineyard" too is a touchstone moment for the harvest poem, as the speaker returns to his family farm in California's central valley and recalls working side-by-side with "a dozen / Families up from Mexico." The poem is a moving elegy to the farm workers Levis knew and what they taught him. However, the exceptions tend to prove the rule of absence: we take both nature and the politics of food production for granted or as outside the realm of lyric poetry. Even when the formal means of a harvest poem persist, such as in the villanelle, which originated as a French harvest song, the traditional content has been stripped bare. However, for indigenous poetic cultures, including those here in North America, the great divide between poetry and (non-metaphorical) human survival hasn't always been so great. In my case, growing up in Arizona, a tradition existed in my own backyard where poetry played an active part in recording a knowledge of how to ethically survive in a fragile landscape.

Singing Up the Corn

In the 1850s, shortly after the beginning of the gold rush, many settlers intent on reaching the California loads elected to take a southern route. Avoiding the long trip by schooner around Cape Horn or the treacherous, snowbound trails over the Sierras, they chose a different passage and braved the heat and dust of the Sonoran Desert.

Ill-equipped and without the knowledge of how to survive in that landscape, many suffered and died along the way. But a few of these settlers, if they were lucky, found themselves saved by an unlikely group: the Pima Indians, or, as they are more accurately known, the Akimel O'odham, meaning River People. The O'odham had lived in what we now call southern Arizona for hundreds of years and developed a close, living relationship with the land that included extensive irrigation and a thorough knowledge of the plants, animals, seasons, and rivers of the region. The Pima were and remain small in number, but their success in living within the desert often resulted, prior to the arrival of settlers, in a surplus of food and water. They often grew and gathered more than they could eat; they did not want for food and their lives, counter to Hobbes, were not "nasty, brutish, and short."

The Pima witnessed the suffering of the settlers, of these newcomers who crossed their lands, and rather than see them as the enemy, they pitied their foolishness and suffering and did their best to help, riding out on horseback in what became known as the "Mercy Patrols," offering food and gourd water to the weary travelers. Here's a version of a Pima poem as translated in the early 20th-century by the ethnographer Frank Russell, which seems to reference those Mercy Patrols.

> Swiftly with a cup of water
> I came running to make you drink.

> I make you drink the water
> and turn dizzily around.
> Among the white cactus leaves;
> Among the white cactus leaves;
> I came running to that place;
> I came running to that place.

If this poem brings to mind the blues, it's no surprise, though the connection to the African-American form is wholly coincidental and not linear or historical, perhaps emanating from a common source of human sorrow. The shared repetitions between the two forms make sure the listener pays attention and the singer gets heard.

Only decades after these first encounters, the Pima found their traditional way of life devastated. Settlers damned the Gila river for their own purposes (agriculture and hydraulic mining) and forever damaged its watershed by extracting wealth that would eventually leave the territory, heading away from its source by railroad toward the East Coast and doing nothing to help, and everything to harm, the indigenous people of the Southwest.

Over generations, the Pima developed a kinship with the desert; they knew how to survive there and they preserved and passed along this knowledge through poetry. Pima song-poems document water insects and aquatic birds. Corn, squash, pumpkins, tepary and lima beans find their way into the poetry which, in often complex ways involving social taboos, addresses the proper way to treat the land and animals and conveys the founding stories of the people. However, to romanticize the Akimel O'odham's traditional relationship to the earth would be limiting, and as an outsider I can only marvel at the immensity of their desert knowledge, detailed in three outstanding books by the scholar Amadeo Rea. In *At the Desert's Green Edge: An Ethnobotany of the Gila River Pima*, Rea documents the continuity of song, religion, and land in Pima culture:

From myth to medicine, the Pimas' metaphor of themselves was as part of the desert, a component of it rather than something separate—and especially not as superior to it. Personal and community health were viewed as part and parcel of the larger natural community. Instances of this cultural self-perception are found throughout the individual accounts of plant species, the folk genera.

Rea continues:

The symbolic roles of plants may be learned from another form of oral literature: song. Only a small fraction of the vast resource of sung poetry has been recorded. Pima songs are precise, tightly structured utterances, often in a language style quite different from ordinary speech.

Precise, tightly structured utterance with a language that differs from ordinary speech. In other words, poetry.

The staples of the traditional diet are present from the beginning of time in the poem of the Pima Creation Story. In the epic, Se'ehe, also known as Elder Brother, decrees that the Pimas should be farmers and makes the first crops from his own body. Elder Brother sings of *haal*, Pima corn:

You look in the fields
And you see the haal is coming out.
The leaves of the haal are like the clouds
And the decoration on the pumpkin
    is like decorated clouds.

To the corn and the pumpkin, add two kinds of beans and you have the four staples there from the beginning, *there* in the poetry. As Rea recounts:

> [...] the People do not just plant the crops and leave
> them to their own devices. The whole process of living
> on the razor's edge of this desert country means singing
> along the entire process from planting to harvest [...]
> the crops are sung along and the rains are sung in.

According to Ruth Underhill, an anthropologist who studied the
T'ohono O'odham (the Pima's cousins to the south) the practices
of the two cultures were very similar:

> Night after night, the planter walks around the field,
> 'singing up the corn.' There is a song for corn as high
> as his knee, for corn waist-high, and for corn with the
> tassel forming. Sometimes, all the men of a village
> meet together and sing all night, not only for the corn
> but also for the beans, the squash, and the wild things
> (quoted in Rea).

Reading these poem-songs might help to point us in the direction
of a useful attentiveness, to show how in another tradition food
and the nature poem have always been naturally entwined.

Despite the marginalization from the canon of poems
about planting, gathering, and harvesting, there are signs that
the ongoing ecological disaster, from drought to rising seas to
famine and species loss, has engendered a return to making food
production and not just food consumption an urgent subject for
poetry. We have been alienated from the source of our sustenance
for too long. Poetry can provide a pathway back to the land. From
Nathaniel Perry's *Nine Acres* and its poems of rural farming (with
titles like "Soil Surface Management") to Ross Gay's celebrations
of urban nature, one senses that for some poets the need to
return to the roots of living has resurfaced. A new generation
of Native American poets, inspired by Joy Harjo and including
Natalie Diaz and Jennifer Foerster, show us the unbroken link

connecting culture to land. In Foerster's "Country of Wildfire," from her magnificent and overlooked debut collection *Leaving Tulsa*, the poet returns to the earth to find that the spirits still have something to teach:

> Returning for acorns, I shuffle through ash.
> Invisible, the women once
> crowded these groves [...]
>
> I step like a thief through larkspur,
> milkweed, listen
> for some form of instruction
> or song [...]

RECOVERY

Janine Joseph

What happens when the body goes slack?
When what anchors us just drifts off toward....
What will remain intact?

Tracy K. Smith, from "The Speed of Belief"

WHAT I REMEMBERED was not the light turning red or the back windshield bursting. What I could remember was that the car in which we could have died was stunning blue.

Stalled again at the open document on my computer, I began a mood board and printed out a picture of my father's mangled Subaru to glue at the center. From where my brother stood to snap the photo, what remains of the trunk resembles an eyelid open over an empty socket. In profile, the car dematerializes after its rear tires.

On the foam board, I cut, pinned, taped, and layered in a clockwise motion an old ring, a postcard, a this, a that, a song lyric, a tear of old blue jeans, a photograph of my father, brothers, and me against a backdrop of Batangas Bay—everything that appeared important to the manuscript I was resuming work on. The composition swelled even more blue.

———•———

Long before I was someone whose floating brain hit and hit the front and back of my skull in a closed head injury—who wrote one word when she always meant another—I was someone who was a kind of collector, a child who kept a binder filled with nouns. On the long, traffic-stopped bus ride home from Colegio de San Augustín, a private Catholic school in Makati, Metro Manila, I gathered what I could from the window and wrote column after column of the sights around me. I commanded myself to never repeat a word so the pages I accumulated became an image-driven map of increasing and deliberate specificity. Some journeys home, I added only a single new word as the sunlight faded. The binder became an irreversible record of my education, as most of our exercises in school were copied onto Magic Drawing Slates that, when lifted, wiped the lesson clean.

When I awoke in California during winter break in 2008, some days after the grey sedan crushed and plunged my father's electric-blue car into the empty intersection, it should not have been such a revelation that, before the words *immigrant*, "*illegal alien*," *undocumented*, *documented*, or *permanent resident alien*, what came back to me was the word *poet*. I was a neck-braced *poet* with purpled thighs and a palpitation in my head. I was a *poet* held down on the bed by a seatbelt of bruises. What I understood about myself in relation to that word, however, began and ended in that moment of awakening. What I knew about poetry and what poems I had already written as part of the manuscript that would become *Driving without a License*, a collection based on my experiences growing up and living in America for fifteen years without (proper) documentation, was still a mystery.

Two weeks after the accident, I flew back to Houston for the second semester of my doctoral studies. I had ahead of me a recovery that involved more CAT scans and MRIs, more appointments with therapists, massage therapists, neurologists, psychologists, and neuropsychologists. I had dizzying days of falling into my closet as I bent to dress. I had ahead of me days of sitting in discussions, the classroom quieting and my hearing going. Of my aphasic prose, my autobiographical narrative professor wrote that he didn't know anything about me.

Had I not been fairly new to the city and the school, I might have chosen to take a leave of absence until—to use an empty phrase—my health improved. But to the students in the graduate program, I *was* new and every person in Texas who got to know the post-accident-me got to know me as someone I did not myself recognize. Even my live-in boyfriend, the one person in Houston who had technically known me the longest, had only been in my life for nine months. At the time, I was also still adjusting to living in America as a *permanent resident alien*—as someone who, for example, could now get carded without distress and follow a body of graduate students into a bar for a night of live readings. I was not, in many ways, the person I was, but I stayed in school and followed through with a decision made by the past me, the *poet*.

I was piqued by the word that was not part of what I repeated when I wandered up and down the hallway of my father's house, explaining to the visitors who were relieved I was not dead, "I seem to be confused." In *What Doesn't Kill Us: The New Psychology of Posttraumatic Growth*, Stephen Joseph asks readers to imagine the overwhelmed, traumatized brain as a snow globe. He writes, "How long the snow remains unsettled depends on how vigorously the globe was shaken." For some time, my various memories, countries and states, and epithets and identities revolved in the blizzard of that waterlogged air. In the writing I produced at school, I could not differentiate verb tenses and within a sentence would compress my life's history and history of selves. As I drove myself through panicked tears on Houston's looping freeways, versions of myself would come back all at once. I would remember a lie I told to an employer or friend and become that undocumented person again. I would stand at the sink, staring at my boyfriend as he watched soccer game after soccer game and ate popcorn in his boxer briefs, wondering why I was not in Brooklyn with the last person I had loved, someone who knew me in the first years I became documented and whose information I had wiped clean from my hard drives the year before my accident in an effort to "move on."

In class once, I read a peer's poem aloud and stumbled on the word *escape*, pronouncing it *es-ca-peh* again and again while the room listened. As the class talked, I falsely remembered a time when I tried to sound out the same unfamiliar word. What I didn't realize was that I was replaying, as if from my own lived memory, the scene from Disney's *Finding Nemo*, believing myself to be Dory, the Blue Tang who suffers from short-term memory loss. Removed from the workshop, I swam past a shiver of sharks and into a chamber. There I was again, struggling to sound out the exit: *ESCAPE.*

———— ◆ ————

From the photos, it seems the driver, at the last minute, pulled his wheel slightly to the right and caused more damage to the passenger side of my father's car. The bumper and trunk disappeared into and through the back seat; the right rear door crumpled and was subducted into the front. Out of which door the firefighters pulled me, I don't know. The last thing I remembered before the accident was the phone call I had made, three days prior, to accept and confirm my interview appointment for the Paul and Daisy Soros Fellowship for New Americans. In the days that followed, I would be told several times that, in a month, I would need to fly back to Los Angeles from Houston. I would have enough time to read through my application materials and travel from Riverside to Houston and from Houston to Los Angeles and back in time to teach my spring classes.

My father suffered a hairline fracture on his collarbone and though the impact and catch by the seatbelt shook my brain, I was discernible enough to my family when we were released from the hospital. I had cracked a number of jokes to the paramedics and doctors in the emergency room and foamed expletives as my cousin drove slowly over the speed bumps in the parking lot. When I laid down to sleep that night, though, some unknowable thing in me loosed its grip and slipped away like headlights around the bends.

———◆———

The second poem that I memorized in graduate school was Tomas Tranströmer's "The Name," translated by Robert Bly. After being shamed in front of my peers for daring to be a Ph.D. student without a single poem committed to memory, I repeated, "I got sleepy while driving and pulled in under a tree at the side of the road," again and again until the first memorized sentence of the prose poem became the second; became the third; became the fourth and fifth; became, "All of a sudden I was awake, and didn't know who I was"; became four whole paragraphs; became the last sentence echoing in my gully-brain: "But it is impossible to forget the fifteen-second battle in the hell of nothingness, a few feet from a major highway where the cars slip past with their lights on." I memorized as I drove to school, imagining myself thrashing in the back seat in the rearview mirror, asking, "Where am I? WHO am I?"

I am someone who stayed matriculated. Who learned, when constructing a mood board, that the proper name of the color of my father's car was Blue Pearl. The name oceanic, already asking me to follow it to its dangerous, vertiginous depths in a single breath.

———◆———

Poet, the scrap of snow that descended first from within the globe and fixed itself on my landscape.

———◆———

For a long while, I stepped over the unrecognizable poems spread across my new apartment's warped floor and tried to convince myself that losing the near-complete book wouldn't be—couldn't be—*a disaster*. Though I could not retain for long much of what I read during my doctoral studies and had lost, somewhere in my overturned brain, much of what I had read before the wreck, Elizabeth Bishop's "One Art" surfaced and bobbed. It was never a favorite poem of mine, but it continued speaking to me for many years, the way Walt Whitman's "Song of the Open Road" did when I was undocumented, always assuring, "Camerado, I give you my hand!" Reaching again through decades and distance was, without reason, a poem.

In Tranströmer's poem, "(a)fter a long while," the speaker's "life comes back to [them]." Their name comes back to them. Trumpets sound and footsteps come running "quickly quickly down the long staircase." The selves sync up. After a long while, it was like the day a friend took me ice skating for the first time and I stepped onto the layer of bright ice and glided one foot after the other—a natural. I could, after a long while, record an endless order of words on a page. The first poem I was able to finish was a ghazal, a poetic form of "stringently formal disunity" with independent stanzas that I could approach a couplet at a time. I could compose a couplet, for example, then disappear into sleep for several restorative hours. If my attention lapsed, or if I woke believing it was a new day, the radif (or refrain) would bring me back. In the form's mahkta (or final, "signature couplet") I could invoke or declare my name in remembrance or as evidence of my presence.

For a long, immeasurable time, however, I could lose a line or image in a matter of seconds, sometimes if I looked away from the screen to glance out the window. Sometimes, I would lose a poem entirely if I thought too deeply about a word. I would surface, small pearl in hand, and the basket and boat would be gone. In desperation, I turned to the existing poems of the manuscript as if they were, like the lists I made as a child, maps that would direct me back to a place I could not find unguided. I attempted poems that were mere imitations of my voice and produced serrated lines that lurched vertically down a disconnected narrative. I opened failed drafts full of discarded images for any point of entry as if backwards was the only accessible route to the self I asserted through language.

I did not expect that reading backwards would be like trying to revisit a country, a state, a city, or a neighborhood, in search of the same exact house. That it would be like the time I entered an old address into the interactive Arcade Fire music video for "We Used to Wait," expecting a nostalgic, musical tour of my immigrant story; instead, I watched, unsettled by the strange silhouette jogging through the neighborhood of my family's first purchased home in the United States. That the journey would be a misstep, eventually steering me to the place where the undocumented speaker of those poems resided, the undocumented self I had been and who I was no longer.

———◆———

"Where am I? WHO am I?" I asked, the questions being the easiest of the poem to remember while I navigated Houston's concentric freeways. For a long while, I was an immigrant to my own body, looking back at my old, pre-accident self as if it were a ceded motherland. It was not through my unfinished manuscript that I was able to return to myself, but it was through poetry that I was able to recover the capacity of the word *poet*. It was the *poet* who made the landscape of my new life familiar, whose metaphors assured me that I could once again make a foreign country a home.

PLACE IN MIND

Peter Streckfus

Shadows

NEUROSCIENCE TELLS US THAT, when we observe another person in physical activity, mirror neurons in our minds fire as if we ourselves performed or experienced the action. If you could see me reach my hand to the wall next to my desk to touch the shadows that move there, the areas of your mind that govern the movement of *your* hand would be activated by your mirror neuron system, as if you yourself reached toward the wall. This is how a child learns motor skills while watching another move. This is how we enjoy viewing the athlete move through space; although we could never move as she moves, watching her stimulates the areas of our minds that govern such movement. But this is only part of what the mirror neuron system does as we observe the physical experience of another. As we view and virtually simulate the other's actions, we also automatically simulate in our minds the abstract feeling or thought states that accompany the action. We interpret, in other words, creating what is known as a "theory of mind" regarding the other. Seeing me move my hand toward the shadows on the wall, your mirror neuron system simulates my action and the thought and feeling that motivate my action, as if you shared those assumed motivations. Our ability to empathize is based on our mirror neuron system. Studies show a similar process occurs in our minds when we read.

When we hear the speaking voice in a poem describe concrete detail, that sensory information in the sentence elicits responses not only in the language processing areas of our minds, but also in our mirror neuron system. We mentally simulate the bodily experience. This is what we mean when we say a reading experience "puts you there." This is the power of concrete detail. We are *placed*. We take on a bodily point of view. And we assume, simultaneously, a theory of mind regarding the point of view and the sensory information it relates. What motivations, what movements of heart and mind accompany the physical experience of the point of view we have taken on? The most interesting and significant difference between the everyday observation of another's experience—passing my doorway, for instance, and pausing quietly to watch me react to the shadows on my wall— and encountering such an experience in a poem lies in the theory of mind, the access to mind that poetic language makes possible.

For example, here are lines twenty-three through twenty-eight of William Carlos Williams' forty-three-line poem "The Descent." You'll recognize the physical experience Williams describes, and yet it is wholly different:

> With evening, love wakens
> > though its shadows
> > > which are alive by reason
> > of the sun shining–
> > > grow sleepy now and drop away
> > > > from desire   .

The concrete image of "shadows" in Williams' lines above is associated with a number of abstractions, "love," "reason," sleepiness, and "desire." The abstractions here, in fact, cast the shadow's physical movement through the scene. The poem does not present branches moving in the light, as I offered above; rather, "love wakens" here, and produces "shadows." Reading these lines, from one to the next, our theory of mind proceeds and is altered, as the speaking voice of the poem presents a mind we would have no way of accessing merely by being present in the physical place. Notice how the second and third of the lines above offers love's "shadows /" as if they themselves were "alive by reason /", animated, souled. And how this momentary reading perception alters as we move through the enjambed "reason /" to the next line, which returns us to the full left margin of the poem, and the concrete world "of the sun shining— /". Thought moves on, as if descending a staircase into the page, and into abstraction: the "shadows" "grow sleepy now / and drop away / from desire   ." As "love," "reason," sleepiness, and "desire" constitute the physical movement of the shadow, they likewise constitute a figurative movement, the movement of metaphor, of analogy, from line to line. We are not provided the physical analogs for "love" or "desire" in this image. Yet the movement of the shadow cast by "love" grounds it in the physical scene. The shadow's dropping "away from desire," however we might interpret that desire, grounds it within the physical scene as well. Though we may not note the plotting of this information in this complex image, our theory of mind alters as we inhabit each line, and as the line of thought proceeds. As we process the concrete details, we process this information as well.

The "shadows," "the sun shining," the dropping away, these render the world in the manner we typically associate with "place" in literature. The six lines above, however, among the poem's forty-three, refer to its only image of the physical world. What is to be said about "place" as subject in a poem such as this? Williams, known for his writing about place, appears to ask this very question in composing the poem. Written in the beginning of his late period, in the 1950s, following a series of debilitating strokes that altered his speech and sight and paralyzed his right arm, "The Descent" observes "place" only partially dependent on the senses. We began, above, in the middle of the poem. Let's move now to its opening lines, one through nine:

> The descent beckons
> as the ascent beckoned.
> Memory is a kind
> of accomplishment,
> a sort of renewal
> even
> an initiation, since the spaces it opens are new places
> inhabited by hordes
> heretofore unrealized,

As a meditation on what place can mean in poetry, "The Descent" "beckons." It calls us to "places" opened by "memory," "spaces" largely composed in abstract terms. "Beckons" and "beckoned" personify the abstractions "descent" and "ascent," which suggest physical movement, one's "descent," one's "ascent" through time and space. Yet the areas referenced here are of the mind. "Memory," which is an "accomplishment," "renewal," and "initiation," opens inhabitable "places" in the mind. The poem continues here, in lines fourteen through twenty-three—the line with which we started:

> No defeat is made up entirely of defeat—since
> the world it opens is always a place
> formerly
> unsuspected. A
> world lost,
> a world unsuspected,
> beckons to new places
> and no whiteness (lost) is so white as the memory
> of whiteness   .
>
> With evening, love wakens

"The Descent" builds relations between ideas ("descent" / "ascent," "spaces" / "places," "kind" / "kinds," "defeat," "world," "white," and finally, "love,") that repeat and modulate until they become volumetric in their abstraction, that become, in their music and volume, a rendering of mind in time and space. There is the "whiteness" we experience in the physical world, and there is the "white" we experience in recollection, having lost our reference to the physical experience. Composed of language that refers to the sensory world and to the world of the mind, ordered as it is on the page, the poem creates "place" in a number of senses. These overlap on the map of consciousness that the poem offers the reader as it moves forward:

> though its shadows
>   which are alive by reason
> of the sun shining—
>   grow sleepy now and drop away
>   from desire   .
>
> Love without shadows stirs now
>   beginning to awaken
>   as night
> advances.

Dreams

The poem, as a place and an event, happens as we enter it, from its very first line to its last. Palestinian writer Mahmoud Darwish, another eminent poet of place, begins his book-length masterpiece *Mural*, written following a life-threatening surgery in his fifty-eighth year, with an image similar to Williams' in its sparseness, a voice in the "spiraling" whiteness of a hospital "corridor," speaking his "name," a sound and a concept to which Darwish returns again and again as he moves between the physical world on which the poem stages its first utterance and the shifting place of the poem itself. Here is that opening, as translated from Darwish's Arabic by Fady Joudah:

> This is your name
> a woman said
> and disappeared in the spiraling corridor
>
> I could see the sky over there within my grasp.
> A dove's white wing carried me toward
> another childhood. I wasn't dreaming
> that I was dreaming. Everything was realistic. I knew
> I was tossing myself to the side
> before I flew. I would become what I want
> in the final orbit. Everything was white:

A sign of language itself, and of the poet as the maker of language, the poet's "name" is the first image of *Mural* we perceive, its first object of the senses—spoken, written, held—and its first object of the mind—we hear and do not hear the "name." Like Williams, Darwish moves in this poem in chiaroscuro, between whiteness and places of shadow, "dreaming" and the "realistic." And, as in "The Descent," the abstractions of *Mural* repeat, renew and cohere into place. Notice the movement of "white" for instance, which opens with the "white wing," moves to "Everything was white," and continues:

> the sea hanging above the roof of a white
> cloud was nothingness in the white
> sky of the absolute.

Sea is offered as sky, the concrete vehicle and concrete tenor of the metonym overlaid abstractly one on the other in a stereoscopy that causes us to see the sea above a white roof, the sky above a white cloud, and the sky as a sea. The stereoscopy multiplies as the period of thought continues into its predicate, "was nothingness in the white / sky of the absolute," figuratively dissolving the view, as if from a window, into the white of abstraction, permeating the physical world through an action of mind. A few lines later in the same stanza, we hear, "I was alone in whiteness, / alone…"

"The sky," its "dove," the "white cloud," these carry the poet as he enters the poem, tossing himself to the side. Three pages later, the "name" of the poet, taken up once more through the voice of the nurse, now vatically merged with the poet's point of view, becomes more pointedly the vehicle for the literary soul in its flight. It carries him:

> be a friend to your horizontal name,
> try it out on the dead and the living, teach it
> accurate pronunciation in the company of strangers,
> and write it on one of the cave's rocks
> and say: My name, you will grow when I grow,
> you will carry me when I carry you,
> a stranger is another stranger's brother.
> [....]
>
> One day we will become what we want

The name as physically written, the "horizontal name," is a "stranger" and a "brother," the written self implied by and created in the poem, and all the poems he has written before. Thus, through his "name," Darwish ascends the place of his own work in this book-length poem, arriving, five lines later, to what one might consider the place of its title, the poem itself:

> So let's go to the highest mural:
> My poem's land is green, high,
> the speech of God at dawn,

"Green," the color of the "poem's land," is associated with the ideal, with paradise, a place of mind, but also with fertile place, a place through which we might walk. Many pages and a number of iterations of this declaration later:

> Green, my poem's land is green,
> the lyricists carry it from one time to another faithful to
>   its fertility.
> And of it, I have
> the narcissus contemplating the water of its image.
> And of it, I have
> the clarity of shadows in synonyms, and the precision of
>   meaning.
> And the similarity in the speech of prophets on the
>   surface of night.

Darwish's highly figurative language brings to the fore the act of writing and the poem as an inhabitable sculpture of language and thought. Carried by "the lyricists" across time, from poem to poem, and here from line to line, the "poem's land" is defined by its relation between, and as a system of, body and mind. Its physical place becomes its ideal, composed and read as it is in a space inaccessible outside the poem itself, with its "reality and myth," its "clarity of shadows in synonyms," its system of "embodiment" and "abstraction":

> And of it, I have the donkey of wisdom forgotten on the
>   top of the hill
> mocking the poem's reality and myth...
> And I have the congestion of symbol with its opposites:
> embodiment doesn't bring it back from memory
> and abstraction doesn't raise it to the grand illumination.

"A poem is a horizon," poet and critic Matthew Cooperman tells us, "what you're looking at and why you look. It is surely a thing and a direction. We read the page, we are a point of view, and the thing we see—the page, the poem—opens before us like a desert or a hearth." The poet offers us the poem for the time of its reading, a material page that "opens before us" as we occupy its physical sensations and build our theory of its mind. We become its "point of view." ("I knew / I was tossing myself to the side /

before I flew," the poet tells us. And so do we know, as we pick up the poem offered.) This offering in Darwish becomes part of the world that frames, stages, and contextualizes the poem's utterance and action. Thus Darwish's own history, and the history under which he composes *Mural* enter the poem. Darwish continues in the very next line:

> And I have the other "I"
> writing its diaries in the notebooks of lyricists:
> "If this dream is not enough
> then I have a heroic wakeful night at the gates of exile..."
> And of it, I have the echo as it scrapes the sea salt
> of my language off the walls
> when I'm betrayed by an archenemy of a heart...

The writing, "the other 'I' / writing its diaries in the notebooks of lyricists," and the reading, "the echo as it scrapes the sea salt / of my language off the walls," the poem's being offered rhetorically and materially to us as readers: all of these may underlie, frame, and press on the world it builds. By titling the poem *Mural*, meaning, originally *wall*, Darwish places the page of the poem, "the sea salt / of [his] language," its very writing and its writtenness, as a physical monument to our own crossing over. As a relational gesture to the world, the poem is a distortion of time and place. We touch and do not touch its walls. We pass and do not pass through it.

Echoes

The time and space it takes to read a long or short poem's many or few lines, the descent of its staircase-like lineation, its literary style, its patterning and shaping of sentences and voice, its allusion to other texts, these are inhabitable spaces in the poem. The very title of Louise Glück's book *Faithful and Virtuous Night* opens place in the mind of the reader. It alludes, of course, to familiar tales of the virtuous knight. The long titular poem of the book is preceded by two poems, "Parable" and "An Adventure," that, also in their very titles, bring us further into the world of such tales, in their symbol and adventure. Here are the first lines of the title poem, "Faithful and Virtuous Night":

> My story begins very simply: I could speak and I was happy.
> Or: I could speak, thus I was happy.
> Or: I was happy, thus speaking.
> I was like a bright light passing through a dark room.
>
> If it is so difficult to begin, imagine what it will be to end—
> On my bed, sheets printed with colored sailboats
> conveying, simultaneously, visions of adventure (in the form
>   of exploration)
> and sensations of gentle rocking, as of a cradle.

Where is the "place" of this poem? Is it, plainly, a child's bedroom? Is it the desk of Glück's implied author, a lonely male artist who struggles with the silence of his gift, as he records these memories? Is it memory itself, its "constituent" parts like "points of clarity in a mist" as she suggests in subsequent stanzas?

> Constituent
> memories of a large memory.
> Points of clarity in a mist, intermittently visible,
> like a lighthouse whose one task
> is to emit a signal.

Or maybe it is the textual story and place of a knight errant, "a bright light passing through a dark room"? Is it the darkness of that figurative room, the night of the title? Glück reports that the voice of this book, particularly the archness of the male speaker that narrates many of its poems, came to her through a desire to enter the world more fully of novels by Iris Murdoch, such as *A Severed Head* and *The Green Knight*. If we note that Murdoch's *The Green Knight* alludes in its title and structure to *Sir Gawain and the Green Knight*, might we describe the latter as the original "place" of the work? Or is the place of this poem, like the land of Darwish's poem, passed by "the lyricists" from one time, one place of mind, to another?

"If it is so difficult to begin, imagine what it will be to end." Here we have an example of the archness of tone Glück describes, and also a shift in address that likewise alters the place of the poem by altering its rhetorical position with the reader, addressing the reader directly, foregrounding its entrance, its "signal," in the world of the reader qua poem and "story." The next lines:

> But what really is the point of the lighthouse?
> This is north, it says.
> Not: I am your safe harbor.
>
> Much to his annoyance, I shared this room with my
>   older brother.
> To punish me for existing, he kept me awake, reading
> adventure stories by the yellow nightlight.
> [....]
> Was this the night in which he read, in which I lay awake?
> No—it was a night long ago, a lake of darkness in which
> a stone appeared, and on the stone
> a sword growing.

If the poem is a land that may pass from one lyricist to the next, to repeat Williams in "The Descent," "the world it opens is always a place / formerly / unsuspected." Williams writes "as night advances." Darwish's *Mural* is set "on the surface of" a figurative "night," as if about to penetrate it. Glück's "Virtuous and Faithful Night" occurs in shared memory, "a night long ago, a lake of darkness." Each of these poems partakes in the modal tradition of the nocturne, the night scene poem, "frequently a threshold poem," according to poet and critic Edward Hirsch, "that puts us in the presence of nothingness or God—it returns us to origins—and stirs poets toward song." As in her previous *A Village Life*, in

Glück's *Faithful and Virtuous Night*, the nocturne is the stage on which the poet "[lies] awake," the site of its utterance. The poem's words, "points of clarity" on that shadowed stage, offer no "safe harbor," yet against the backdrop of darkness offer a clearer place for the world of the senses to mingle in the world of mind, for the articulation of consciousness to take precedence over the world of things.

You and I

In *Citizen: An American Lyric*, Claudia Rankine likewise creates place through the articulation of consciousness. Yet the everyday world in which we wake and speak necessarily comes more to the foreground in these essay-poems. While darkness and whiteness in Williams, Darwish, and Glück connect primarily to inner states—movements of mind, soul, and memory—the consciousness that Rankine articulates speaks to the darkness and lightness of skin, a fact of the body permeated by the abstraction of race. Defining itself through *you*, its vehicle for self and other, the speaking voice of this work addresses the reader, placing "you," poem by poem, in moments during which another's theory of mind about your darker skin results in your erasure. Needless to say, this interlocutor usually sounds as if he or she is white—to him or her, you are invisible, or you are hypervisible. The residue of these moments builds in your body. *Citizen*'s subtitle immediately places us: the land of these aggressions and microaggressions is the United States, physically, poetically, and socially, grounded in nonfiction accounts compiled by Rankine. Yet, despite *Citizen*'s documentary sources, the stage on which its actions take place is saturated in the light of abstraction. Consider the book's opening paragraphs:

> When you are alone and too tired even to turn on any of your devices, you let yourself linger in a past stacked

> among pillows. Usually you are nestled under blankets
> and the house is empty. Sometimes the moon is missing
> and beyond the window the low, gray ceiling seems
> approachable. Its dark light dims in degrees depending
> on the density of clouds and you fall back into that which
> gets reconstructed as metaphor.
>
> The route is often associative. You smell good. You are
> twelve attending Sts. Philip and James School on White
> Plains Road and the girl sitting in the seat behind asks
> you to lean to the right during exams so she can copy
> what you have written. […]
>
> You never really speak except for the time she makes her
> request and later when she tells you you smell good and
> have features more like a white person. You assume she
> thinks she is thanking you for letting her cheat and feels
> better cheating from an almost white person.

Although "you are alone and too tired even to turn on any of
your devices," meaning the tablet, the phone, the laptop, the
above passage is filled with literary *devices* that stage its events in
figurative and abstract terms, "a past stacked among pillows," the
sky is not a sky, but a "low, grey ceiling"; "its dark light dims" and
"you fall back into…metaphor." The "route" here is "associative"
because the poem presents not a literal physical space, but a place
of mind, of memory, the poem itself. The "landscape" of the first
section of *Citizen* continues in this mode, blurring the senses,
sending the mind into itself:

> The rain this morning pours from the gutters and
> everywhere else it is lost in the trees. You need your glasses
> to single out what you know is there because doubt is
> inexorable; you put on your glasses. The trees, their bark,
> their leaves, even the dead ones, are more vibrant wet.
> Yes, and it's raining. Each moment is like this—before
> it can be known, categorized as similar to another thing

and dismissed, it has to be experienced, it has to be seen. What did he just say? Did she really just say that?

In this case, self "doubt" constitutes the place in which the poem occurs. The landscape is purely figurative, yet it is at the same time concrete, putting the reader into the bodily experience of the mind unable to decipher its senses. As a study of failures of intimacy between friends, acquaintances, and strangers, speaking as one side fails to imagine and understand because of the other's skin, *Citizen* places the reader with the poet in the presence of nothingness, to draw once more from Hirsch's definition of the nocturne. In Rankine's hands, that nothingness becomes a place of erasure, an existential night that has no proper song. At the same time, it is a source of the poem's meditation. Disorientation and self-reflection resound:

> When you arrive in your driveway and turn off the car, you remain behind the wheel another ten minutes. You fear the night is being locked in and coded on a cellular level and want time to function as a power wash. Sitting there staring at the closed garage door you are reminded that a friend once told you there exists the medical term—John Henryism—for people exposed to stresses stemming from racism. They achieve themselves to death trying to dodge the buildup of erasure. Sherman James, the researcher who came up with the term, claimed the physiological costs were high. You hope by sitting in silence you are bucking the trend.

"It's a question," Rankine says, in an interview on *Citizen*, of the failed intimacy on which the book focuses, "of language as it arrives from one body to another. It becomes the thing in between two bodies." The poem, then, like the failed interactions it presents—and like its vehicle, the apostrophic *you*—is a "thing in between" persons, a place and an entry into one's self. The poem is "an environment," says Rankine: "It's the thing that opens out to something else. What that something else is changes for readers. So what's on the page—it falls away." As Williams' page becomes a shadow staircase for a descent into memory, as Darwish's becomes the wall we ascend into his vision, as Glück's becomes the story of the night itself, Rankine's page, in its merging of the nocturne's figurative space with nonfiction narratives, becomes a portal through which we might investigate American difference. As such, the poems of *Citizen* bring into stark contrast our capacity and limitation. The power of the mirror neuron system to put us in the positions of others is not automatic. Our theories of mind regarding others are always our own, fraught with and restricted by our abilities to imagine and understand the other's position. The poem, as a textual place, may allow the concrete reality of the other further constitution, through the abstract presentation of the mind, its leaps of figurative language, its presentations of thought and feeling. The poem is an instrument of imagination and understanding, of empathy, an expansion, an opening "out to something" and someplace "else." Yet "what that something else is changes." As in the physical world, this system through which you and I as readers inhabit the other's experience is always each our own—less a mirror and more an echo, a shadow, a dream. The poem becomes, finally, our own place in mind. Sometimes, we change our minds. And we enter a new world.

IF YOU NEED ME, MOTHER IS THE POEM WHERE I'LL BE

Sabrina Orah Mark

IN THE DREAM the sign over the old, black door reads **MOTHER**. It is trimmed with the hair of the missing. The hair is thin and blond, unlike my **MOTHER**'s hair or her **MOTHER**'s hair. "When we talk about the writer's country we are liable to forget that no matter what particular country it is, it is inside as well as outside him. Art requires a delicate adjustment of the outer and inner worlds in such a way that, without changing their nature, they can be seen through each other" (Flannery O'Connor). I reach up and touch the hair, and when I do the old, black door creaks open. I step back. My **MOTHER** places her hand on my shoulder. "Thank god you are here," I say, turning around, but it isn't my **MOTHER**. It is Flannery. "Your mother," says Flannery, "is dead." "To know oneself is to know one's region. It is also to know the world, and it is also, paradoxically, a form of exile from that world" (Flannery O'Connor). "Shut up, Flannery," I say. "Shut up, shut up." In the dream I want to call her a stupid peacock but I can't remember the word for peacock so I call her peas.

The *Chevra Kadisha* is a holy society of men and women who prepare the Jewish dead for burial. Shards of pottery are placed over the eyes to mark the body a broken vessel. "For dust thou art, and to dust shalt thou return" (Genesis 3:19). If it pleases you, feel free to read this essay as the shards of pottery I fear being placed over my **MOTHER**'s eyes. I don't think I will survive her dying.

———◆———

In graduate school one of my professors told me I write too many poems with **MOTHER**s inside them. In the same workshop, he told us poets are often in the habit of dragging lines around with them, like corpses. Lines that don't really belong anywhere. Lines that should be buried. But we drag the lines around with us. With the hope that maybe this time it will fit inside the poem. No. Maybe this one inside this poem? No. We prop the line up and beg it to live. We rouge its cheeks. We put our hands up its torso and open its face. One of my corpse lines was "too much architecture, not enough rain." Disappointing, I know. I think the line had something to do with freedom. If only I could etch it into the side of a skyscraper made entirely out of dew. But even **MOTHER** knows this is impossible. Especially **MOTHER**.

———◆———

Ever since I became a **MOTHER**, I have written one poem, and about twenty stories. The last line of the only poem I've written since my sons were born goes, "I'm sorry, Son, / I'm just a poet. I hope this is enough. / If it isn't I'll burn down the house / and give you the ashes." The endings of most of the stories I've written involve bodies climbing over bodies or being swallowed.

———◆———

My **MOTHER** and my father—neither of whom have ever gotten over anything in their lives—are often in the habit of telling others—specifically their children—to "get over it." I have never gotten over anything in my life. This too is a place. This too is a kind of poem.

———◆———

"One has to be very careful what one takes when one goes away forever, something seemingly useless might become essential under specific circumstances" (Leonora Carrington). I wasn't careful when I left poetry for storytelling. All I brought with me were these lousy notebooks filled with words like "roses" and "liver" and "king" and "rot" and "boy" and "heaven." I will have to go back. I ask my **MOTHER** what useless thing she would take with her if she was to go away forever. She wants to know, what do I mean by "useless?" "Like a photograph?" she asks. And then she begins to worry: "What about the necessary things will they have the necessary things where I'm going?" "Forget it," I say. "This is all too much," she says. "Plus I think the stock market is crashing."

———◆———

I say to my sons bath time, or dinner time, or don't throw the apple at your brother, or helmet, or get down from there, or socks and shoes, or please be careful, or brush your teeth, or go to bed. Once I told my older son that those squirrels over there once were boys, but they didn't eat their dinner. "I love squirrels!" he hoorayed. There is a hole where the **MOTHER** words go. One day I will find the hole and pull the words out, one by one, mud caked and sleepy. I will wash them and lay them all out in the bright sun, and out of them make a poem that will break all the children's hearts if only (for once) they would listen to me.

(Forgotten) rumor has it that a famous poet once referred to me as Claudia Rankine's "tail." I think it was meant to be an insult. As an undergraduate at Barnard, I had taken all her classes, then worked for her, then lost her when I went to Iowa, then followed her to Georgia, then almost followed her again to Houston, but didn't, then lost her again, then found her again among the cheering crowds. She is my poet **MOTHER**. All I ever wanted was to be close enough to her to hear everything she ever said. When I met her "I was still in the very beginning of being human" (Jorie Graham). When I saw her last December for a quick tea (almost 20 years after we first met), we hugged, and out of her purse she started pulling gifts for my two sons: a periscope and a superhero and a tiny police car. Impossible not to read each of these toys as a metaphor for what her poetry is after.

One Sunday afternoon, a woman knocks on our front door. She is frantic. Her father has just had a heart attack. They don't think he will make it. "Oh my god," I say. "Come in, come in." She stands in our livingroom. My sons are staring. "How can we help," I ask. She needs money for gas. The hospital is in another town. I give her $20, and a weird smile flashes over her face. It isn't gratitude; it is something else. I notice her front teeth are rotten or rotting. My husband enters, and the woman waves the $20 bill like the flag of a disappearing country. I can tell from his eyes she's been here before. "How's your **MOTHER**?" he asks. Last time it was her **MOTHER** who was dying in the exact same way the father is now dying. The hospital is always in another town. She is gone before it dawns on me entirely that she's lying. I've been had.

Later that evening, I find out she goes up and down the streets knocking on doors. Her parents dying over and over again. In a far off hospital. It looks like they will never make it. She will never get there in time, but she'll try. At first I am angry, and then I realize this frenzied scam artistry might not be all that different from writing.

———◆———

There is a Brown Thrasher that repeatedly flings itself into our living room window. We have done everything: covered the windows with black paper, hung scarecrows, soaped the glass, cursed it out, taped up raptor silhouettes…nothing works. We could remove its nest, but we don't have the heart. The thrasher has been fighting with her reflection for months. And even when her reflection is obstructed she still keeps hitting the window because this route (nest to glass) has become like a necessary heartbeat. It's miserable. I can't decide whether to name this occurrence "What Is a Poem" or "I Miss my **MOTHER**."

———◆———

For my 40th birthday I wanted two things. #1 to clean my entire house. #2 to have a word with Gertrude Stein's **MOTHER**.

———◆———

About the value of critique, Claudia Rankine once said to our workshop, if the whole room is looking in one direction it's probably a good idea to look at what they're looking at. You don't have to believe in it, or care. But it's probably worth your time to turn your head, to know what has caught everybody else's attention. After I visited her class at Pomona, she told me I look up at the ceiling too often when I speak publicly. I do. I'm probably searching for a heaven above, or Claudia, or my **MOTHER** or some other inconceivably vast thing. Once, when our tea date was drawing to a close, she looked at me with a gravitas I know only Claudia to possess, and very slowly, and very deeply asked, "how do you spell woohoo?" And with the same precision I forced on myself when I spoke to her as an undergraduate about Paul Celan or Toni Morrison or J.M. Coetzee or Aimé Césaire or Gertrude Stein, I spelled the word the only way I knew how: *w-o-o-h-o-o*. That night she gave the most magnificent poetry reading I have ever attended. She moved the whole gigantic audience to tears. She read from *Citizen*, a collection that breathes in the sadness of the world, and breathes it out as poetry. At one moment, before she read one of her anecdotes-gone-poem, she confessed to changing the "real" ending to make it a happier ending. "I believe," she said "in repair."

———— • ————

When I was arranging my first collection, *The Babies*, the brilliant poet and pianist Oni Buchanan gave me the best advice. She said each poem should somehow contain a window or a portal or a hole or a trapdoor through which the poem that follows can enter. Nabokov calls these the "nerves" or the "secret points" or the "subliminal coordinates by means of which the book is plotted." Just between you and me, I've already plotted the coordinates of my new collection. It is a perfect drawing of my **MOTHER**'s face.

ON BLACKACRE

Monica Youn

BLACKACRE is a legal fiction, an imaginary landscape. Just as we use "John Doe" for a hypothetical person, lawyers use "Blackacre" as a placeholder term for a hypothetical plot of land. Every law student in the Anglo-American system encounters the term in the core course on property law, and in trusts and estates law. So a typical hypothetical on a law school exam might start: "John Doe, possessor of a fee simple in Blackacre, wishes to transfer his interest to Jane Roe, in exchange for her property Whiteacre…" The sequence of fictional properties continues with Greenacre, Brownacre, Redacre, and Blueacre. First coined by Sir Edward Coke in 1628, Blackacre—with its echoes of *Bleak House*, of black-letter law, of blight taken to gothic extremes—is an inside joke among lawyers, a password marking one's initiation into a centuries-old tradition of legal indoctrination.

"Blackacre" is the title sequence of my most recent book, which also contains poems titled "Whiteacre," "Greenacre," etc. I think of each "____acre" as a landscape, a legacy—the allotment each of us is given to work with, whether that allotment is a place, a span of time, a work of art, a body, a destiny. We never start with a blank slate—each acre has been previously tenanted, enriched and depleted, built up and demolished. What are the limits of the imagination's ability to transform what is given? On any particular ____acre can we plant a garden? Found a city? Unearth a treasure? Build a home?

———◆———

When I was trying to write the poem that became "Blackacre," I was trying to write something painfully private, painfully personal—about my "barrenness," my desire to have a child who would be genetically "mine," my increasingly irrational pursuit of that desire, its long-drawn-out failure, the fallout of recriminations and regrets, and my eventual decision to have a child by other means. I've never been comfortable with autobiographical material, and for years I circled the topic, trying innumerable false starts, wanting to approach the issue straightforwardly but failing at every attempt.

Any kind of direct treatment seemed inadequate, untrue. My "experience" of infertility was a tiny kernel rattling around in a confusion of cartilaginous walls: vestiges of my Catholic upbringing, my Korean-American background, my legal training, my socialization into normative codes of class and gender and sexuality, the stories and lessons and phrases that chorus in my brain—all the semi-dismantled interpenetrating structures through which I filter and process sensations, emotions, thoughts. The resonating echoes from these half-ruined structures were as much the subject of the poem as any originating "experience."

My attention kept shifting away from the blank page and toward a space already furrowed with black text, the near-rectangle of Milton's great sonnet "On His Blindness." It was a field already trenched and planted and harvested that I would try to force into yielding another crop, using whatever technologies of fertilization, gleaning, grafting that I could devise. A perverse endeavor, maybe, but one that felt right to me.

———— ✦ ————

Sonnet 19 is a poem that I've always obsessed over, a poem that I recite under my breath while waiting for subways and elevators, a poem in which I'm constantly finding new depths and patterns. Mulling over the question of my infertility, the words "spent," "useless," "denied," "chide," "need," "wait" kept thudding in my mind. Using Milton's poem as the frame for my own poem "on my barrenness" somehow became the only workable solution.

It's not that blindness and barrenness are in any way commensurate, not by orders of magnitude both quantitative and qualitative. But there's a structural similarity in the way Milton tries to rationalize his blindness and the way we talk about infertility. In Milton's poem, serving God is a universal good, and he mourns his inability to make an active contribution to that good. But Patience cuts short his flow of regrets, telling him that the good does not depend on his direct involvement; that he participates in the good even if he cannot claim a personal stake in it. We never hear how, or whether, Milton replies to these assurances; Patience gets the last word, both literally ("wait") and rhetorically.

Similarly, we often treat parenthood as a universal good (although one that many opt not to pursue). Of course, there are many ways to participate in that good without a personal (*i.e.,* genetic) stake in it—adoption, the use of egg and sperm donors, etc. But that assurance—that nongenetic parenting is the perfect equivalent of genetic parenting—can't explain our culture's no-holds-barred pursuit of genetic parenthood: IUI, IVF, egg-freezing, surrogacy, and other assisted reproductive technologies, the edge of desperation that shows itself in conversations about the biological clock. Some of the most progressive and enlightened couples of my acquaintance have spent money and time they could barely afford on successive rounds of IUI and IVF and hormone therapies and homeopathic remedies and acupuncture—a dead-end street I travelled down for years.

What motivated me to engage in serial renunciations, purifications, penetrations, to submit to measures that were painful and humiliating and carcinogenic and expensive? How can I make sense of my own desperation? Was it egotism—the temptation to trace one's own features and traits in a younger (and more adorable) self? Heteronormativity taken to extremes? Family pressure? Fear of death? Self-abnegation? Some primordial biological imperative buried deep within the lizard brain?

———◆———

I'm a mother now. I love my son, I can't imagine loving him more. When I was writing "Blackacre," I was determined to finish it before my son was born. Surveying Blackacre from this vantage point—from across the border of parenthood—the topography and features of the landscape are resonantly familiar to me. But I can be glad that I don't live there anymore.

THINKING DETROIT

Hayan Charara

THE PAST OF MY POEMS is usually called Detroit. But because I left the city for good in 1996, and return infrequently, the city exists for me predominantly as memory, and a lot has changed over the past two decades, so much so the Detroit I write about may not, in significant ways, correspond to the Detroit of the here and now. In *The Alchemist's Diary*, my first book, I describe the city as "a shithole" "where boys / are manufactured into men," where "Fords and Chevys, the carcasses / of car makers' assembly lines, / [are] torched and overturned," where "rats cried for escape," and where "I was first called a sand nigger." Yet I also bestow on Detroit the epithet of holy city, a nod to its stubborn refusal to die, its insistence on rebirth. And in a poem titled "Dandelions," a lone dandelion rising out of a crack in an asphalt parking lot symbolizes the city and its people. The dandelion is a weed, of course, a thing unwanted, that gets yanked out. But with its bright yellow petals, it's easy to mistake it for a flower. The dandelion insists on being

> a show of survival, of getting through,
> of coming close to not making it,

and then, all of a sudden,
life where we never expect it.

Detroit is also where I witnessed, on a highway exit ramp, a man holding a sign that asked, "Why doesn't Jesus turn asphalt into bread?" It is where I heard the city's longtime mayor, Coleman Young, explain Detroit's decades-long decline by noting, "Neighborhoods collapsed because half the goddamn population left!" Detroit embodies the inextricability of the profane and sacred—a shithole, a holy city.

My take on Detroit—its complexity—arises out of facts, those which any researcher, professional or amateur, can find supported not only in other poems by other poets, and in novels, films, essays, history books, and government statistics, but also by simply speaking with someone who has lived or still lives in Detroit. You could also visit the city and see for yourself. However, I have to concede that despite the facts, the city of Detroit, as I know it, as it appears in my poems, is probably more imagined than real. Lately, I've been thinking about this a lot (probably because I have surpassed the milestone of living more years in other cities than in my hometown), and I have come to a few realizations, one of which is that I can hardly tell the difference anymore between thinking about the past and remembering the past. In fact I am beginning to wonder, when it comes to thinking and remembering, if there is any significant difference between the two.

Most people, myself included, view thinking as tied to the present moment, as a here-and-now practice, whereas memory resides in the past—remembering as a practice with the capacity for time travel. Our everyday language reinforces the dichotomy. We tend to "think back to" rather than "think on" or "think of" an earlier time. We *re*member and *re*call events and people from the past, the "re-" prefix a reminder of the returning, the going back. This division between past and present is not quite right, though. A return to an event or idea via memory is not a return to the original encounter. The "re-" prefix so often used in the vocabulary of memory belongs as much to the new and now as the old and then. When we "*return*," "*recall*," "*remember*," "*remind*," we must also think of things that occur "afresh," and "anew," and these necessarily invoke the present moment, the right now.

In the strictest sense—literally speaking—every thought occurs in the past. Whatever I think at this very moment—or speak or write—the moment, perceived as the present, occupies a space already a fraction of a millisecond gone (the time it takes for the sensory experience of an act or thought to travel to and register in the brain as the here and now). Every moment experienced as "now" takes place "then." However, our brains simply cannot sense this infinitesimally small lapse of time. Maybe, then, we should regard memory (remembering, thinking about the past) as something that happens simultaneously in the past and present. This is what I do. You can do what you want.

Obviously, no single image or set of related images can possibly embody an entity as complicated as a city, a truism for cities both in the actual world and memory, cities of the past or present. Oddly enough, I found in the work of my forebears, Philip Levine and Lawrence Joseph, a Detroit all too familiar to mine, even though decades separate the Detroit of our poems and pasts. This speaks to endemic problems, often largely ignored or worsened by inept, inadequate, or misguided policies and politicians. It also brings attention to the way the past works—a city, or anything else for that matter, should be unchanged in the past. What happened then, happened once, is set in stone. Except—both in the real world, and in the imagination, the past is anything but static. While the *actual* changes Detroit undergoes may be too slow or, for those who must bear the brunt of its ills, nonexistent, the Detroit of my memory-thinking is constantly changing, in some respects more often and more dramatically than in actuality. Which brings me to another problem I think a lot about—truth. I take truth to be an endpoint—at least an intention—of my poetry, and while no pursuit of truth is entirely innocent, mine follows the path of a poet, not a philosopher. In other words—or, in Richard Hugo's: "The words should not serve the subject. The subject should serve the words. This may mean violating the facts."The poet, Hugo tells us in *The Triggering Town*, "owes reality nothing and the truth about...feelings everything."

While I never tell lies in my poems, I do violate the facts— innocuously, I believe. Worse than allegiance to the truth about my feelings over the facts, however, is my reliance on memory to arrive at truth. In its service, except to persuade, memory can be nearly worthless. Most lawyers will tell you—the one I'm married to tells me all the time—that eyewitness testimony (or "memory") may indeed be one of the most effective, persuasive kinds of evidence, but it is also possibly the most unreliable. In this way, the past mirrors a work of literature: open to multiple readings, interpretations, and, more importantly, open to misinterpretation. In the law, certain verifiable forms of evidence applied to eyewitness testimony (DNA in a criminal investigation, for example) show that even the most self-assured, without-a-doubt, under-oath memories turn out to be simply impossible. Like other poets who aim for truth, I don't place my hands on a Bible and swear to tell the truth, the whole truth, and nothing but. No poet—nor any witness in a court of law— ever swears to tell the facts, either. Other forms of speech—in particular, I'm thinking of legal and political speech—come with formal (public) rituals and oaths. Elected officials swear to do this and that; persons about to be married do the same. Poets have no such rituals. They do, however, engage in other rituals and commitments—the practices and pacts a poet makes with craft, with a reader, with his or her own censors—but these come about voluntarily, and they vary from poet to poet. If the facts can be disregarded or altered, and truths (definite or indefinite) depend on or emerge from feelings, then do I owe my subject any allegiance? What do I owe the city of Detroit, which, a quarter-century after abandoning it, I still call my hometown?

The easy answer, which I had to learn, which every poet must learn: nothing at all. Louise Glück puts it this way: "The artist's task, then, involves the transformation of the actual to the true. And the ability to achieve such transformations, especially in art that presumes to be subjective, depends on conscious willingness to distinguish truth from honesty or sincerity." While poetry may depend on actual experiences, "honest speech" does not lead the poet, or the reader, to discovery. Honest speech is "the degree to which and the power with which the generating impulse has been transcribed. Transcribed, not transformed." The poet's work is not to transcribe but to *transform* experience into truth. The poet's experience serves as a "lightning rod," but the truth isn't necessarily found in the lightning bolt. The poet must transform the experience so it may lead to a discovery. The poem that does this is one that "sounds like honest speech," but, Glück reminds us, sounding and being honest are not the same. The "authentic" voice is the one that rings true. "The true, in poetry, is felt as insight," Glück writes. It does not have to be lived, either. "It is, instead, all that can be envisioned." The advocacy here calls for an inventive mind, and a bold mind. The poet can—Glück seems to be saying the poet *must*—transform lived experience. It has to be "changed—heightened, distilled, made memorable." She also advocates for "the true," which is the thing in a poem "felt as insight"—it is "*all* that can be envisioned." The emphasis is mine. *All* that can be envisioned requires, I think, a long-term, continual commitment to the truth—to return, again and again, to a previous realization or discovery, to a subject (to a city, for example—and if not a city, then to another subject, another *object* of attention until it becomes, in the ideal, an obsession). A poet may never get to "*all* that can be envisioned," but each return (to the poem, to its subject) is a step in that direction. This, Glück contends, is the "advantage of poetry over life." I would add politics and law to the list of things over which poetry has an advantage.

Poetic speech, it should be obvious, is not political or

legal speech. Nor is poetic practice akin to its legal or political counterparts. Plain and simple, poetry is not politics, or law, or, for that matter, journalism or history. Much as I write about Detroit, and what has happened to it, and to its people, my poems on the subject, concerned though they may be with truth, are not public records. They are private ruminations that come to be only barely, occasionally public. And, yes, I aim for them to speak a truth, and I believe many do, but no matter how apparent a truth in them may be, no matter how authoritative the poems or the truths in them, they are never authoritarian. You can undo them. But even if you don't, I have no doubt that eventually I will. I will try, at least.

Though I have spent more years living in other cities than in Detroit, I keep going back—that is I keep *thinking* about the city. Nostalgia—the pain, the yearning to return home—only partially, and inadequately, explains why I go back. I do so because I am, every few years, someone new—not a better human being, necessarily (though hopefully), but simply someone with another, different perspective through which to make sense of the world—my world, in particular. Because I have changed, so has my past. A colleague of mine, lecturing on Aeschylus' *Agamemnon*, remarked that one of the frustrations of Greek tragedy is that no one has a second thought about a horrific crime or transgression until it is too late. Agamemnon may not be able to go back in time to the moment before he decides to murder his daughter; he seems incapable of this task, even in memory. But I am not Agamemnon, and having managed to avoid such darkness, most of us aren't. We can go back—we must go back—and when we do, we can rethink our pasts, and we return from the journey with either knowledge or pain, which is a kind of knowledge. Either would be fine. Both can be made into one of the many truths available to us over the course of a lifetime. I am convinced—more than I have ever been, probably because a little older I hope I am a little wiser—that this is necessary if only (but not only) because the truth possesses an extraordinary capacity for disappointment. Once made—you can say *discovered*, if you wish, or *realized*, or *arrived at*, but I'll say *made*—the truth wants to be exclusive; it does not wish to share space with other truths. But anything experienced in isolation ultimately gives way to an aching for something more, something else. With the truth, this is the beginning of its undoing. And to undo, we must first go back before going forward.

The poems of my first book try to make sense of the city, its meaningfulness, by way of presence, rootedness—the images concrete and definite: "Interstate 94, at milepost 210," "the city beside the strait," "Hart Plaza," "Eight houses from the birthplace of Henry Ford," and so on. In *The Sadness of Others*, written nearly a decade after I left, I go back to the city, but I think-remember Detroit differently. Having settled into a new life, in New York, a city and a life so much unlike those I knew in Detroit, I ache for something new, something more. The city is transformed in these poems because I underwent transformation. No doubt—I can say this now—my mother's death loomed over this ache. She had been dead almost a decade—she died only months after I left home, left Detroit—and her death, the most literal, permanent embodiment of transformation, made it nearly impossible for me not to view almost everything in those days through this lens. And so the poems in *The Sadness of Others* turn to more reflective renderings and become more concerned with absence than presence—the images, the speech, the truths, less definite and more liminal, occupying the space of transformation, which inhabits both sides of the boundary separating past from present.

When past and present become enmeshed with one another or indistinguishable from each other, where do you stand, and what do you do?

You can forgive

the past. Or you can
forget it or curse it.
Either way,
it doesn't matter.
Soon enough, you'll sleep
in another city,
dream of bridges
with different names,
and somehow even the air
that rises above
the sewer grates
will smell like lilacs
in spring.

This is a kind of reconciliation with the past—*kind of*, because the terms of the agreement, the settlement, allow for acceptance or rejection, for reinvention, for wholly altering the past, or even, as a last resort, for a mild embrace. Perhaps reconcilement is not quite right. A more accurate way to conceive this may be as a re-visioning of how to struggle with the past. Re-visioning allows us to do what could not be done when our actions, thoughts, and feelings first happened—to stop the forward march of time and consider them slowly, repeatedly, carefully, with all the benefits of hindsight and distance. This allows us to unmoor the past from time and place, to unfix the past.

This thinking appears in *Something Sinister*, my most recent work: "The past is a strange land. // Go because you can. / Go because you can / come back." Though I did not until recently come to this realization (that we can not only journey to the past, but find it new each time we visit, and bring back with us something new each time we take leave of it), I must have had some inkling of it early on. "Thinking American," a poem written on the occasion of leaving Detroit, ends

Listen,

when I say Detroit, I mean
any place. By thinking American, I mean made.

We live in places. Regardless of where on earth, and when in time we live in them, and regardless of the extraordinary diversity of these places and of humanity across space and time, our joy and grief, our pain and happiness, remains much the same. How we encounter and reencounter those joys and pains also remains much the same. Whether in Houston or New York City, London or Madrid, on a trail in a forest or at a table in a coffee shop, when I think of Detroit in the years 1972 through 1994, which are all gone, or when I think of the house I grew up in on Carlin Street, which is gone, or my mother, gone, and everything else in the past which is always on the verge of coming to mind, when it comes, all of it, whether I want it to or not, it is always there, always here, and never the same.

HOMING IN: THE PLACE OF POETRY IN THE GLOBAL DIGITAL AGE

Philip Metres

MY WIFE AND I went shopping for smartphones recently, beholding these modern votives with equal parts wonder and worry. We, digital immigrants and introverts who tote a decade-old "flip" phone only for emergencies, see the benefits of these magical devices—the fairy tale power of a digital genie, released with the mere swipe of a screen. But what genie will we unleash when we bring this technology into our lives? Doesn't the servant, in the end, always change the master?

Despite the fact that digital technologies offer global connectedness, they also appear to isolate us further into our own self-created reality, dislocate us from the non-digital world. And the greater our privilege, the more we can cordon off the real, the stronger our myopia. As "Luxury, then, is a way of / being ignorant, comfortably," Amiri Baraka once wrote. Yet privilege does more than damage our vision; it starves the heart. In the Biblical parable of Lazarus and the Rich Man, the rich man's flaw is not merely being unable to see Lazarus in pain right outside his gate; after his death, when he looks up from Hades, he clearly recognizes Lazarus next to Abraham in heaven, and begs

Abraham to ask Lazarus for a bit of water to cool his torment. The rich man knows Lazarus by name, but even in hell, does not see fit to address him directly.

In our global digital age—with its information flood, its attenuation of attention, its transmogrification of subjectivity, its obscuring of our connectedness—what can poetry and the arts do? The artist's challenge is not merely to chronicle the hectic present, but to develop an understanding of how we find ourselves at this time and place, to explore what binds us to each other, and to ask Leo Tolstoy's question: "how, then, shall we live?"

Poetry's oldest and least-marketable power, paradoxically, offers us a secret vitality. Poetry's slowness, its ruminativity, enables us to step back from the distracted and distracting present, to ground ourselves again through language in the realities of our bodies and spirits, and their connections to the ecosystems in which we find ourselves. The form of a poem is one that forms us, holding us in its thrall. To dwell with singular lines or phrases, lines that puzzle or clarify, carries us back to the ancient practices of ritual chant and shamanic trance, fundamental to the ecstatic possibilities of communion and healing. In the words of C.D. Wright, *pace* Horace: "Some of us do not read or write particularly for pleasure or instruction, but to be changed, healed, charged."

Such grounded visionary practice is both exercise and meditation, a parallel to prayer. The work of the imagination invites us to slow down, pay close attention, to visualize, to wonder. Poetry tunes us to ultimate things.

Poetry is not a mere throwback, some atavistic practice for the vestigial few. On the contrary, poetry's discipline of entering us into our minds and bodies—our restless bodies, our roiled souls—is an ancient practice that invites grace to enter our brokenness, to hold us together, to waken us again. The Sufi poet Rumi wrote, "the wound is the place where Light enters you," seven hundred years before Leonard Cohen sang, "There's a crack in everything. That's how the light gets in"—thus proving Thomas Merton's thesis that "that which is oldest is most new."

While poetry tunes us to ultimate things, poetry also can act as a technology of embodied inquiry, a way of locating ourselves and others within contexts heretofore outside of our understanding, yet which include us within their operations. Michael Davidson has proposed that "perhaps poetry, in its proximity to affective states, is the dreamwork of globalization." Poetry and the arts indeed can help us perform what Fredric Jameson calls cognitive mapping, "enabl[ing] a situational representation on the part of the individual subject to that vaster and properly unrepresentable totality which is the ensemble of society's structures as a whole." I love this strange quote; Jameson, a postmodern Marxist theorist, has in mind a materialist totality, and that we are subjects (and objects) in the system of late capitalism. Yet Jameson's phrasing is mystical, inviting us to consider not only human structures, but also planetary, cosmic structures. Perhaps, even, the unrepresentable Divine.

That's why I love the term "cosmopoetics" to describe art that performs cognitive mapping. It suggests both cosmopolitanism—the philosophy of global human solidarity—and also something cosmic, where the universe offers us traces of a great Totality. When I look at my own writing—which began only as a blind reaching-out into the epistemological dark—a cosmopoetics, a geographical imagination, seems to have taken shape. Like many poets, I began writing to make sense of what was happening to me and around me; as my interests have orbited further outward, I was challenged—and the language challenged me—to reach beyond comfortable frames of understanding. Each place became a portal to new worlds. Traveling to my grandparents' houses in Brooklyn or Rhode Island, or climbing inside the ancient step pyramid at Chichén Itzá, or after college, living in Russia for a year, were quantum leaps where my language flailed to reach for some sort of handhold.

The questions of travel, as Elizabeth Bishop called them, have often been at the center of my writing. Travel exposes us to otherness (other cultures, other histories, other people), and exposes us as other to ourselves. Yet, as Mary Louise Pratt argues in *Imperial Eyes*, the trope of "anti-conquest" in Western travel writing—in which an innocent Westerner encounters other places and cultures—becomes a strategy of representation that enables one to "seek to secure their innocence at the same moment as they assert European hegemony." So many writers have exploited their travel experience as yet another subject to plunder, the imagination as a marauding imperial Columbus. That's why in one poem in *To See the Earth*, I cite my Russian mentor, Dimitri Psurtsev, who once remarked after reading some of my poems, "this is your version of Russia, not Russia."

When I speak of "cognitive mapping," of cosmopoetics, I am talking about an essential human endeavor—to connect our apperceptive physicality to our surroundings. I love getting lost, because getting lost also entails a new kind of knowing. Just when you think you know where you're going, you're lost. When you see you're lost, you're going to find something larger than the self. Yet cartography and its abstractions are deeply political, and often have extended exploitative power arrangements, carved people and peoples apart for the aims of empires. That's why I'm wary of broad claims about the representativity of my representations. *To See the Earth* is "my" creation story, *Pictures at an Exhibition* is "my" Russia, *A Concordance of Leaves* is "my" Palestine, *Sand Opera* is "my" Iraq. Or rather, this is where "I" come from, this is the Russia in which I lost and found myself, the Palestine that absorbed me, the Iraq that carries me.

Sand Opera began as a daily Lenten meditation, working with the testimonies of the tortured at Abu Ghraib, to witness to their suffering; it has become an attempt to find a language that would sight/site (both in the sense of to render visible, and in the sense of locating in the geographical imagination) the war itself, constantly off-screen. War is so distanced that the closest most Americans get to it is when they encounter a veteran or refugee.

That it was illegal for eighteen years—from 1991's Operation Desert Storm until 2009—to take photos of flag-draped coffins of U.S. military suggests the level of censorship during war. This policy is designed not only to abstract the enemy, but also to render the cost of war invisible and suppress domestic questioning. More recently, our contemporary program of "targeted assassination" by drones has yet to be made fully visible to the American people.

My desire in *Sand Opera* is to make the Iraq War and the wider War on Terror visible, to make a visible and audible map of it, a map that we would carry in our eyes and ears, in our bodies and hearts, to replace the maps of pundits and demagogues. In a strange way, I see my practice paralleling St. Ignatius of Loyola's notion of "*composición*"—often translated as "seeing in imagination" or "mental representation." *Composición* comes from the Latin *compositionem*, meaning "putting together, connecting," but the word's roots suggest that imaginative visualization involves placing oneself with (com + position). In Ignatius' Spiritual Exercises, we come closer to God through *composición*, which can both locate us in our own lives (what he calls the daily *examen*) and bring us to far-flung places, to stand with others. For *Sand Opera*, I wanted language to make visible the ruptures of violence, through the black bars of redaction and fractured syntax, but I also found myself drawn to the strange images that show (and do not show) the operations of war.

Throughout the book, for example, unexplained drawings of rooms appear, with language floating on a vellum page above them. These are renderings by Mohamad Bashmilah, a former prisoner from Yemen, of what have come to be known as black sites—secret prisons where the United States and its allies would illegally hold and interrogate detainees. These drawings are the renderings of one who has been "rendered," sundered from everything he knew. To witness them is to enter the mind of a person utterly dislocated, yet rigorously, obsessively, trying to locate himself:

Black Site (Exhibit I)

Whenever I saw

a fly in my cell

I was filled

with joy

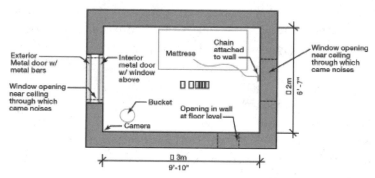

though I wished for it

to slip   under the door

so it would not be

imprisoned itself

Sand Opera also contains a diagram of a proper "Muslim Burial" from the Standard Operation Procedure (SOP) manual for the Guantanamo Bay prison. The SOP notes the importance of the treatment of the body—the enshrouding process, the prayers that should be uttered—and how the body should point toward Mecca. Alongside the testimonies of prisoners who saw the Qu'ran thrown into the toilet, we are struck again by the gap between our measure of cultural sensitivity and our manipulation of that knowledge for cruel and degrading acts.

Poems are a momentary home, ways to home in. Their architectures, their forms, inform how we perceive and feel insides and outsides. In *Sand Opera*, we stumble among the broken syntax of the tortured in Abu Ghraib prison; stare at the thick walls of the vellum-paged "Black Site (Exhibit I)," trying to read the words on the next page seeping around the prison cell; we confront the words of a bereaved widow of a soldier who has the chance to enter the military tank where her husband died, in "Home Sweet Home," nested inside another poem, based on a letter of a Marine lamenting his own entrapment in a war where he can't fight the evil he faces.

Cosmopoetics is ultimately not just about mapping, or even seeing. It's also about listening, about a radical vulnerability to the other. As Isaiah writes, "morning after morning / He opens my ear that I may hear." *Sand Opera* is the sound of my listening. These poems carry forth voices that have opened me—the Iraqi curator Donny George Youkhanna, sharing slides of lost art from his cherished museum, abused Iraqi prisoners and U.S. military at Abu Ghraib prison, a recipe in Nawal Nasrallah's Iraqi cookbook, the detained Mohamad Bashmilah, a drone operator who isn't sure who he's killing, an Arab-American living through the paranoid days after the 9/11 attacks, and my daughter's coming to consciousness in a world where war leaks through the radio and television. The words of my daughter at the end of the poem "Hung Lyres" embody what I hope I can continue to open myself into:

What does it mean, I say. She says, it means
to be quiet, just by yourself. She says, there's

a treasure chest inside. You get to dig it out.
Somehow, it's spring. Says, will it always

rain? In some countries, I say, they are
praying for rain. She asks, why do birds sing?

In the dream, my notebook dipped in water,
all the writing lost. Says, read the story again.

But which one? That which diverts the mind
is poetry. Says, you know those planes

that hit those buildings? Asks, why do birds sing?
When the storm ends, she stops, holds her hands

together, closes her eyes. What are you doing?
I'm praying for the dead worms. Says, listen:

How can we map these connections and distances without losing our focus on what's directly in front of us—this tendency toward *hyperopia*, that longsightedness that is another kind of myopia? I've thought a lot about all the ways that my obsessions with distant wars and places and people have frayed me to loose ends, distracting me from intimate joys and domestic peace. At times, I've wondered if I've engaged in the poetic equivalent of the father scrolling through his phone while his child finally balances on her bike and glides down the sidewalk, in perfect rhythm with herself and her conveyance. How to hold the sight of my daughters' faces, dearer to me than any faces on this dear earth, alongside the sight of someone else's daughter's face—first seen on Facebook—pulling schoolbooks out of a bombed house in Gaza, to continue studying another day? How to hold and be held by my beloved wife, and also teach my classes, catch up on emails and messages, mow the lawn, take out the garbage, and also find time to click a microloan to a Gazan farmer named Ahmad, who needs to buy some hens for his egg business? How do we carry our others and ourselves on this fragile planet?

Antonio Gramsci once asked himself so poignantly: "[is] it really possible to forge links with a mass of people when one has never had strong feelings for anyone, not even one's own parents, if it is possible to have a collectivity when one has not been deeply loved oneself by individual human creatures. Hasn't

[this]...tended to make me sterile and reduce my quality as a revolutionary by making everything a matter of pure intellect, of pure mathematical calculation?" Gramsci's question is an old theme, as old as Diogenes' idea of cosmopolitanism. The cosmopolitan idea that we are all connected and that a person on a distant part of the globe is as dear as our neighbor has always engendered the profoundest critique of the cosmopolite—that he is one who loves everyone in the abstract but hates (or ignores) all particular people. It's a real danger I have occasionally blundered into, blinkered by vanity or distracted by novelty.

Poetry is one of the ways we might try to home in—to claim our own ground—not our digital platforms but the raw earthiness of our own bodies, our beloveds, our kin, our distant next-door (human and sentient) neighbors of the communities in which we live and ones to which we're tied. Like any other technology, poetry contains powers that both distract and focus us; it is a danger like any power. Yet it is one of the ways I answer the question—how to ground myself in my own body, my breath, exercising something I have no other word for but *love*, that radical opening of self to the other? "For we are put on this earth a little space," William Blake writes, "that we may learn to bear the beams of love."

I'd like to circle back to the smartphone for a moment. It's strange to think that the very smartphone that enables you to Google Map your way in any strange city in the world doesn't advertise the often deplorable conditions for workers assembling these phones. Nor does it divulge that the rare earths that go into its construction (exotic elements such as tantalum, tungsten, tin, and gold) may have come from—and fueled conflict in—places such as the Congo. And once a new model emerges and we've worn out the phone, where does this material go when we've thrown it out? Whose child will be paid pennies to pull out its innards? Who will inherit its poisons?

I trace my awakening to this question from my early days at Loyola Academy where, in a freshman religious studies class taught by the improbably-ancient Father Steenken, we watched

"The Wrath of Grapes"—a documentary exposé on pesticide exposure to migrant workers—and the filmic adaptation of Ambrose Bierce's "Occurrence at Owl Creek Bridge." Ignatian spirituality—from social justice conscientization to existential exploration of a condemned man's longing for freedom—lit my imagination and dilated my empathy. What I long to write and to encounter is art that can help us make a quantum leap in our moral imagination. As a poet, I long for Isaiah's fire, for a "well-trained tongue, / That I might know how to speak to the weary / A word that will rouse them." To make poems that will open not only our eyes, but awaken us, pry open our hearts and souls, induce μετάνοια (*metanoia*)—transforming how we spend our breath on this earth.

I'd like to end with a poem of mine, called "Compline," that is also a prayer:

That we await a blessed hope, & that we will be struck
With great fear, like a baby taken into the night, that every boot,

Every improvised explosive, Talon & Hornet, Molotov
& rubber-coated bullet, every unexploded cluster bomblet,

Every Kevlar & suicide vest & unpiloted drone raining fire
On wedding parties will be burned as fuel in the dark season.

That we will learn the awful hunger of God, the nerve-fraying
Cry of God, the curdy vomit of God, the soiled swaddle of God,

The constant wakefulness of God, alongside the sweet scalp
Of God, the contented murmur of God, the limb-twitched dream-

Reaching of God. We're dizzy in every departure, limb-lost.
We cannot sleep in the wake of God, & God will not sleep

The infant dream for long. We lift the blinds, look out into ink
For light. My God, my God, open the spine binding our sight.

ON WRITING FROM THE NEW OCEANIA

Craig Santos Perez

Write *from*

FROM indicates a particular time or place as a starting point; *from* refers to a specific location as the first of two limits; *from* imagines a cause, an agent, an instrument, a source, or an origin; *from* marks separation, removal, or exclusion; *from* differentiates borders. "Where are you from?" In the preface to my first book of poems, I wrote: "On some maps, Guam doesn't exist; I point to an empty space in the Pacific and say, 'I'm from here.' On some maps, Guam is a small, unnamed island; I say, 'I'm from this unnamed place.' On some maps, Guam is named 'Guam, USA.' I say, 'I'm from a territory of the United States.'"

> *from* excerptus: "pluck out" *from* ex- "out" + carpere "gather" or "harvest"

From also indicates an excerpt or a passage quoted from a source. My own passage and migration *from* Guam to California often feels like living an excerpted existence; while my body lives here, my heart still lives in my homeland. Poetry is a way for me to bring together these excerpted spaces via the transient, processional, and migratory cartographies of the page. Each of my poems, and each of my books, and seemingly every breath I take, carries the *from* and bears its weight and incompleteness.

Write Oceanic

The imagination is an ocean of possibilities. I imagine the blank page as an excerpt of the ocean. The ocean is storied and heavy with history, myth, rumor, genealogy, loss, war, money, the dead, life, and even plastic. The ocean is not "aqua nullius." The page, then, is never truly blank. The page consists of submerged volcanoes of story and unfathomable depths of meaning.

Each word is an island. The visible part of the word is its textual body; the invisible part of the word is the submerged mountain of meaning. Words emerging from the silence are islands forming. No word is an island, every word is part of a sentence, an archipelago. The space between is defined by referential waves and currents.

Oceanic stories are vessels for cultural beliefs, values, customs, histories, genealogies, politics, and memories. Stories weave generations and geographies. Stories protest and mourn the ravages of colonialism, articulate and promote cultural revitalization, and imagine and express decolonization.

Write Archipelagic

An individual book is an island with a unique linguistic geography and ecology, as well as a unique poetic landscape and seascape. The book-island is inhabited by the living and the dead, the human and the non-human, multiple voices and silences. The book-island vibrates with the complexity of the present moment and the depths of history and genealogy, culture and politics, scars and bone and blood.

A book series is an archipelago, a birthing and formation of book-islands. Like an archipelago, the books in an ongoing series are related and woven to the other islands, yet unique and different. Reading the books in a series is akin to traveling and listening across the archipelago.

Because Guam is part of an archipelago, its geography inspired the form of my *from unincorporated territory* book series. Additionally, the unfolding nature of memory, learning, listening, sharing, and storytelling informed the serial nature of the work. To me, the complexity of the story of Guam and the Chamorro people—entangled in the complications of ongoing colonialism and militarism—inspired the ongoing serial form.

The first book of the series, *from unincorporated territory [hacha]* (2008), focused on my grandfather's life and experience on Guam when the island was occupied by Japan's military during World War II. The second book, *from unincorporated territory [saina]* (2010), focused on my grandmother's contrasting experience during that same period. The third book, *from unincorporated territory [guma']* (2014), echoes and enlarges the earlier books through the themes of family, militarization, cultural identity, migration and colonialism. Furthermore, *[guma']* focuses on my own return to my home island after living away (in California) for 15 years. I explore how the island has changed and how my idea of home has changed. I also meditate upon the memories that I have carried with me, as well as all that I have forgotten and left behind.

The titles are meant to mark and name different books in the same series. Just as an archipelago has a name, such as the Marianas Archipelago, each island of the archipelago has its own unique name. The names can be translated as [one], [elder], and [home]. My first book was given the name, [*hacha*], to mark it as the first book, first island, first voice. While one might expect the second book to be named second, I chose the name, [elder], to resist that linearity and instead highlight genealogy, or the past.

The third book, which means house or home, was an attempt to weave together time and space (the house or book as spatial and temporal). The fourth book, *from unincorporated territory [lukao]* (2017) includes themes of birth, creation, parenthood, money, climate colonialism, militarization, migration, and extinction. The Chamorro name of the book, [*lukao*], means procession.

My multi-book project also formed through my study of the "long poem": Pound's *Cantos*, Williams' *Paterson*, H.D.'s *Trilogy*, Zukofsky's *"A,"* and Olson's *Maximus*. I loved how these books were able to attain a breadth and depth of vision and voice. One difference between my project and other "long poems" is that my long poem will always contain the"from," always eluding the closure of completion.

I also became intrigued by how certain poets write trans-book poems such as Duncan's "Passages" and Mackey's "Songs of the Andoumboulou." I employ this kind of trans-book threading in my own work as poems change and continue across books (for example, excerpts from the poems "from tidelands" and "from aerial roots" appear in both my first and second books). These threaded poems differ from Duncan and Mackey's work because I resist the linearity of numbering that their work employs.

Write Cartographic

I use diagrams, maps, illustrations, collage visual poetry as a way to foreground the relationship between storytelling, mapping, and navigation. Just as maps have used illustrations (sometimes visual, sometimes typographical), I believe poetry can both enhance and disrupt our visual literacy.

One incessant typographical presence throughout my work is the tilde (~). Besides resembling an ocean current and containing the word "tide" in its body, the tilde has many intriguing uses. In languages, the tilde is used to indicate a change of pronunciation.

I use many different kinds of discourse in my work (historical, political, personal, etc.) and the tilde is meant to indicate a shift in the discursive poetic frame. In mathematics, the tilde is used to show equivalence (i.e. $x \sim y$). Throughout my work, I want to show that personal or familial narratives have an equivalent importance to official historical and political discourses.

Cartographic representations of the Pacific Ocean developed in Europe at the end of the 15th century, when the Americas were incorporated into maps: the Pacific became a wide empty space separating Asia and America. In European world maps, Europe is placed at the center and "Oceania" is divided into two opposite halves on the margins. As imperialism progressed, every new voyage incorporated new data into new maps.

As I mention in the preface to my first book, the invisibility of Guam on many maps—whether actual maps or the maps of history—has always haunted me. One hope for my poetry is to enact an emerging map of "Guam" both as a place and as a signifier.

The "actual maps" in my first book are, to me, both visual poems and illustrations of the rest of the work. In my imagination, they function in two ways: first, they center "Guam," a locating signifier often omitted from many maps. Second, the maps are meant to provide a counterpoint to the actual stories that are told throughout the book. While maps can locate, chart, and represent (and through this representation tell an abstracted story), they never show us the human voices of a place. I place this abstract, aerial view of "Guam" alongside the more embodied and rooted portraits of place and people.

"Song maps" refer to the songs, chants, and oral stories that were created to help seafarers navigate oceanic and archipelagic spaces. Pacific navigational techniques are often understood as a "visual literacy," in the sense that a navigator has to be able to "read" the natural world in order to make safe landfall. The key features include reading the stars, ocean efflorescence, wave currents, and fish and bird migrations.

Scholars and navigators describe this technique as "moving islands" because in these songs, the canoe is conceptualized as remaining still, while the stars, islands, birds, fish, and waves all move in concert. Islands not only move, but islands also expand and contract. For example, if you see an offshore bird associated with a certain island, then you know that island is nearby (thus, it has figuratively, expanded).

With this in mind, I imagine that poems are song maps of my own journey to find Guam across historical and diasporic distances. I imagine the reader is in a still canoe, reading the songs in order to navigate the archipelago of memory and story. In this way, books and words become moving islands, expanding and contracting, inhaling and exhaling.

IN THE COUNTRY OF WAR

Jehanne Dubrow

A YEAR AND A HALF into our marriage, we've barely unpacked his boxes—still making room in the closets for uniforms, PT gear, black pairs of steel-toed boots—when my husband phones me from his blue and gold office in the ROTC building on campus. As he says the words *individual augmentation*, I bite the inside of my lip—something I still do whenever I encounter a new military euphemism like *coercive interrogation, enemy combatant, kill box*. After the 2003 invasion of Iraq, he explains, Navy personnel are being given temporary duty assignments to help fill Army vacancies abroad. *Advancement*, he says, *opportunity*. Already I can see him, not in the engine room of a ship, but riding in a Humvee like an actor from a Hollywood blockbuster, wearing Kevlar and carrying a rifle. It is one thing to imagine him in the haze-gray passageways of a destroyer or aircraft carrier; these are places whose hazards I understand. A ship contains flammable, explosive, sometime nuclear dangers. But even a desk job in Baghdad's Green Zone will force him to enter the landscape of IEDs, snipers, and RPGs. He will be killed, I sob into the phone, *you're going to fucking die*.

Months later, my husband mentions over dinner, casually the way one says *please, pass the wine*, that plans have changed. There will be no individual augmentation. Not this time. But my fear remains, and I begin to draft what eventually becomes my third collection, *Stateside*, a book about the before, during, and after of a deployment. At the time, there are very few women writing about what it means to be married to the military. While the soldier poet has long been a recognized figure, the military wife represents an entirely new voice in the evolution of the war lyric. And over the past decade, in response to our sustained engagements in Iraq and Afghanistan, a small group of military spouses have begun to expand the literary conversation about war to include a modern, female viewpoint.[1] The military spouse, who traditionally has remained silent, embodying patriotism through her fixed, unmoving station on the home front, has begun to develop a literary presence.

The contemporary, American soldier poet continues the tradition of witness, which we find in the work of the great English-language poets of WWI, particularly Wilfred Owen and Siegfried Sassoon, as well as in the writings of Vietnam-era poets such as Yusef Komunyakaa and Bruce Weigl. Recent collections—Brian Turner's *Here, Bullet* and *Phantom Noise*, Hugh Martin's *The Stick Soldiers*, and Kevin C. Powers' *Letter Composed*

---

[1] The U.S. Armed Forces have only recently begun to move away from the performance of strictly traditional gender roles; therefore, this essay takes "soldier poets" to mean men and "military spouse poets" to mean women. Although it may soon, contemporary American war poetry doesn't yet include significant examples of female veterans publishing collections about their experiences in combat. We are also still waiting to see male dependents publish poems about their wives' military service. And, with the repeal of DADT and the Supreme Court's recent recognition of marriage equality, no doubt we'll soon see poems written by LGBTQ veterans and their spouses. Finally, because this conversation is in its first wave, we need to see work from poets of color writing about their experiences, both as soldiers and as civilians.

During a Lull in the Fighting—travel to our 21st century wars in the Middle East, using urgent, sensory detail to lead readers through the exotic topography of battle; these books argue that war itself is a foreign country, a contained area with its own fierce dialect and customs. The soldier poet strives to reassure us that he has indeed "been there," his poems achieving authority through emotion and through the use of exact, acutely-seen images. When women appear in these texts, they are erotic because they are remote, as when the speaker in Kevin C. Powers' "Letter Composed During a Lull in the Fighting" writes to a woman stateside: "I tell her I love her like not killing / or ten minutes of sleep." The female figure is often an unchanging presence; she represents the peacetime of the United States, her body unscarred by combat.

Unlike the soldier poet, the military spouse is unlikely to have walked the alien landscapes of war. Her poems are positioned in the United States, situating her beloved in the sand-blown geographies she has only seen on the evening news. Through verse she attempts to picture him there, either in danger or perhaps enduring the boredom of boot-shining and standing watch. The soldier poet offers eyewitness accounts. But the poet who is married to a soldier, a sailor, an airman, has a more complex task; her poems thinking across time zones, barriers of cultures and speech. She too is an embattled poet, one who demonstrates that the country of war has tremendous reach, touching even those without stripes on their sleeves or service ribbons on their chests. Before the soldier leaves for combat, his tongue is altered by the necessary jargon of his community, a language that is constantly changing to reflect the current technologies, conditions, and regions of battle: *self-licking ice cream cone, fobbit, hajji, secret squirrel*. But a spouse's tongue is altered too. She absorbs the same foreign speech. *Whiskey Tango Foxtrot*, she says, meaning "what the fuck," *negative* to mean "no." Her poems assert that the country of war is not just elsewhere but also *here* in line at the post office, at the cross walk near the library, or in aisle three of the grocery store.

Mornings, I sit in my kitchen and stare at a photograph taken on my wedding day: my husband in his dinner dress whites, my outline draped in silk. I've written about this image before. In a poem, I say: "He's dressed in the uniform / of war, our wedding photograph / a shot of cream and navy." In an essay: "We stand in front of a picture window, turned half away from the camera, so that the viewer's eye sees still-life instead of portrait: shoulder boards and miniature metals, the lustrous folds of damask, our figures in chiaroscuro." My gaze keeps returning to these two people, our forms balanced in the composition, the tall window behind us, which is the larger world, its light spread evenly across both our faces.

The military spouse poet tries to create the same kind of images, the perspectives of soldier and wife equally illuminated on the page. In "Gratitude," from her book *Clamor*, Elyse Fenton envisions her husband, a medic, nursing a wounded soldier:

> By the time you arrived
>
> there were already hands fluttering white flags of gauze
> against the ruptured scaffolding of ribs, the glistening
> skull, and no skin
>
> left untended, so you were the one to sink the rubber
> catheter tube.

Fenton transcribes the soldier's experience, recounted during a long-distance call. She synthesizes the facts of war with her own intimate knowledge of her partner, the poem moving between exposition and imagination. "When you tell me this over the phone hours later I can hear rotors / scalping the tarmac-gray sky, the burdenless lift of your voice," writes the poet, her language both precise and lyrical.

In many ways, the military spouse assumes the duties of the soldier poet. She must convey the *been there*-ness of her husband's story, overlaying it with her own perspective, trying to approach the beloved psychologically as well as physically. Fenton pictures her husband inserting the catheter, "And I love you more for holding the last good flesh / of that soldier's cock in your hands, for startling his warm blood / back to life." Here, the poet moves uncomfortably close to this tableau vivant. Her husband's hands on the wounded soldier's penis are nurturing, almost sensual. Beneath the gaze of the female poet, it is the men who become symbols of erotic longing as well as subjects of intellectual scrutiny. Fenton struggles to comprehend her husband's military service, which has made him other, paradoxically one who carries both a gun and a bag full of medical supplies. As much as "Gratitude" is a poem about what happens during combat, the text is also deeply concerned with the efforts of the civilian to get what the soldier is going through and to transform him into a less frightening figure.

The title poem from Victoria Kelly's debut collection, *When the Men Go Off to War*, offers an escapist fantasy of what happens on a military base once the men are sent overseas. As if in a vividly drawn dream sequence, "the houses fold up like paper dolls, / the children roll up their socks and sweaters / and tuck the dogs into little black suitcases," all the dependents floating away. Rather than following the deployed men to Afghanistan or Iraq, the women in Kelly's poem pursue their own strange journeys, eventually landing in "in places like Estonia or Laos," where like a "strange carnival" they settle for a few months, befriending the locals and attempting to forget the realities of military marriage: the shadow of death, the temptation of infidelity, "how people fall in and out of love." And, just before their husbands' billets end, the women return to America, tethering their homes to the earth again. When the husbands arrive stateside, their wives appear unchanged, mouths bright with red smiles. "What have you been doing all this time," ask the men, comforted when they're told, "Oh you know, the dishes," a response which leads the husbands to believe that "some things stay the same."

While *When the Men Go Off to War* evokes the can-do attitude of a WWII propaganda poster (*We Can Do It! Victory Waits on Your Fingers*), its narrative subverts our expectations; this is not a poem about the solace or satisfaction that wives can derive from supporting their soldiers. Instead, Kelly reminds us that these women have interior lives. Their days are more than PTA meetings, casseroles, and trips to the commissary. Readers may be inclined to view military spouses as women trapped in the Mamie Pink glow of the 1950s, but Kelly's poem shows us that these wives are not defined by the world of the base. Their intellects allow them to venture beyond the ordered grid of military housing, each lawn kept cropped, an American flag waving from every front porch. The country of war is a felt presence in the text, but it does not define the wives who remain independent, covertly separating themselves from their husbands' immersive experiences in battle.

How hard the military spouse poet must work to justify her voice in this literary conversation. She has a very narrow lexicon; she is expected to speak about war in hushed, deferential tones, reverent about her husband's sacrifices, and pious about the duties asked of her. The military spouse must invent terrain she has never walked, envisioning war (as any other civilian might), while also charging the landscape with feelings that go beyond abstract sentiments of concern, fear, or anger. She loves a man in uniform and is, therefore, implicated in his choices: to follow orders, to follow a blip across a screen, to push a button.

Making her task even more difficult is the fact that war is often sensually packaged, desirable as Richard Gere dressed in his summer whites and carrying a young Debra Winger in his arms. I sleep beside a man who does not fit the trope of the *baby-killer* or *war-mongerer* and yet, on one ship, he was responsible for the Aegis Combat System, which uses computer and radar technology to track and guide weapons that destroy enemy targets. The Aegis—I've written about it. How could I not, with its irresistible allusion to Greek mythology? "[N]amed for a shield Athena wore / when she was angriest, and therefore / beautiful, the golden scales of it // like snakes writhing?" I wonder: Can my poems represent my husband as a real and nuanced human being while acknowledging that his work unnerves me? How do I explore the country of war simultaneously at a great distance—the imaginative leap—and within the intimate bed of marriage?

In his provocative treatise on the addictive nature of combat, *War Is a Force that Gives Us Meaning*, Chris Hedges speaks of the "seductiveness of violence," comparing war to the "ecstasy of erotic love." When I write about military marriage, I too feel the allure, the romantic myth of the officer and the gentleman. But art can also be a powerful opportunity for anticipatory grief, a way to imagine death and mourn even when catastrophe isn't imminent. In 2006, for example, I draft a sonnet in my living room while the television plays muted in the background. My husband is somewhere nearby, perhaps taking a nap or else walking the dog. He isn't deployed. He isn't in danger. Flipping through the channels—*news, news, sitcom, reality show, news, soap opera, news*—I keep stumbling on scenes set in foxholes, jungles, death camps, the tan hues of deserts. Then I am crying. Who, I ask myself, am I seeing on the screen?

Like so many of his colleagues, my husband can recite long passages of dialogue from *Patton* and *Mister Roberts*, the scripts of American cinema a way of speaking about his service without addressing it directly. But my language is iambs and metaphor, my tradition the sonnet's fourteen lines, the ceremonial turn of the volta. The poem I begin to write that afternoon as I sit in front of the television, "Against War Movies," uses film as a way to enter the country of war, marrying my husband's vernacular to my own. Here, the sexy abstraction of cinema becomes personal, the landscape of combat brought into the wife's living room where she can project her husband into battle scenes from *Platoon*, *M*A*S*H*, and *Stalingrad*. And while I write the first twelve lines in a day, it takes a year to arrive at the closing couplet. "Each movie is a training exercise," I realize, "a scenario for how my husband dies." To discover, as a poet, the sonnet's end—the pleasure that comes with lyric closure—is one thing. But, as a wife, to describe my husband's death on the page is to risk the possibility that one day the doorbell will ring and I will open it to find a casualty assistance calls officer standing there. *Ma'am*, he will say, *may I come in?*

After *Stateside* is published, I read at civilian and military institutions around the country, often encountering receptive audiences, but also meeting those who want my poems to be different than they are: more patriotic or more critical; more supportive of U.S. foreign policy or else more visibly antiwar. Sometimes my poems have too much of a feminist perspective for a military audience, or else are too hermetically domestic for a liberal, academic readership—too much in the bedroom and not enough on the marble steps of the Capitol.

One autumn, I visit the U.S. Naval Academy, meeting with literature students and reading alongside Brian Turner, perhaps the most successful and celebrated soldier poet of our time. In every classroom, the students want to hear more about Brian's years as an infantryman: What was it like to detain prisoners? To shoot at enemy combatants? To come home from Iraq? Finally, a professor notices my silence. How many of you expect to see combat? Every hand shoots up. Only ten percent of you will experience battle, the instructor says. Now, how many of you hope to be married or in a long-term relationship? Every hand goes up again. Yes, and most of you will, the professor nods. So who has a question about what it's like to go to war and to leave the one you love behind?

Later that day, Brian and I are ushered to the indoor stadium where we will speak to the entire plebe class. Students stomp in, the bleachers filling with thousands of bodies dressed in white. They are anonymous, starched uniforms slouched and leaning in their seats, some of them already falling asleep, exhausted from a day of workouts, classes, training, drills. Brian and I climb the rattling stairs to the stage that has been erected for our event, taking turns talking into the mic. I am wearing a red dress. And when I begin to read my first poem—*I see my husband shooting in* Platoon—I can picture myself as I must look from the back of the stadium, a blur of scarlet, feminine and diminutive. But then, my voice reverberates, echoing as if from a continent away, crossing the metallic barriers of the space, louder and more resonant than I have ever imagined I could sound.

BONE WILL ADAPT TO LOADS OF PRESSURE: THE BODY & POETIC SPACE

Emilia Phillips

T HE NIGHT BEFORE the horse necropsy, I called my father to tell him what I would witness. "Are you sure you can handle something like that?" he asked. "Have you ever *seen* anything like that?" What should I say? Should I tell him about the time during my freshman year of college when I walked into my mother's house to find blood all over the floors and walls in the dining room, my stepfather cleaning his gun and face in the bathroom, our dog Gibson's body wrapped in trash bags in the trunk of the Camry? I couldn't bear to bring up the death of my brother, my father's son— only ten-years-old—the ventilator pumping his chest even after they pronounced him dead. How I'd held my grandfather, his shoulders and neck in my lap like a child, when he died. "No," I lied. "But I can do it."

He told me to get some liniment oil and rub it up my nostrils. "That's what crime scene veterans do," he said. "For the smell."

My father is a fingerprint expert, an ex-cop who worked his way up from patrol to the head of the forensics unit without a college degree, who spent time training at the Forensic Anthropology Center, also known as the "Body Farm," at the University of Tennessee. There, bodies donated to science are allowed to decompose in unique circumstances, allowing researchers to monitor and measure mortification rates, data that later helps investigators determine time and cause of death. "They are donated cadavers, helping, in their mute, fragrant way, to advance the science of criminal forensics," Mary Roach writes in *Stiff: The Curious Lives of Human Cadavers.* "The woman lies in a mud of her own making. Her torso appears sunken, its organs gone—leaked out onto the ground around her." The only thing my father has ever said of his time at the Body Farm has been an ominous, sneering mention of "the smell." In recent years, he's worked as a contractor with the military, and intelligence agencies stateside and in the Middle East, spending the bulk of his career in war-torn countries like Iraq and Afghanistan. He's recently quit his job. "Bureaucrats," he says, and that's all he says, in his mute, seething way.

———— ◆ ————

During the semester, it's hard for me to find time to write, but it's also the semester—my conversations with students, my engagement with their work—that really makes me want to write. These experiences compel me into poems, to look back with new eyes, to make my own, to balance my desire to speak with my desire to be silent. Poems can contain—no, embody—both speech and silence. They give speech and silence a form, a body. When I'm busy, like I am in a semester, I find that the only time I can write, that the only time I can give body to my thoughts through poetry is when my own body is in motion, when I'm huffing it across campus, walking my dog at the arboretum, taking a train into the city, driving my car. There's something about the movement, the sense of going forward, that allows me to access my ideas that sitting at a computer or holding vigil over the blank page will never offer me. My father's work is that which concerns itself with proofs and evidence, and, therefore, with fact.

My work holds out for mysteries, for the ineffable, examining *what is* for *what could be*, and, besides, fact is an absolute zero we can approach but never fully reach or define. It's that liminal space I'm interested in, which is why perhaps I negotiate the body in many of my poems, the way that it continually reminds us that it's more complex than the brain it contains can even fathom.

———◆———

I spend the evening grading student short stories, and I don't make it to the store for liniment oil, but I do hold out for the hope of a poem. In my dash to get to my university's equine campus the next morning, I stop by Walgreens and get a Sprite and anti-nausea medicine (just in case), some gum, and Burt's Bees peppermint lip balm, the latter of which I smear up my nose. When I make it to The Barn I realize I'm inappropriately dressed. The gravel arrowheads its way into the tender parts of my feet through my teaching flats, and the dew soaks the cloth until they are squelchy.

I have no idea where I'm going after I park the car. The biologist's directions say *up past the parking lot, behind the main barn*, but there are several barn-like structures, all nearly identical. I find a woman in riding breeches and boots, and I ask her if she knows where the necropsy is taking place. I've imagined a large sterile room with a sloping floor and heavy metal drains, everyone in smocks diligently taking notes. I think, too, of the waivers I had to sign when I had the last excision of melanoma, along with a lymph node dissection and the removal of parotid and salivary glands, in September 2013, and the facial reconstructive surgery, the "wound revision," in January 2014. The operations took place at Virginia Commonwealth University's MCV Hospital, a teaching hospital. If the surgeons desired, they could allow students to watch my surgery, to take notes. I never knew if they did.

"Oh, it's right back here," the woman says, pointing to the gravel drive, its curve around a building. "I'm headed there myself. I'll show you the way."

As we make our way to a back field, a crowd of students and faculty stand silently along the fence line, at a distance from a horse trailer, a large grey gelding, the veterinarian, and the horse's owners. "They are going to euthanize the horse after its owners say goodbye," one of the equine faculty whispers to me. We watch the family—two adults and a teenage girl—kiss the horse's nose, stroke its withers, hug it around the neck. At this distance, in this hush, it seems like a distant film, a magic lantern of grief.

"The most startling part of the whole day will be when they give it the anesthesia. It keeps it from being in pain, but it will fall over. It's sometimes quite alarming."

———————◆———————

Death was a part of my imagination from early on. I had early occasions to imagine it. Down the street from the first house I remember, a single-story cube on Lyndon Avenue in Red Bank, Tennessee, a cemetery stood just back from the road. At night, as I laid in bed, I imagined that ghosts would rise from the graves and come to our house, smash through my window or else float through the walls. Sometimes I even imagined them rising through the floorboards like radon. My mother often watched *Unsolved Mysteries* after I went to bed, and although my room was down the hall, I could hear the narration of brutal murders. Robert Stack's voice haunted me so much that I would run to the den and beg my mother to turn it off, sobbing and clinging to her leg. The terror I felt through imagining what was hidden to me and what could be is much the same I feel now whenever I'm writing. Drafting a poem, especially poems that build their nest in mortality, feels a lot like running full speed at the horizon and not knowing if I'll fall off the edge of the world.

When my father worked third shift, his spare radio would remain on in the kitchen, and my mother would stay up half the night listening to it, to hear what was happening, to listen to my father's voice. *This is badge 490.* She learned the incident codes, and therefore knew when somebody had died, when shots were fired. When I slept my parents turned a radio on in my room, perhaps to block out the police radio, but I could still hear it like an ocean tide somewhere out in the dark world, those competing frequencies not unlike the voice of the poet and the voice of the poem, distinct yet entwining.

Years later, after the divorce and my father's move to the Automated Fingerprint Identification System (AFIS) unit in the forensic department and his volunteering on the Hostage Negotiation Team (HNT), I told him about my bad day at school, and he said, "At least it wasn't a body stewing in a house for a week." When I was eleven or twelve, he picked me up from my mother's one Sunday and drove me to the police department so that he could fingerprint me. "I can find you this way," he said. He had my orthodontist make a dental impression of me so he could keep it on file. "Bite the soft part of the car door if you're ever kidnapped," he said.

———— ◆ ————

There are four experts leading the necropsy: the former faculty veterinarian, the current faculty vet, the equine nutritionist, and one of the biology professors who specializes in comparative anatomy. When Mike, the former faculty vet, slices a back leg off, I am startled by the beet-purple color of horse muscle. The leg is just as beautiful, chiseled into hard muscle, removed. A student drags the leg away from the rest of the horse—the crowd parts to let her through—the nerves still firing the muscle to move. "The horse had melanoma," Mike says as he moves to the horse's genitalia. He hands the tumor to me, a black hunk, dense but spongy, still warm from the body, slick.

One year after I watched my half brother die from complications related to a rare genetic disorder called propionic acidemia in a bed at the Erlanger Hospital PICU, I was diagnosed with melanoma. The uncertainty of the body after these two events made me feel like I was standing on a thin ice sheet beginning to crack. It was at this time when my poems moved away from the cold, clinical rendering of the body through the projected lens of forensics, as I'd done in my first book *Signaletics*. Instead, the body became intimate again, a setting from which I looked out, the place of my point of view. Instead of writing about *the* body, I began writing about *my* body.

Three years ago, even two, I wouldn't have been able to come to the horse necropsy without feeling the sympathetic string of my body chimed by the violence against muscle, bone, and organs of the horse. I would have re-lived my pain, the muscle memory of trauma.

Writing poems and lyric essays through my ordeal with cancer—and, urgently, I might add, as I feared for my life—allowed me to create new, surrogate bodies in which to live for a time, these poetic forms becoming near-corporeal forms, places to inhabit, to feel safe inside. In doing so, I found that my poems became more charged even as they became more plainspoken—they were naked, unbending. They also allowed me the space to consider the ways in which my body has always been in danger—from others, from illness, and from my self. They became a radio tuned to my fears staticked by hope.

———◆———

For weeks I've been trying to write a poem—even poems—about the horse necropsy, all its implications, how calm I was, almost meditative, as I watched Mike lift the stomach full of sweet feed and carrot, its giant wine-colored heart about as large as its brain. The 2016 presidential election happened, and I found myself mute, struck dumb by the flood of hate crimes, the violent rhetoric seemingly empowered by the president elect. Finally, over a month since the election, I found some footing in a draft, found the poem, with a title borrowed from Gerard Manley Hopkins. Here's the opening:

DEEP CALLS TO DEEP

Until I reached the paddock
where the gelding grey

collapsed, back hooves
clacking like stones to

fire, I didn't know of the melanoma
buried like a rotten black

bulb in his cheek & neck. I came
only to see his viscera

tagged & marked, some,
like the penis, knotted

with tumors metastasized
from the initial onyx

jewel, sunk in a bucket for later
jars, a class next fall.

It's still too new, too raw, for me to judge it, to know if it's good—if it's *there*—but several revisions in, I started to realize that the poem wasn't so much about the horse, or even the serendipity of its melanoma, but that it was a poem about fear, about witnessing something beautiful, sovereign, fragile gutted, maimed, and being unable to cry, to wretch, so consumed as I was with fear, which is a bodily concern, fight or flight, a hum along the nerves, a firing squad in the brain.

———•———

In the aftermath of November 9th, the devastating news hollowing my ear, shaping my brain, I keep picking up two books: *Poems and Prose* by Gerard Manley Hopkins and Italo

Calvino's novel *The Baron in the Trees*. Hopkins' invented metrical form of sprung rhythm is meant to imitate human speech which, like all wind instruments, is dependent upon breath; it manifests itself with a stress at the beginning of each foot and an alliterative structure, inspired by the Welsh form of *cyngehedd*, as demonstrated by this excerpt from "Inversnaid."

> What would the world be, once bereft
> Of wet and of wildness? Let them be left,
> O let them be left, wildness and wet;
> Long live the weeds and the wilderness yet.

Beyond the poem's sentiments of keeping the world wild, undeveloped by humans, its allegiance to this breath, to the tongue's fluid movements between similar sounds so that it doesn't have to stray far—echoing, echoing—from its position in the mouth, the poem maintains its sense of wildness, of the unhampered body, unrestrained speech. Say aloud the first sentence here, and you'll hear what I mean:

> What would the world be, once bereft
> Of wet and wildness?

The *wh*- in "What" and the *w*-s in "would" and "world" allow the lips and tongue to remain in the same shape and the same position in the mouth respectively, broken only by the closing of one's teeth on the *-t* of "What" and *-d* of "would" and "world," the conductor's stroke upwards of the tongue to the back of the teeth for the aspirated "the," falling into the aspirated, lip-released "be." Ultimately, however, all of the sounds are formed using the front of one's mouth, until the retracting tongue on the *n* of "once" and the rising, mid-mouth second *e* in "bereft." Hopkins is phonetically economical, playing to the structures of the body that make the spoken poem—mouth, tongue, throat, lung. In doing so, Hopkins attests that the body is the ultimate setting for the poems—its maker, and its instrument.

Calvino, on the other hand, reminds us of the body as point of view, its dependency on physical space to render understanding and its ability to submerge itself into the greater setting, as with this passage in which the young baron has climbed up into the trees, realigning his point of view.

> Now it was a whole different world, made up of narrow curved bridges in the emptiness, of knots or peel or scores roughening the trunks, of lights varying their green according to the veils of thicker or scarcer leaves, trembling at the first quiver of the air on the shoots or moving like sails with the bend of the tree in the wind. While down below our world lay flattened, and our bodies looked quite disproportionate and we certainly understood nothing of what he knew up there […]

———◆———

The poem about the body is a poem of place and, likewise, I would argue that all poems about the body are as forensic as they are intimate, as clinical as biased by perception. Ultimately, however, we must remember that poems about the body are naturally attended by the body's risk of existence, its likelihood of undergoing violence and trauma, to be revised by those experiences. The poet, therefore, should be mindful of this in approaching the body as subject matter, of grafting the physical body into the body of the poem. The form should always be one in which the body feels safe, so that the poem doesn't become a stage of voyeurism and provocation, hands reaching in and pulling out the heart—animal or human.

A PLACE FOR GHOSTS

Abigail Chabitnoy

WHERE ARE YOU FROM? A simple enough question, but what if we change the terms? *Where do you come from?* It's the effect of the least variation, a change in form, that draws me to language. In my great-grandfather's native tongue there is a question, *Kinkut ilaten?* The answer depends on the translation. *Do you know your relatives? Do you know who your relatives are? (What are all of you?)* I grew up in Pennsylvania, in a hilly neighborhood between pockets of dense wood, where the fog settles thick on the roads and between homes at night. It wasn't on the way to anywhere, and only neighbors drove its wide streets. My parents have lived there since the house was built, just after their first child was born. I went to school in Pennsylvania. *Where are you from?* It should be a simple question. And yet, I never know how I'll answer. My response depends on context, how I orient myself. When traveling, even just to Denver, I might say I'm from Fort Collins, where I've lived for the past five years. Outside the state, I might say Colorado. Only in Fort Collins will I answer Pennsylvania. And yes, there are trees in my poems, thin crooked limbs like the woods that weave through the suburbs back east. I can't imagine growing up in a landscape without trees.

And yes, my poems settle on the page almost like fog, the way they anchor to and pull from edges, the way they percolate. Like fog, yes, or like ghosts. Where am I from? Who are my relatives? (The same question?) I come from ghosts. And in this lineage, place too is a family ghost.

My father's family is from the Aleutian Islands, a volcanic archipelago stretching west from the Alaskan Peninsula over a thousand miles and crossing the international dateline to contain both the westernmost and easternmost points of the United States. The "seams of the world," synonymous with "fog, rough smoking islands of basalt, volcanic ash and green grass, rain, sleet, sometimes snow, terrible winds and seas, sometimes unbelievably blue skies and fluffy clouds and a stillness broken only by the sound of the seabirds, the gentle wash of surf on black sand beaches." On the Islands, there are hardly any trees. At least, that's what I've read. I've never been. (And records only place my family on three of those islands, maybe four. And while each were once distinct, the Russians did their part to muddy the water.)

The stories of my great-grandfather, Michael Chabitnoy, have come down through my family as through the fog that recoils each morning. He was an orphan at the Woody Island Baptist Mission in Alaska where a traveling priest selected him to join ten other children to attend the Carlisle Indian Industrial School in Pennsylvania. This was 1901; Michael was fifteen years old. School records list his father's cause of death as "traumatized." His mother died of a "bad heart." His brother died of whooping cough, and his sister had not survived infancy. Michael did not return to Woody Island after Carlisle. We don't know why. (We don't know if he could.) His records show an aunt on Unalaska. A cousin says his parents died in a boating accident shortly before another aunt on Woody Island sent him to Carlisle. While my family enrolled with a Native corporation on Kodiak when the Alaska Native Claims Settlement Act was passed (Woody Island uninhabited by that time and Kodiak just a narrow channel across), genealogical records indicate Michael was born on Unga, but previously his family was from Unalaska. Eight hundred and twenty-four miles. Perhaps home was already a ghost.

————◆————

For reasons practical and otherwise, I've never gone to the Aleutian Islands. The logistics alone are easy enough to hide behind. Kodiak is 411 miles from Anchorage. One could fly there in an hour, it being one of the easier destinations on the archipelago to reach, though it would cost as much as my ticket to Anchorage. Or if you prefer the scenic route, you could drive four and a half hours from Anchorage to Homer, then take the ferry to Kodiak. (Another ten hours.) Unalaska is trickier, though the success of the reality show *Deadliest Catch*, following the perils of commercial crab fishermen out of Dutch Harbor, make this island perhaps more approachable. It depends how you define the terms. The surest way to get there is by private plane. (Price will vary.) Or you could wait for the ferry, the Alaska Marine Highway, which travels to Unalaska once a week, over two days from Kodiak. An investment, sure. But no more so than other trips I've taken. So why have none of us returned?

Everyone wants to see a ghost until it's time to lift the sheet. After leaving Carlisle, Michael settled in Lebanon, Pennsylvania, and died shortly after my grandfather was born. No stories from his childhood, from his home, were passed on to my grandfather and his brother. No one has gone back to the Aleutians. And yet these islands, with their wind and fog and disheartening weather, their bursts of green and calm, haunt me, haunt my poems. The landscape is my great-grandfather, his family, his sister Nikifor. It is the space they occupy. A space of possibility outside of time and body where they dwell still. A place I can speak into and entertain an audience with family I've never known. In my poems, place becomes a space for ghosts. To go to these places, I fear, would be to fix them in a less permeable state—to turn the ghosts to bones. But the landscape haunts me nonetheless.

I've always been afraid of the sea. To this day, I don't like to put my head under water. I suppose I'm afraid I won't be able to resist the current, or the weight that might press me under. Large waves form unexpectedly. But to be *on* the water is another matter: in a kayak or canoe, a fishing boat on a windy lake—even just on a paddle board in a reservoir, the water pulsing beneath me. I still fear the current will be stronger than my own barely developed skill, am still aware of what might be below me, even if nothing more than a depth I can't follow. But I feel at home in a way I hardly do on land. The closest I've come to experiencing this feeling on land is on the outskirts of Anchorage, in the Chugach Mountains to the east and west along the Tony Knowles Coastal Trail looking out past the bay in the direction (nearly, at least) of the Islands. I imagine navigating such vast space in an iqyax built to my own body on a landscape that leads its own course regardless of my doings. The first Russians to stumble across the Unangan people noted their skill in the water. I wonder how I'd stay upright in the waves, what it would be like to live half one's life on the water. Would you keep the islands in sight? Solid land, a more constant landscape? And in a landscape so vast it's been said one can travel for days with no notable change in major landmarks, how is one's progress mapped? Perhaps progress is the wrong word. Perhaps one doesn't progress through the archipelago any more than one progresses through a poem. One simply settles, like the fog. Or the fog settles in the body.

I've never been able to go to a place, however moving, and write it. Only once at a river I wrote a poem that barely references the river, focusing instead on my inability to write it. "In Communion with the Nonbreathing" is an apostrophe to my great-grandfather, Michael, who was never at this river until I brought his ghost there through the poem. It's a poem full of holes. Or perhaps it's a raft of otters, a chain of islands condensed to fit the page. It begins,

> I went to the river   Michael to see if you would
> speak to me   but   you
> weren't there   and the water   was to hide across
> and I wasn't big enough   to make a boat

Giving in to the river's refusal to speak, its insistence on absence, the poem continues,

> to make my body a boat there was a boy and I
> couldn't fit him   in my body so   I
> talked to no one   sent eyes air born to spy but
> there was no other   body   Tell   me which shore
> did my father call home   do my fathers called
> home   dead   Slips of the tongue
> are telling   are telling   And there's nothing for
> it but the way I came   return me to the sea infinity

But it was in my own removal I fell short. To stand where one can see the mountain (or the water) is to be of that landscape, is to carry that landscape. Like a fog it settles in the dips and curves and curls out until it can't be separated from the air it has displaced—as though the air were static and not itself a presence. To write to the land is almost an apostrophe, except the land is only as absent as I am from the landscape.

Place isn't just a physical entity. It's not just the ground, the trees, the dirt. It carries with it its history and a memory of what occurs or has occurred. It isn't a single point of focus, but the landscape and one's orientation to it. The body too in this way becomes of the landscape that is moved through and moves. My relationship to place is muddied by policies meant to break the mountain down to a few isolated sites. An anthropologist might trace it through forensic evidence, the hard matter that decays slowly. Bones and teeth. But to step outside my own body, to write into other bodies or assemblies of bodies, is to hold the state of those bodies suspended between an actuality where they are gone (in some cases brutally slaughtered) and the possibility of their infinitude. I trace my way back to Kodiak through blood, records of birth and death, but also story—familial, collective, individual. All these roads, these waters, seep with relatives. Real and imagined, tangible, permeable. Like the fog that settles in the hills in Pennsylvania, the fog that settles on the sea between islands.

———◆———

What is it to be of a place? To be removed from that place? To carry that place? *Kinkut ilaten?* I write of displacement. It's difficult for me to claim a place I've never been. There's never a simple answer. But as another Aleut once told me, exasperated by my need for impossible precision, to be Aleut is to be of the water. It's not a place or orientation that is fixed, but fluid. I've never been home, but each time I'm in water I recognize the landscape and my body settles in itself; it stills. Each stillness is a poem, is a moment of attention where I can see otherwise. Place fills me like the poem, as something I can't contain and am forever trying to write toward, or from. The line shrinks and swells like ocean waves. Whereas I fear that to physically stand in such places—on Kodiak, Woody Island, Unalaska—would fill me with silence, the poem holds open a space of possibility, a place of suspension, wherein I can speak with my relatives. And while I hold the possibility in my heart that these places still sing, and sing my own poems back, internally I'm battling an overwhelming cynicism of an upbringing removed from that landscape, in which that landscape is nothing more than the ground, the trees, the dirt, and the water is not even the same.

I've never been to the islands that haunt my poems. I've never pulled fish from the waters, never ridden those waves or felt the cold spray, the wind so strong no man could walk against it. I've never been to this place where my world begins. Still that landscape rolls in like a fog, and through its slippery sheen every place is changed, is sent floating. Each poem is a wave, a shore, a piece of the landscape, *is* the landscape. An island to the archipelago. To write place is to be in the company of ghosts, to carry home with me always, like the fog that settles in my bones.

TAPPING THE GLASS:
ON POEMS, AQUARIUMS & FORM

Nicky Beer

One seal particularly
I have seen here evening after evening.
He was curious about me. He was interested in music;
like me a believer in total immersion [...]

Elizabeth Bishop, "At the Fishhouses"

THE VOLUNTEER at the Georgia Aquarium recites his catechism in a tinny, miked voice: *Who can tell me what makes a mammal a mammal?* I train my eyes upon the tank—nearly two stories high and just about as wide, a massive field of blue. Dull-white, textured with moony grey pockmarks, beluga whales float in the color, reflecting it without absorbing it. It's a religious blue, a Virgin Mary blue. I see the characteristic smiles of the whales, unwavering benevolences that counteract the aesthetic chilliness of all the blue and white. Giant klieg lights set above the tank pour celestial shafts into the water, creating a grove of illumined columns the whales swim in and out of, as if they were choosing from a series of available annunciations. The children directly in front of the tank are kneeling.

———•———

From childhood, I've been transfixed by poems and aquariums alike—I can't remember a time when I wasn't gazing deeply into one or the other. Aquariums' darkened galleries, voyeuristic tunnels, and slowly-drifting fish-bodies make for intimate, cerebral spaces. We move through mysterious galleries and have our wayward thoughts thrown back to us in flashes of silver, again and again. Poetry's use of lineation and juxtaposition similarly steers the mind deeper into interior, unconscious territories. The forms of prose are designed to recede entirely into the background so that their narratives may remain in the foreground. By contrast, the forms of poetry are meant to charm, tease, and occasionally confound their readers. In poetry, "form" implies containment. It encompasses the battle between white space and type, patterns and arbitrariness, rigidity and spontaneity. It's the ego negotiating between the superego of craft and the id of improvisation. And form is at its best when it is revelatory, when it illuminates its interplay with poetic content. It's not unlike the small tank where what you thought was a piece of a coral fan turns out to be a mantis shrimp. A rock you initially overlooked is a snoozing eel.

———•———

British naturalist Philip Henry Gosse was the first person to codify and promote the term "aquarium" to describe the confinement of aquatic animal and plant life to glass tanks for observation, specifically through his bestselling 1854 book *The Aquarium: An Unveiling of the Wonders of the Deep Sea.* But consider this: in the years before the publication of *The Aquarium*, he became deeply involved with the Christian sect the Plymouth Brethren Movement, which forbade "reading novels or poems as well as going to the theater or singing temporal songs." Is it any wonder, then, that Gosse would develop an obsessive relationship with the ornamentations and dramas of the creatures of the coastal ocean, and turn this into an evangelical mission to popularize the home aquarium? His son describes the routine of his early study of British marine life, a constant genuflection to the sea:

> He was accustomed every day at low tide [...] to go down to the shore, and for several hours before and after the lowest moment to examine the weedy rocks, the loose flat stones under which molluscs and crustaceans lurked, the shallow tidal pools, and the dripping walls of the small fissures and caverns. [...] After some hours of severe labour, he would tramp home with his treasures, arrange them in dishes and vases with fresh sea-water, and then proceed to a scientific examination of what was unique or novel.

Imagine you were forbidden *War and Peace*, *Beloved*, "Wild nights—Wild nights!," "Those Winter Sundays," *Hamlet*, and Prince. Wouldn't you, too, turn to the movement of the lionfish, whose florid contours and supple spines seem a riot of creative spontaneity? Could you channel your excitement for the revelation of an acrostic or Golden Shovel into the sight of a flatfish almost perfectly blended in with the ocean floor? Could looking into those artfully lit tanks, their carefully-curated kelp and worms, replace the anticipatory hush of the curtain's rise? Could stroking the sticky, clasping tentacles of an anemone in a touch pool stand in for the erotic first stroke of a new-opened title page? Could the form of the aquarium, in its galleries and grottos, stand in for the arts' implicit promise: *we are here to thrill you*?

———•———

We go to poetry for how it dislodges us from our complacency with language, just as we go to aquariums to be dislodged from the predictability of our terrestrial element. Amy Lowell's "An Aquarium" exemplifies the sensual, strategic Imagist aesthetics for which she is best known. It is the fifth and final section of the sequence "Towns in Color," the last poem of her 1916 book

Men, Women, and Ghosts. The sections of "Towns in Color" take as their subjects different sites of commonplace yet arresting public urban display, such as the sight of the "row of white, sparkling shop fronts [...] gashed and bleeding, / it bleeds red slippers," or the "big lunch room [that] is coloured like the petals / Of a great magnolia, / And has a patina / Of flower bloom / Which makes it shine dimly / Under the electric lamps."

The majority of "An Aquarium" unspools down the page in a single, narrow-columned stanza, and is rendered in the kind of vivid strokes one might associate with the interiors of Matisse. The denizens of the tank, or tanks, are "silver shiftings," "grey-green opaqueness sliding down," and "Sunshine playing between red and black flowers / on a blue and gold lawn." There is little narrative drama to distract us beyond "a sudden swift straightening / and darting below" mid-poem; the image-heavy phrases and the short lines keep the reader's attention narrowed and focused, like the contraction of a keyhole. The real surprise of Lowell's use of form, though, comes in the short coda that concludes the poem, the sequence, and the book. After the long absorption of the previous stanza in which the reader is completely immersed in the movements and interplay of fish, light, and shadow, the poem's gaze abruptly breaks and shifts:

> Outside,
> A willow-tree flickers
> With little white jerks,
> And long blue waves
> Rise steadily beyond the outer islands.

The description may seem understated, particularly in comparison with the showiness of the fish we've been observing, but the shift in perception is vast. Suddenly, we are looking beyond the tank, beyond the window, and even beyond the city, across the vastness of the sea—and this move is contained in the poem's smallest stanza-tank. The poem has taken us through a kind of odd, refractive journey in which we have stared deeply into the urban aquarium's captured wildness, perhaps as a means of escaping the city, only to have our point of view vaulted, as if by catapult, beyond the city, beyond dry land, out into the unexplored regions of the ocean; we moved from city street to aquarium building to aquarium room to aquarium tank, as if purely for the sake of this brief, transcendent journey back into unexplored, unconquered space. Thus we see one of the great ironies of the aquarium's form: we often use it to imprison the non-human with the hopes of escaping the confinements our own human context. Even more: the aquarium takes the massive, the alien, and shrinks it down to a manageable, human-sized scale. And what better way to describe the function of poetry?

———◆———

Compared with the sprawling audacities of its coastal American counterparts in places like Boston, Baltimore, and Monterey, the aquarium in San Sebastián, founded in 1928, is modest. Aesthetically, it's of a piece with the tasteful elegance of this Old World seaside resort city—the stately boardwalk of the La Concha promenade, the scrupulously-maintained gardens of its plazas, the grandly-ornamented Maria Cristina Bridge spanning the Uremea River.

In a subterranean, sparsely-attended exhibit, I sit on carpeted risers in front of the wide glass. Moray eels cut slow, grim paths through the frivolous carnival crowds of the other fishes like doomsday priests. Though the low-ceilinged corridors, the racket of the school groups is approaching. It's a sound that's likely the same in all languages—the high-pitched, exuberant traffic of the young voices, punctuated with the alternately cajoling and sharp reprimands of the teachers and chaperones shepherding them. Then the sound changes. Not abruptly or uniformly—a slight shift in a current. One of the children has started singing. Another child picks up the song, and another and another, until dozens of voices are carrying it. The tune is unfamiliar. The language could be Spanish, Basque, French, or something else entirely. No words or meaning, only with the music itself. Sometimes it has a folksong quality, sometimes it's like a hymn. It sweetly drifts, keeping time with the blue, unhurried cadence of the fish.

The indecipherable, affecting song of the children makes me think of how the sonics of a poem can work on us in such subtle but profound ways. Mark Doty's "A Display of Mackerel" lavishes its visual attention upon the repetitive, coruscating shapes of the fish laid out on the supermarket's ice, stilled in death, yet still lively to the eye. Yet the poem's sonic life makes us see the fish with our ears, so to speak—the vowels and consonants of successive words throughout flash and reflect one another, as in "Iridescent, watery / prismatics," "oily fabulation," "unduplicatable, doomed," and, most literally, "all, all for all." In the last stanza, by the time we reach the poem's final word, "gleaming," a visual signifier, its vowel sound has already been forecast by "seem," "even," and "be." That "gleaming" becomes both echo and inevitability. Our experience of the fish, as Doty has orchestrated it, is as much musical as it is visual. Though I went to the aquarium in San Sebastián to abandon myself to the act of seeing, to become, as Ralph Waldo Emerson calls it, the "transparent eyeball," my visual memory of the place is heightened and transformed by how it is overlaid by the children's wayward, spontaneous song.

———◆———

The painter Helen Frankenthaler says that "...a really good picture looks as if it's happened at once, though I think very often it takes ten of those overlabored efforts to produce one really beautiful wrist motion that is synchronized with your head and your heart...and therefore looks as if it were born in a minute." In a really good poem, we are not seeing the "overlabored efforts" that made the work possible; when we read "One Art," we're not conscious of the sixteen drafts which preceded its completion by

Elizabeth Bishop, nor are we conscious of the twenty-odd years which lay between the beginning of the composition of "The Moose" and its end. The glass disappears—we see only the sleek, scaled shape swimming past.

Technological improvement accounted for the late 20th century's rise of aquariums, providing "the ability to maintain crystal-clear water and the ability to display huge aquatic vistas without obstructions," according to Vernon N. Kisling's *Zoo and Aquarium History*. And what is artistic craft but the technology of invisibility? Poetic form, too, relies on invisibility. As much as we are conscious of the chimes and repetition of the villanelle, when it is truly successful, we are forgetting its form as well. One can spot a sonnet simply by how it lies on the page, and yet the great ones momentarily make the essence of their form disappear, render their rhymes and meter invisible. The constriction of its form is a hypnosis, lulling the reader into an unconscious state that allows the beauty and truth of the poem to penetrate more fully. Such is the paradox of poetic form: at its best, it manifests to fuel its own vanishing.

———•———

Like Lowell's "An Aquarium," Pimone Triplett's "Narcissus and the Aquarium Guide" also makes use of the long, short-lined single stanza. Here, we are in the realm of the contemporary public aquarium; where the human presence is implicit in Lowell's poem, it is speaker and subject here, and almost naggingly present in the last lines of the poem, with its "crowds / And hours / children screeching / More time at the touch pool." And something in the shortest lines suggests a kind of nipped-in quality, like a woman in a too-tightly-laced corset. They make one subconsciously gasp for air. Even the first sentence of the poem squeezes its reader with disordered, near-Shakespearean syntax:

> Truth to tell, he was for floods
> Of love long due, since lapped

> At him always the model lake's
> Waves in verge, arriving
> Whipstiched, bent
> With hunger.

The reader flails a bit in the language before catching hold of the grammar; if reading the poem out loud, you might be initially unsure of where to space the breaths to negotiate that sentence. And here, in a poem spoken by an aquarium guide whose day is defined by the audible gasps of the guests—adult and children alike—and the ceaseless, visual gasps of the fish swim-pacing their tanks, we enter its space by gasping as well. The next sentence reveals that the speaker, too, is gasping: "I saw him first / at noon." You can't help but grin at the wit of that jealous enjambment: *I saw him first!* And the short, simply-constructed sentence sets up the real terms of the poem: love (or lust) at first sight.

The poem proceeds with the guide describing his[1] desire for the Narcissus figure, intensifying with his returning visits to gaze into the tank. Until the time comes when the man does not return, and the speaker is bereft. The poem concludes at "day's end" at that cacophonous touch pool, where

> I tried to teach how it takes
> One anemone, splitting,
> Asexual, some real work,
> To get up, walk away from itself.

It is in these last lines that the pathos of Triplett's form truly makes itself known. The poem has come to us in a single stanza—unsplit, so to speak, enacting the tragedy of the speaker's situation. He could not "split" himself from his vision of this man

---

[1] The gender of the speaker remains unspecified in the poem. However, I believe the narrative is more resonant if the speaker is male: as Narcissus fell in love with his own male reflection, the speaker, too, "mirrors" Narcissus' actions by falling in love with another man.

who, unlike Narcissus, succeeds in tearing himself away from the vision in the aquarium that so enchanted him. The guide is left with surfaces that no longer reflect the face of his beloved—only his own. One could argue that the mythic Narcissus with which we are familiar makes the safer choice: to fall in love with one's own reflection means one can never be abandoned.

———◆———

Before I even join the line at Denver's Downtown Aquarium, I'm hustled in front of a green screen, where I'll be photoshopped against undersea backgrounds and given the option of purchasing the photos at the end of my visit. Other screens apprise me of the day's feeding times, as well as my opportunities for photo ops with grinning, fish-tailed nubiles called the "Mystic Mermaids." After purchasing my ticket, I enter the escalator to the exhibits through a giant open shark's mouth. I'm ferried up through a tunnel-like structure arched with metal bands mean to suggest the animal's ribs—which sharks do not, in fact, have—which are ornamented with lights. At the top, presumably, I am shark-shat out.

I try to be good-humored about the aggressive commercialism of the Downtown Aquarium. The signage is garish, and burbling sound effects and music are pumped in everywhere—even the restrooms; the nadir of the aesthetic is the animatronic orangutan in its "Rainforests of the World" exhibit. But it's the small Giant Pacific Octopus—one of the most animated specimens I've ever seen—that wins me over. I watch her push herself against the walls of her tank and shoot herself across its length like a fleshy parachute. She flings her arms around a clump of kelp with romantic abandon. Her caregiver tells me her name is Jackie, and that she's been with them six months. He's plainly fond of her energy, too, and can't keep the admiration out of his voice when he tells me "She'll siphon the heck out of you—she'll get you from a few feet away!"

I'm reminded of another octopus who "got me," and changed the course of my poetry. I'd gone to the Tennessee Aquarium in

2005 with my family, excited to see the new exhibit of seahorses and weedy seadragons. Yet as I turned the corner, I caught sight of an octopus with its entire underside sprawled against the glass in an audacious and showy display. I stood before the tank in a kind of reverie, all thoughts of seahorses abandoned. The memory of the episode nagged at me for a couple of years. Eventually, from this single encounter grew one poem, and then another, and another, eventually becoming my second book, *The Octopus Game*. And this, really, is the macrocosmic version of how poetry works for me: something in the world suddenly shocks me out of my assumptions and carefully constructed plans, and the encounter pesters me until I write it. The poem, in other words, becomes a *place* to re-immerse in the original moment of disruption. But in a larger sense, doesn't the drafting process reflect our desire to reconnect with the moment when we first "woke up" to poetry? I think of Philip Henry Gosse tirelessly picking his way through the low tide of the British seacoast, seeking out those specimens that would doubtlessly unconsciously transport him to his original moment of falling in love with the sea. And in his intense study of these specimens in his tanks at home, he summons something new out of the old urge that drew him to the water. And so we have poetry in a nutshell (clamshell?)— the compulsion to reconnect with the primal poetic moment, which leads to an obsessive immersion in language, which in turn engenders something utterly new.

———————— ✦ ————————

The aquarium in Nick Flynn's "Aquarium" seems more like a subject of conceptual video art—were are asked to imagine that we are "unable to see this aquarium [tank] directly," and that we are watching it elsewhere on a remote screen via two cameras set up to film the single fish in it. It is as though the fish has been divided into the "real" fish and the "filmed" fish, and the filmed fish is further subdivided by the two cameras. The language of the poem, too, seems to split and echo over the first eleven lines: "*Is it a clown fish? / A clown fish? Sure, a clown fish*," "it is in / another room & you don't know where that room is. You are in your room [...]," "a box within a box, a glass / within a glass." The poem then leaps backwards into a memory of youth, the speaker reminiscing about how "we" would fool around in parked cars with girls named "Mary & Mary."

Interestingly enough, the form of Flynn's poem seems to work against these echoes and mirrors. The poem is in a single stanza rendered in medium-length lines, but shorter, truncated lines are scattered throughout the poem—eight in total. The first four are right justified, the last are left-justified. It is as though these fragments are reaching across physical and conceptual space to one another, longing to be complete, always failing. The isolation of these truncated lines seems to countermand the sense of familiarity one might derive from a reflection or echo; they are consigned to remain unmet and unanswered.

The speaker directs us out of the memory of youth and back to the filmed fish in its tank by instructing us to "remember that / aquarium"; the imagined aquarium has now become memory, too. In the last eleven lines of the poem, we experience a blurring between our imagined voyeurism, the memory of the Marys, and our consciousness of selfhood:

> [...] One fish swims
> inside its tiny ocean—Mary smiles at Mary, not
> at me. We think this world must be broken into
> fragments, we think memories are dispersed
> throughout the brain & that the brain itself is
> dispersed. We
> think we began from a bang, but the bang never
> stopped. Mary watches
> Mary, waiting to see what will happen—the night
> has to end somewhere. *Communion*. Communion
> is the word.

With the twice-invoked "Communion," Flynn leaves us with a final echo. Here, communion is not something which has happened, but something we wait for. Our fragmented selves and memories long to be drawn together in it. Even in this "Catholic town" with its double Marys in parked cars, the communion longed for is less religious and more existential—a longing for a feeling of wholeness that never, in this poem, quite arrives, but is anticipated, hoped-for. The poem ends on its final fragment of a line, the word "word" reaching out into the expanse of the blank page, the infinite, empty tank.

———•———

In an interview about his collaborative aquarium photography project with his wife, Diane Cook, the landscape photographer Len Jenshel observes that while we tend to identify with and project ourselves upon the animals in zoos, "in an aquarium… you don't identify with fish or even jellyfish as other individuals, as other subjects or other selves like oneself. Rather, the way you identify with them is almost as *thoughts*." And later, he describes the dark, collective experience of the aquarium as a kind of "public dream." At the Georgia Aquarium, I learned that those holy belugas—all belugas, really, as well as other whales and dolphin species—engage "unihemispheric sleeping." Because they are conscious breathers, meaning that they do not breathe automatically as other mammals do, they cannot be fully immersed into an unconscious state when they sleep. When their equivalent of sleep happens, they drift in the water with only half of their brains shut off; the other is "awake," maintaining respiration and staying alert to potential threats. It's something like a trance state. I like to think this is the state by which we encounter poems and aquariums alike, half our rational selves attuned to what's in front of us, the other half drifting, suggestibly unconscious, open to wide, dim-lit dreams into which anything might swim.

LOCATING SILENCE

James Allen Hall

1. (48° 51' N, 2° 21' E)

INSTRUCTIONS: Fill in the blank on the left with the name of the city, then use our globe or wall maps to find the latitude and longitude. Write in degrees and seconds.

Example:

_____ is the capital of France.

(_____, _____)

———◆———

I approached the globe with reverence, singing in my head, *He's got the whoooole world, in his hands.* On its stand, the world-in-manageable-miniature was unstable, wobbly. I could see where the North Pole had been chipped and repainted with white-out. I liked to imagine the fallen world, tumbling under the desks, rolling between the legs of my fellow fourth-graders, coming to uneasy rest.

Earlier that morning, the prettiest girl in class had summoned my desk's neighbor with a kick to his leg. When Robert Cronin turned, Kimberly asked him if he had any extra lunch money.

The blue of his eyes lit up like the Baltic Sea. "Sure. I'll give you lunch money for what's between your legs." Her blush hushed to anger.

———•———

Turn a few degrees, turn to the night I dream Robert repeating his demand into my ear. He's standing behind me. The space between each word lets the syllable cool on the skillet of my ear before the next one lands and sizzles. My palm opens for his crisp dollar and he is leading me into the thicket behind Woodward Elementary. I watch myself move forward with him. The trees *whoosh* close, almost wordless with what they know. What I am disappears behind.

I don't have to tell you: what I was never came back.

———•———

It had never occurred to me that our bodies were exchangeable, that I wanted another boy to want me, that I wanted to be humiliated by his wanting. That this located me in my body for the first time. That it located me on ground I knew was untenable, unfixed as any world.

In between the now-narrowed latitude of the real and the longing of the dreamworld, I learned an uncharted, powerful silence. It held my pulsing desire, Kimberly's disgusted rage. I fell in love with it, not knowing it had a name.

2. (39° 43' 19.92216" N, 75° 47' 18.93851" W)

"This is what divided the country," Mrs. Hixson droned, using a ruler to tap the map roughly along the Mason-Dixon line. "But all you kids need to know about the Civil War is that we lost," she said. Shaking the overwhelm of her curls, her eyes big beneath her tinted eyeglasses. "We lost," she repeated.

I wanted to console her.

But then the bell rang to bring both the class and the school day to a close.

We never looked at that map again.

3. (,   )

Across the sidewalks that traversed the playground, up through the sandy hills that abutted South Cass Street, through the thinning thicket and to the paved gravel street, I followed Danny Roland's tall willowy figure, staring at his broad thighs which bloomed into his ass. It was only when he looked back at me that I caught myself. "What are you doing?" he said, his mouth fixed somewhere between grin and grimace. I looked down, fixed in the crosshairs of shame. "We lost," my teacher's voice echoed out over the slide and the see-saw, out over the black tarmac of the basketball court. "What are you doing?" he said again, and "we" broke apart into separate selves, a war between us. I lost. I lost.

4. (27° 33' 35" N, 80° 39' 47" W)

Every morning of my childhood, the ritual lining up from oldest to youngest boy in front of the door. We turned to face our mother, who bent down to button our coats. "Remember," she said, her face earnest, her fingers nimble down our torsos, "They found Adam Walsh in pieces." Then sent us out the door to school, which was directly across the dead-end street from our house.

Five minutes later, my brothers and I were sorted into our home-rooms, standing with our hands over our hearts, reciting The Pledge of Allegiance. I would stop to listen to my classmates' voices in the throbbing hum, hunting for the sound of each boy or girl I knew, unthreading them singular. Safe.

Which precipitated the first time I was sent, unpatriotic boy, rebel mute, to the principal's office where I was told I had to be taught a lesson.

I was made to take down the flag every day that year from the pole out in front of the school, taught to fold it into a tight triangle, lay it gently away in its little dark box. I did this wordlessly, gladly, putting the body of my country to rest.

5. (poem, line)

And so it was that when I discovered poetry, I discovered where all those silences went to be used. "No one likes the child /" Susan Mitchell says in "Smoke," and I feel bad for the kid until speech snaps back across the line break, "to point the gun at them." That's a silence that allows tone to shift, for a voice to be sad, to proclaim some kind of loss, and then to give reason to feeling.

We lost, my teacher said / the civil war // and was I more / numbed or angry // that she erased reason / in service of feeling? What other / erasure did I learn // to keep quiet inside of me?

I distrust the memory that says Mrs. Hixson's lesson occurred the same afternoon that Danny Roland caught me checking out his butt. It couldn't have happened that way. But the drama I am says *yes*. Folds one layer on top of the other. Makes them share a border. Memory insists on tying one coordinate to another. To create an exact replica of a feeling in time. Like a poem does.

6. (break,)

I thought I was putting feeling down

for you to find it: a poem. Here, in this line. The effable

scorched into serifs and syllables, the digraphs

transmogrified from plosives and mutes. What I was

doing was making a place for the silence

I'd grown up with: the desire, the elegy

for a dead boy I thought was my twin,

the road of my childhood, severed by woods

(29° 0' 44" N, 81° 19' 52" W) in which, one summer,

the neighborhood cats—all of them—wound up

dead, the way in class we played Hangman,

one kid noosing another, how good I was

at King and Queen, balancing erasers on our heads,

tagging each other out, chasing through the maze

of desks, how expert I became moving

my plump body out of reach, zigzagging

away from anyone's touch, how I always won

Dodgeball though I was the largest target,

thinking of myself that way: *target*,

intent on leaping into invisible space,

having learned to make myself

unfindable territory. How I pored

over the story of Atlantis. How I loved

the limit of x as it approaches... How I loved

(25.000° N, 71.0000° W), longing to pilot

airspace that defied knowing. I could fly there,

if only the machinery around me ceased,

could stop holding me safe in gunmetal cage.

———•———

It is hard to live in a line break, to cohabitate with resonant and trembling doubt. Enjambment manifests a stay against the resolution of syntax and its bridegroom, sense. In that pause, all is possible because the line pilots us into an airspace in which the radio can't transmit but can only crackle. The line break is alive with possibility, electric with danger and uncertainty. The place where "I dwell in Possibility," as Emily Dickinson writes ("a fairer House than Prose").

In dodgeball, I became good at making space because I could feel the reason behind the throwing-boy's force; my pleasure lay in thwarting his desire to eradicate who I was. On the playground, when my friend caught me looking, I felt my failure was that my silence had stumbled into recognition, a kind of speech. I yearned to live unmarked, a witness in invisible space, not knowing that this yearning marked me as well.

In a poem, we map real-world silences and the wellspring of complex feelings. And it's there, in the building block of a poem's DNA, that contemplation is possible, the pleasure of sound and sense converging before one of those rushes ahead of the other, looking and laughing back, stopping quick and jutting out its backside, saying with that silent gesture, "Go on and gawk at my ass," striking sense dumb with wanting.

———•———

I wrote, "In a line break, I am safe." But that's not true.
~~In a line break, I am~~
~~safe.~~
Safety is an imaginary place.

The line break: most dangerous place in the poem, where the machinery of language fails and the sea comes closer, where illogic threatens to subsume us, where coherence strips off its coordinates. Come.

Live here with me.

FAMOUS MUSHROOM

Mark Wunderlich

L AST YEAR, the Poet Laureate of Winona, Minnesota, invited me to give a reading. I was born in Winona and grew up a few miles away, just across the Mississippi in rural Buffalo County, Wisconsin. My parents had never heard me read my work, and for the first time I had written a book whose overt subject matter was palatable to my parents' sensibilities; there was little sex in the book, and it contained overt religious themes married to a consideration of what it means to have roots in the rural Midwest. I assumed the reading would be a small, rather cozy event with a few interested strangers, my parents and the organizers. I accepted immediately and without too much thought.

When July came, I flew from my home in Upstate New York to Minneapolis and made the three hour drive south to Fountain City. "City" is beyond exaggeration; the town has a population of about 700. An immigrant Wunderlich from Germany was one of the early settlers in the town in the 1830s, and my family has lived there ever since. When you drive from Minneapolis south along the Mississippi, the landscape changes from rolling fields of corn and soybeans dotted with cattle and farm buildings, to the swampy bottomlands of the river basin. You enter into the area called the Driftless Zone where limestone bluffs hem the valley.

The hilltops are black-green and shaggy with cedars, the tan rock face of the cliff fronts pocked with caves. Bald eagles are legion, and near Pepin and Maiden Rock and Stockholm I counted more than a dozen, the rough cones of their nests caught in dead trees at the water's edge, the birds' curved flights inscribing the sky overhead as they set out to fish the river—a hazard as I careened around to take them in.

Arriving from the north, I drove through the town of Fountain City, with its three tiered streets, the Dugway cutting up from the river to the bluff ridge. I know this place as well as any in the world. I passed through Germantown—the name of the far end of town with its small workman's cottages piled on the steep bank and hung over the railroad tracks, and past Eagle Bluff, the highest elevation on the Mississippi and which Mark Twain reports on in *Life on the Mississippi*. Fountain City gets a passing mention, and the bluff is described ironically as a place where angels might go to roost. I have made this entrance into the town thousands of times. This set of bluff and river, the houses and three church spires sometimes appears to me in dreams, indelible and narrow, bound as it is on either side by cliffs, the river the only plausible escape route. Even now, typing this on a summer morning in New York, I can call up the dank smell of the river in summer, the cool sour air of the barroom interior of the Monarch Tavern, creosoted railroad ties baking in the sun down by the tracks. If I posses any treasure in this world, it is the depth of my connection to this place. Recalling the finer details makes my chest ache a little with a potent mix of longing and ambivalence which is one of the primary feelings of my adult life. *Heimweh*, is the German noun for it—literally "home-pain," but that translation somehow misses the softer edges the Germans managed with their poignant compound noun. I have not lived in the town since I was eighteen, having spent years in New York City, Los Angeles, San Francisco, Tucson, Provincetown, and most recently the Hudson Valley. Fountain City will always be the place I long for, though in the gulf the years have opened between my childhood and adult life, it is now a place I can never quite occupy whether I am physically present there or not.

When I arrived home, I hugged my parents hello. The newspaper was out on the kitchen table. Prior to my arrival, I had been interviewed by the three local papers, and the first article had appeared. From his La-Z-Boy, my father says dryly, "You made the front page, Kiddo," before adding, "Below the fold." Indeed, there was a publicity photo of me and the image of my book cover, with a nice story about a poet returning to his roots. The lead story? "A Cactus in the Family: 70-Year-Old Cactus Thrives at Area Nursing Home." My father's characteristic delivery had the familiar mix of lessons from my childhood: achievement is fine, but nobody likes a braggart. *Pride goeth before destruction, and an haughty spirit before a fall.*

At the beginning of the school year in his seminars at Columbia University, poet Richard Howard would remind his students that calling yourself a famous poet is like saying you're a famous mushroom. Howards' admonition was aimed at skipping the track of the aspirations of young poets who can easily get caught up in the competitive cycle of publications, prizes, and connections. Writing well, making complex art, and having a life of the mind differs from achieving public recognition. The headline from the *Winona Daily News* gave with one hand, and gently slapped me down with the other.

——— • ———

Eight years ago, my father was diagnosed with a brain tumor. In the time leading up to the diagnosis, he had started dragging one leg when he walked, and when tired his face drooped on one side making him look inordinately sad. Normally a man of dogged patience, he became stubborn and almost sub-lingual. "Works good," became his most-used phrase. "What works good, Pop?" He mostly couldn't say. One day in October while out in the marsh hunting ducks, he lost his balance and went into the water. The details of his rescue are hazy, but he remained in the water up to his chest until a farmer found him and hauled him out. He may have been there for hours, mired in the soft mud of the Trempcaleau River while his Labrador, William, paddled around him. Only after this did he agree to see a doctor. Surgery was performed to remove the tumor, and he was treated for cancer with relative success, but in the intervening years he has suffered strokes, seizures, and a bad fall. Radiation therapy has also taken its toll, and my father can no longer walk unassisted. He struggles to understand and to be understood, and spends much of the day sleeping in his chair. What was once a vigorous life, much of it spent outdoors in the woods and fields and on the water, or working with horses and dogs, is now circumscribed, and whether or not he would attend the reading would depend on how strong he felt that day.

I had convinced my parents that the bookstore hosting the reading wouldn't be open until a half-hour prior to the event, so there was no point in arriving earlier. On the day of the reading, my father felt well enough to attend, and so we began the process of getting him into the car. When we arrived at the Blue Heron, I pulled up in front and got out to help my father, positioned his walker, got him safely to the door where my mother took over while I went to find a place to park.

When I entered, I was greeted by a wall of noise. The room was packed. Faces came into focus. People smiled at me from out of the past, and I smiled back, reaching for names. I scanned the room for my parents, and found them at a table near the door, my mother deep in conversation with friends while my father looked a little stunned but content, as someone patted him on the shoulder and spoke loudly in his direction. The bookstore owner came buzzing toward me, asking if I had more books; the thirty he ordered had sold out, and he needed as many as I had.

I made my way slowly through the room, greeting people. Faces I hadn't seen in decades swam into view; people said hello and hugged me, shook my hand. My high school German teacher was there, as well as my fifth-grade homeroom teacher. There were members of my family church—a dozen? more?—and three classmates from my school waved from the back. My father's friends from the American Legion Hall had come. My godmother beamed at me, and family friends whose faces had aged, but whom I would know anywhere, all said the same thing, "I'm sure you don't remember me." Of course I remembered them—how would I not? These were the people who raised me, fed me, taught me, ushered me through my formative years. Much of the work they did in the world was aimed at making possible a moment like this—they had done their best to give me what I would need to be a successful adult.

When the organizer announced that the reading was about to begin, no one could hear him. The din of animated conversation was fueled by people's uncertainty of what to expect. For most of the audience, this would be their first poetry reading. I helped him settle the crowd, and after a kind introduction, I took the podium.

How often does a writer read to an audience made almost entirely of people who have known him since birth? As I stood at the podium I was moved and unnerved. The poems I had chosen to read were not just about my home town; some of them name people my audience would know. The central poem in my book *The Earth Avails* is called "Driftless Elegy." The poem was my attempt to describe my own sense of alienation from this very place and from the people who were now looking at me with a mix of excitement and guarded anticipation. The poem has echoes of Robert Lowell's "Skunk Hour," a sour treatise of his own estrangement from a coastal New England that seems to represent, in its singular broken characters, the psychic wounds left on the poet. Was this what I thought of my audience? Were they representations of my own bad feelings, or were they real people with struggles of their own who had somehow found their way into my poem? I wince whenever I read again of Lowell's "fairy decorator" brightening his shop for fall. Was it possible

I was about to wound someone tonight? Lowell seems to have bargained that the enormity of his own psychological pain was penance enough for any damage he might do to others. Was I just as egotistical?

When I read "Driftless Elegy," something in the atmosphere changed. The audience settled into a quietude you recognize when a roomful of people aims their attention at a single target. As I began to read, the audience reacted. There were nods and smiles. Several times I had to pause to let laughter die down. When I described an event people had been part of, their faces acknowledged it. When I named someone they knew or remembered, they would laugh with recognition. There was mild shock at the mention of a local strip club—the subject of countless private gossipy conversations, but a thing not often spoken of in a public place. The poem which had been read to maybe a hundred urban audiences was, for the first time, not exotic or foreign or tragic. This was not a melancholic reflection of a disappearing rural life, but documentation of what it feels like to live in a place literature and art have largely passed over. Read to this audience, the poem transformed. There was no nostalgia here, no urban cliché invoking the death of small town America. The town I elegized was alive with the daily experience of the people who live there, and who had come to listen to a writer tell them about themselves.

In the days that followed, as I ran errands for my parents, or as I moved through town, people recognized me. They had seen my photo in the newspaper. Some had attended the reading. I was asked again and again if I was the poet they had read about or heard on public radio. My parents' phone rang for days as people called to discuss what I had said and done. When I came home from the store, or from taking the garbage to the dump, my parents wanted to know whom I'd seen or who had mentioned the reading. "How's the famous mushroom?" my father would ask.

All of this was a heady experience, and I felt enormous gratitude and a sense of luck for having had it. Yet something bothered me. Despite my deep roots to this place and its people, I have lived my adult life exiled from it. Growing up queer in the rural Midwest, I knew there was no life for me there; I would have to leave, and I would most likely have to move to a city. In an urban place I could make friends, find a society in which I belonged, and live a life of culture and books and like-minded comradery. I could fall in love. I could be safe from gossip and casual violence. Certainly I was often home on visits, but when I was there, a silence surrounded me and the life I had set out to create. I had sidestepped the conventions of the public-private life heterosexuals have always been afforded—marriage, children—having chosen to live in the traditional queer American places of New York, San Francisco, and Provincetown—not just by choice, but out of necessity. If I was going to thrive, there were certain things I didn't want to worry about.

Why was I being welcomed back now? When you leave a small town for the larger world, your departure is often greeted with a mix of resignation and resentment. "Didn't like us, did you? Needed a bit more excitement? Don't let the screen door hit you on the way out." The fate of the small town homosexual was not going to be mine—laughed at or derided, lonely and alone, trying to make do with vacations to Florida, or trips to Minneapolis while dutifully tending to aging parents. The script was written long before I was born, and I wouldn't be part of it. I wouldn't be Lowell's "fairy decorator," brightening "Skunk Hour" as a target of scorn.

Everyone likes a success story. My return to my hometown was met with delight because I had made myself into something recognizable. Reading in my home town had changed me. I had looked into the past and reported on the present. I have gone into the world, but I brought my home town with me, along with everyone in it. They sit with me now as I type these words into a machine. I am alive in a multitude of places, though I know with certainty that most of those places no longer exist.

MY BACKYARD, BUT NOT WHAT HAPPENED TO MY BODY

Molly McCully Brown

GROWING UP in the middle of nowhere means you spend a lot of time in the car: ten miles to school or the grocery store, thirty-five to the movie theater or a decent restaurant, nearly sixty to the nearest place you might want to buy clothes. You drive the same stretch of rural highway so many thousands of times you stop really seeing it: mile markers and exit signs, the constant purple rise of the Blue Ridge in the distance yawning in and out of fog. For years, I sped past Colony Road and the government issued sign for *The Central Virginia Training Center* (CVTC) nearly every day without much interest. I knew vaguely that the CVTC was a residential facility for people with serious disabilities, and that it had a complicated history, tangled up with Appalachia, and eugenics, and the Great Depression. In high school, grappling with my own cerebral palsy, I sometimes thought about it glancingly, the way you consider something that *almost* relates to you but doesn't exactly. Mostly, though, the facility was just another feature of the place I was raised: red clay hills, Baptist church, bakery, Training Center. All of it familiar and forgettable as my own hand.

I was eighteen the summer that changed, home in Virginia between my sophomore and junior years of college, taking a theology class at the university about an hour north of my hometown. Initially, I devised a day trip out to the boondocks of my childhood as an attempt at a diversion for a close friend who was going through a difficult stretch and needed a distraction. We bought cheeseburgers at McDonalds, put her dog in the truck, and turned the radio up loud. The plan was to go south and do a drive by tour of my one-stoplight town, and then continue on into Bedford where we'd heard there was an attraction called *Holyland USA*, a kind of homemade theme park someone had built featuring all the stations of the cross. The trip was supposed to be easy and amusing, a chance to spend time with the idiosyncrasies of a landscape I loved.

I don't remember, now, why we decided to turn off the highway at Colony Road. Because we'd never been there? Because the honeysuckle was blooming over the gate and looked beautiful? Because the dog was whining in the cab and needed to be let out? I do remember seeing the former Colony for the first time. After the wrought iron gate, the road forked in two directions. One led to the facility proper, the other to its sprawling cemetery. Like many things in central Virginia, the Training Center sits on a huge amount of land, the acreage around it much greater than you could practically ever use. As the facility fell into disrepair in the many years after its founding in the early 1900s, instead of being rehabbed or knocked down older buildings were simply abandoned, new construction rising around them on all the available land. That day we first visited the place, the CVTC struck me as the strangest combination of ghost town and functioning operation: at once the center that it is now, and the shadow of everything that it had been—built up around its own troubling history in the most literal of senses.

The Training Center as it exists now makes little explicit concession to that dark past, when it was called The Virginia

State Colony for Epileptics and Feebleminded. On the facility's website, a page marked *history* includes, just after a discussion of the Colony's first post office, a single paragraph acknowledging that for a period, acting in accordance with Virginia law, "the facility embarked on an ill-advised program of involuntary sterilization, combined with routine appendectomies, of so-called '...defectives with cacogenic potentialities.'"That's all there is. No details about the men and women who once filled the infirmary beds, or the salpingectomies and vasectomies performed without their consent or even their knowledge.

That July day, we drove slowly through the Training Center's grounds, my wheelchair rattling like the bones of an animal in the truck bed. The buildings were a mix of brick and white clapboard, the older ones slouching like ragged hollow ghosts next to the Center's contemporary facilities, marked with black numbers that no longer seemed to indicate any kind of order. We didn't talk much but I hung half my body out the passenger side window looking at the white-washed porches and the cloudy windows—in which sometimes a stray curtain still hung—and counting the *crossing for handicapped pedestrians* signs. Occasionally we saw a maintenance truck, but whoever lived at the CVTC seemed shut away inside. No one stopped us to ask who we were.

Eventually, we parked down by the cemetery and got out. I pulled my wheelchair from the truck, but quickly abandoned it. The wheels stuck in the gravel and the clay. I leaned on my friend's arm, or put my palms to the dirt where the hills were high to keep my balance. We picked our way toward the outlying buildings and the flat grave-markers lain into the hill. The headstones were dated as early as 1911 and as late as the past few years. Some people had died in old age, but many more were young: twenties, thirties. On one section of the hillside the graves belonged entirely to infants and children. A metal placard read: *Dedicated to those whose lives and care we held in trust 'as seedlings of God we barely blossom on earth; we fully flower in Heaven.'* I felt very aware of my own disabled body, then: my feet and ankles turning in underneath me, my perpetually contracting hamstrings and swollen knees, the steady, constant pain radiating from my lower back into my toes. I remembered hearing about the doctor who told my parents, when I was born in 1991, that I would probably never live independently, might never even speak. I felt time and space collapse: sixty-five years ago, born in my hometown, I might have been sterilized in that Colony, or dead.

I wasn't ready to write about The Colony at the time—I could only hold it at a kind of suspended distance—but once I'd been there, I couldn't get it out of my head. Something about seeing the old pieces of the place, still standing there on the soil where I was raised, in the mountains I *always* recognized and claimed, even when the landscape of my own body felt foreign, kept tugging at me. Two years later I graduated from college and moved to Texas. I spent my time teaching creative writing to inner-city grade school students and feeling very much at war with my own difficult body, which hurt all the time and made me feel ill-suited for my job and, frankly, for life in the world. I felt more than a little like I'd muscled through a childhood and adolescence marked by surgical intervention and constant physical therapy in pursuit of some bright and "better" future, only to find myself staring down the barrel of an adulthood that looked just as thorny, lonely, and medically uncertain. Increasingly unmoored and casting around for something that felt sturdy and like it mattered, I turned, as I always do, toward the hills and valleys of my home. I started doing research into The Colony's past, and almost immediately I began to hear a chorus of ghosts. Then, I began to write.

There are remarkably few records from the years in the 30s and 40s at the height of The Colony's sterilization practices. Patient accounts are, of course, especially few and far between. In a rare newspaper story from the early 1990s, a reporter describes tracking down a former Colony patient who was released as a young woman and then spent her entire adult life trying to have children. Essentially, he had to sit at her kitchen table, look at her in her wheelchair, and tell her her own story: *This is what was done to you. This is the great shroud over your life, and you didn't even know about it.* Reading it, I wondered how her face had altered then, and if she'd gotten up and turned back to her stove, her sink, her dishes, turned away.

The more I read and the more I contemplated, the louder I began to hear the imagined voices of other women in The Colony. Women who were epileptic; women who were brilliant, but whose bodies left them unable to move or speak, and so who were assumed to be witless; women whose childhoods were stripped from them. Women with their faces pressed to dormitory windows and their heads bowed in a modest chapel. I came home from teaching and wrote for hours, eating handfuls of dry cereal out of the box because I didn't want to pause to make dinner. In just a few months, I found I'd produced a claustrophobic little manuscript in the voices of these women, organized into the handful of rooms in which they would have lived. The poems were haunted and interior, intended less to stand in for the records of real patients' lives that don't exist than to call attention to the devastating fact of their absence: all the remarkable thoughts, feelings, and discoveries that are lost to us because they happened inside the heads of women who were committed behind Colony walls, who were called *feeble* and *idiot* and *insane*, who were denied their ability to be a part of society, to have a stake in the future of the world.

I'm tempted, here, to say something along the lines of how, in writing about The Colony, I found myself at home, again, in my body and the world. But the truth is, I'd never been especially at home in either. I'd always been a gunner, though, foot on the gas and eyes on the horizon, ambitious about a future that promised to be better than whatever present I was in. I went to college at sixteen and, after two years, I left my tiny Massachusetts liberal arts school for a big California University and all the opportunity it held. I pushed myself to graduate by twenty, even though I was happy there and could have easily stayed another year. I made myself alone on purpose. Somewhere along the way, I developed the sense that if I was ambitious and extraordinary enough—if I did everything flawlessly and never stopped moving—I could outrun the truth of my body, leave it behind in the wake of all my excellence.

But no matter where I was, my brain fired stray signals across the same flawed circuit, and my tendons pulled too tight, and my joints ached a little louder every year. I hurled myself from one city to another, one achievement to the next, but the great trick of it all was that with every milestone I passed, it got harder and harder to ask my body to lie to itself. And so I found myself, at twenty-one, having run as far as I could manage. I wrote about The Colony when I had no choice but to sit still and listen. I lived in my body; I turned my eyes back toward where I was raised.

The wildest thing is that, when I did, I found woken up in me a shocking stab of kinship, a profound awareness of a lineage I'd never paused to feel or consider before: this sense that my body, as much as it divided me from my family and friends and most of the world, also *tied* me to a huge group of people who had lived before me, and were living alongside me. Here was this real shared heritage, made all the more poignant and complicated by the fact that so many Colony patients were denied the opportunity to have their own biological children, and by my consciousness that only an accident of time was responsible for the fact that I had *written* the poems in front of me and not lived out one of the lives they detailed. Here was the messy truth of it after all, a truth I had finally found only in stanza and metaphor and line: I had no choice but to make a home in the place of my body, but it turned out I had never been going it alone.

LONE TREE, FAR AWAY

Shane McCrae

L ONE TREE, IOWA, is a small town about 9 miles southeast of Iowa City. As I wrote that first sentence in my head—as I considered and reconsidered it and maybe half a dozen sentences like it, and I spent about an hour, actually, I'm amazed to realize, thinking about that sentence before I sat down to write it, *that* sentence, but maybe I spent so long thinking about it *because* I hadn't yet sat down to write it, and yes, now that I'm thinking about it, about the process of writing itself, what I mean is just this: I write prose in my head like I'm writing a poem, and I write prose at a desk like I'm writing prose. As I wrote and re-wrote that first sentence in my head, not once did it occur to me that Lone Tree might be farther than 9 miles from Iowa City. I lived in Iowa City for 7 years, and I drove from Iowa City to Lone Tree and back dozens of times—I ought to know how far apart they are. But I don't. Or, at least, I didn't. I know now because I Googled it. Lone Tree, Iowa, is a small town about 16 miles southeast of Iowa City.

For years now—I started when I was about 25, 10 years after I started writing poems (I got my driver's license late)—I've driven, whenever I've had the chance, by myself to, and really mostly

through, various small towns within an hour or so of wherever
I've happened to be living, which, right now, is Oberlin, Ohio,
itself basically a small town. I've done this thinking I was seeking
the towns themselves, and the weird, impossible nostalgia I feel
in them—impossible because I've never lived in any of the towns
I've driven to, nor ever in any town like them, at least not before
I lived in Oberlin, which, even though it *is* a small town, is still
bigger than any of the towns I drive to. But lately I haven't had
the time to drive as often as I used to, and I've come to realize it
wasn't the towns themselves, nor even the impossible nostalgia, I
was seeking. It was the act of driving itself.

Drives lull babies to sleep. Everybody knows that. Drives lull
adults to sleep, too—even when they're driving. There's a certain
driftiness achievable only behind the wheel. And this driftiness
has something to do with writing poems—or maybe it would be
more correct to say that this driftiness has something to do with
the state of mind necessary to the writing of poems. I've never
done drugs, and I've never drank alcohol. And I really don't know
exactly what it is, if anything, writers in particular are looking
to find with and through drugs and alcohol (and I hate writing
about this stuff at all because I feel like such a square), but I
think maybe some of them, at least, are looking for this driftiness.
It is a driftiness—and I think this is particular to driving (and
maybe, you know, the drugs and the drink)—in which one is
extra-receptive. Which only makes sense, right? Receptiveness is
good for driving.

But it's a paradoxical receptiveness, one in which a 16-
mile drive can seem only 9 miles long. The driftiness one can
achieve while driving does not, in other words, incline one to be
especially *per*ceptive—at least not as we usually understand the
word. When one drives, if one attains the particular driftiness
I'm talking about, one becomes extra-perceptive of certain
immediate things—the road itself, trees and big branches and a
box of old clothes that fell out of the back of a pickup on its way

to Goodwill, and people or animals or objects in motion that might intersect with the road. That's a list of important stuff! But it doesn't include, for example, time and distance, which become distorted and difficult to measure accurately. In a letter to Paul Demeny, Rimbaud wrote that "the poet makes himself into a visionary by a long derangement of all the senses." And isn't that—it is, I'm sure it is, but in a mild, or maybe easy, but not lesser way—what I do when I drive, what everybody does? Our senses become unusually focused and thereby deranged, and we become temporary visionaries behind the wheel—we just don't recognize ourselves as visionaries because we forget: visionaries see *less* than other people. A visionary doesn't see everything in the room—a visionary sees the one thing in the room nobody else sees. For a long time, and maybe I still believe this, I thought that was what a poet was supposed to do, too.

So I drove to Lone Tree a lot trying to trick myself into becoming, at least for the twenty minutes or so it took to drive there from Iowa City, a visionary. But I never thought about what I was doing, what I was *really* doing, when I was doing it—I just thought I was driving to Lone Tree to get a little sad. I thought I had a special, kind of weepy, affinity for Lone Tree and towns like it, even though I never once had a conversation with anybody in Lone Tree, nor ate at the one restaurant in Lone Tree. I thought it was the place itself, and not the people in it, that made me feel misty and diffuse and poetic. But it wasn't the place or the people. I loved Lone Tree because I could get out of my head driving there. I loved Lone Tree because it was just far enough away for me to forget how far away it was.

A POETICS OF TECTONIC SCALE: THE GREAT DISTANCE POEM

Katy Didden

THERE'S A NEIGHBORHOOD PARK in Seattle that I love: Lake Dell, Leschi. It juts out from the side of Leschi hill in a narrow panhandle, and it doesn't look like much from the street, but if you follow the path behind a row of Madrona trees, you arrive at a lookout with a sweeping view of Lake Washington, where, as Marianne Moore writes, *the wind makes lanes of ripples.* When the sky is blue with a few bright clouds, and the afternoon light blurs the North Cascades to one dark green, you can see Mount Rainier in the far distance. Though the mountain has been fixed in place for millennia, it remains one of the most unstill objects that I can imagine—unstill, and unsettling.

The mountain is always there, but you can't always see it, and you can't always predict this by the weather. I've seen it in sharp detail on gray days, and barely visible, like a pink mirage, on hazy days. When it's invisible, you start to think it could be anywhere, and when it's out, it floats on air—you can feel it shift the cells of your body from single to double space. It's not unusual to see people stare at Rainier, a little stunned, as if they were facing an enormous, wordless creature, alive and breathing, in the eerie stillness before it strikes: a mammoth, a dragon, a giant octopus of ice.

———•———

The summer after my junior year in college, my friend, Carol, and I sublet a room across from Greenlake in Seattle. I worked the closing shift at Guido's Pizza, so I had the mornings free. I used to walk to the top of the alley behind our house to get a view of Mount Rainier, and I'd sit there, holding a paperback copy of Marianne Moore's *Complete Poems*. I would read "An Octopus," Moore's homage to Big Snow Mountain, and then I'd stare at the mountain itself. Since then, poetry and the Pacific Northwest have been closely connected for me. In fact, I cannot look at the mountain, *its vermillion and onyx and manganese-blue interior expensiveness*, without hearing lines from the poem in my head. If it is not, as Wallace Stevens once wrote, that the poem "took the place of the mountain," it is something close to that, a kind of evolving inter-relationship, an unfolding of text and tectonics.

In her book, *The Creative Habit*, Twyla Tharp claims that our imaginations are "hardwired" to a preferred focal length: "All of us find comfort in seeing the world either from a great distance, at arm's length, or in close-up. We don't consciously make that choice. Our DNA does, and we generally don't waver from it." I love how Tharp locates the process of art-making in the body, like reading anatomy in a signature. I also like how this distance is, for the artist, what you're able to *perform*, to re-tell for others. I wish I were a poet of the close-up or middle-distance. As soon as I read Tharp's description, though, I knew my creative DNA was of the "great distance" variety. That perspective activates my imagination, which is why so many of my poems take place in dramatic landscapes like Patagonia, Death Valley, and Iceland.

It would be easy to say the long view stirs an inner restlessness, and that any view of the mountains makes me want to see what's beyond the next ridgeline, to move, to climb, to leave the known behind. In my pursuit of the poem mountain, I *have* moved across the country a lot, from one graduate program or teaching job to another. But as much as I'm addicted to the promise of possibility, I hate leaving people and cities behind, and this feeling of loss is why the "great distance" perspective feels like fate, the story I'm born to tell. What the great distance represents for me is less a restlessness so much as a willingness, as though the view makes setting new directions possible.

My poetic process mirrors my affinity for distance. Like Moore herself, who wrote "An Octopus" only after she'd returned from her visit to Rainier in July 1922, and after she'd read guidebooks about the mountain, I tend to write about places I've only visited or come to know through research. Both the act of looking back and of gathering information are like reading a topographic map. For me, great distance writing means tuning in to those memories or ideas that some mysterious energy elevates above the sea of thoughts.

Maybe this approach resembles Wordsworth's "emotion recollected in tranquility"; maybe any discussion of the great distance perspective invokes the Romantic poets, and the sublime. Think of the moment in *The Prelude* when young Wordsworth unties a boat from a willow tree, and rows out on a silent, moonlit lake. While he gazes out at the horizon, he watches as "a huge peak, black and huge / as if with voluntary power instinct / upreared its head." Or think of Keats, in "On First Looking into Chapman's Homer," who compares his discovery of Homer to eagle-eyed Cortez, staring at the Pacific, "silent, on a peak in Darien." When I start to think about the great distance poem in terms of craft, several questions circle in my mind—what techniques do poets use to convey scale? How do poets create the sensation of a vantage point? Does that vantage point reveal anything about how poets conceive of seeing itself, and our relationship to visual technologies? What does it mean not just to look, but to *perform* looking? How do we invite readers to that looking?

Not surprisingly, there is a strong correlation between the Romantics' great-distance poetics and their contemporary visual culture. This was the age of spectacular devices such as eidophusaikons, dioramas, camera obscuras, and Claude glasses. It was also the age of one of my favorite visual phenomena: the panorama. Panoramas were enormous, 360-degree paintings set inside a viewing rotunda; patrons ascended a central tower to gaze at city scenes, historical events, or dramatic landscapes. Panoramas offered viewers the illusion of finding a single vantage point that could reveal an entire landscape. In turn, this perspective affected the way that people encountered nature. As Stephan Oettermann notes in *The Panorama: History of a Mass Medium*, "more than just the aesthetic counterpart of a natural phenomenon, the panorama was both a surrogate for nature and a simulator, an apparatus for teaching people how to see it." Taking a cue from this, maybe we could name poems where a solitary speaker confronts the beauty and terror of a massive landscape "panoramic," especially those poems where the centrality of the speaker, and the act of looking, is important.

Consider Shelley's ode, "Mont Blanc: Lines Written in the Vale of Chamouni," and how Shelley begins the poem by asserting the presence of the human mind: "The everlasting universe of things / Flows through the mind, and rolls its rapid waves." Shelley describes the landscape with glorious intensity; frequently, he also depicts himself looking:

> Dizzy Ravine! and when I gaze on thee
> I seem as in a trance sublime and strange
> To muse on my own separate fantasy,
> My own, my human mind, which passively
> Now renders and receives fast influencings,
> Holding an unremitting interchange
> With the clear universe of things around.

I'm intrigued by how Shelley's stance of looking is essential to the meaning of the poem, as he invites us to watch him in the trance of his own "separate fantasy." It's a fascinating move, and it points to what I think is the main way Shelley builds a sense of distance: tone. Addressing the Mountain directly, Shelley gives the illusion of authoritative certainty, of stability and predictability in the "everlasting universe of things." He also claims that poets have god-like power: "And what were [the mountain], and earth, and stars, and sea / If to the human mind's imaginings / Silence and solitude were vacancy?" Shelley questions why it is we associate remote mountain peaks with this "unremitting interchange / with the clear universe," and assigns humans the power of affirming presence in nature. Still, when I read the poem, I often feel like I am listening to a man shouting at a cliff, from a cliff.

Perhaps this is similar to the effect Oettermann describes when he writes of the famous painting by Caspar David Friedrich, *Traveler Looking Over a Sea of Fog*: "his painting includes a figure seen from the rear and thus simultaneously shows a panorama and a visitor to it [...] What is presented in Friedrich's landscape paintings is not a panorama per se, but rather a view of the world as panorama." Even though Shelley talks about the interrelation of nature with his own mind, by showing himself looking, and by performing shouting, he maintains a sense of separateness, or even dominion, in the way the world stretches out before him— an attitude that feels less persuasive now.

Moore's "An Octopus" shares some things in common with "Mont Blanc," including serpentine glaciers (Shelley notes how "the glaciers creep / Like snakes that watch their prey"; Moore's ice-fields have "the concentric crushing rigor of the python"). But Moore's "An Octopus" is a poem of a different species. I can think of few other poems that are as lush, as disorienting, and as epic in scale than "An Octopus." Reading it, I feel an awe not unlike what I feel seeing the mountain itself. This is not because

Moore gives a photo-realistic description of the mountain (who would recognize "the glassy octopus symmetrically pointed" as Mount Rainier, out of context?). But it does come from the way she moves through the poem.

As scholars like Tom Gunning, Jonathan Crary, and Ross King have argued, the spectacular devices of nineteenth century visual culture were pre-cursors to cinema. This helps me to think of Moore's poetics as the next step: as cinematic. This is not to say that the panoramic perspective disappears—I don't think the evolution is that linear. But cinema introduces new ways of accessing the "unremitting interchange" with the universe, and adds new perspectives to the aggregate of looks. The camera-lens model of perspective is a radical departure from a person standing at the panorama's fixed distance. Instead, we have Moore looking, at multiple angles, from multiple distances, through multiple lenses, and splicing together separate takes into a coherent whole. Consider "An Octopus":

> "Picking periwinkles from the cracks"
> or killing prey with the concentric crushing rigor of the
>   python,
> it hovers forward "spider fashion
> on its arms" misleadingly like lace;
> its "ghostly pallor changing
> to the green metallic tinge of an anemone-starred pool."

Moore not only blends multiple voices into this poem, citing quotes from sources as varied as *The National Parks Portfolio*, the *Illustrated London News*, Cardinal Newman's *Historical Sketches*, and W.D. Hyde's *The Five Great Philosophies*, but she also jump-cuts between diverse creatures, from diverse ecosystems (periwinkles, pythons, spiders, anemones), that serve as animating metaphors for the mountain. What's curious is how this multiple-looking, while it is Moore's signature technique, actually dislocates the speaker—she is no longer at a fixed point in space or time.[1] Maybe this disembodiment is why Moore's cinematic description is particularly apt to capture the "ghostly pallor" and shape-shifting of the mountain that disappears in veils of clouds.

Moore builds scale by way of syntax and juxtaposition, with tumbling, Whitmanian lists:

> Big Snow Mountain is the home of a diversity of creatures:
> those who "have lived in hotels
> but who now live in camps—who prefer to";
> the mountain guide evolving from the trapper,
> "in two pairs of trousers, the outer one older,
> wearing slowly away from the feet to the knees";
> "the nine-striped chipmunk
> running with unmammal-like agility along a log";
> the water ouzel
> with "its passion for rapids and high-pressured falls,"
> building under the arch of some tiny Niagara;
> the white-tailed ptarmigan "in winter solid white,
> feeding on heather-bells and alpine buckwheat;
> and the eleven eagles of the west,
> "fond of the spring fragrance and the winter colors,"
> used to the unegoistic action of the glaciers
> and "several hours of frost every midsummer night."
> "they make a nice appearance, don't they,"
> happy seeing nothing?

By using a long sentence structured as a paratactic list, Moore asserts a democratic equality between "a diversity of creatures." She levels humans with non-humans—the mountain guide is as oddly curious as the chipmunk, and the water ouzel is a tourist in its

---

[1] *In Cinematic Modernism: Modernist Poetry and Film* (Cambridge UP, 2009), Susan McCabe discusses how the medium of film appealed to modernists, because of how it suggested disembodiment: "The body could be deliriously elsewhere, uncannily absent, yet viscerally present" (1).

own right, venturing towards a "tiny Niagara." In this way, Moore troubles the paradigm that humans are the center of the universe.

Moore performs another sleight-of-hand with her descriptions, one that contributes to the sense of Rainier's enormity, as she moves between instantaneous actions (the chipmunk running, the water ouzel building, the ptarmigan feeding) and long-term actions "the mountain guide evolving from the trapper." She invokes the winter, spring, and midsummer habits of these creatures, implying that the speaker has observed this environment through multiple seasons. Furthermore, Moore builds scale by alternating between close-ups and establishing shots, from the tiny "nine-striped chipmunk," to the sweeping, "unegoistic action of the glaciers." In doing this, she suggests that the thing observed, the mountain, is too large to capture at one glance, from one angle. Curiously, it is precisely the movement between those two positions (close-up and panning shot) that gives us the sense that we're traversing a great distance.[2]

The sense of scale in "An Octopus" also comes from the magnitude of Moore's poetic process, and how you can see the evidence of this process in the work itself. I've read "An Octopus" hundreds of times and I'm still bewildered by the density of Moore's descriptions and allusions. She assembles a vast network of voices (integrating quotes from sources as various as articles on fashion, guidebooks, and treatises on Greek philosophy), and creates an avalanche of ongoing, simultaneous, and shifting perceptions. Though Moore provides extensive notes for "An Octopus," they are less a guidebook than peculiar maps meant to lead readers far afield. She immerses us in language differently, as orderly tracks of iambs give way to new methods of orienteering.

---

[2] I've written more on Moore's use of cinematic techniques in this poem, and her use of colors and anachorism in "The Poem That Won't Leave You Alone" project for *At Length* magazine: http://atlengthmag. com/poetry/the-poem-that-wont-leave-you-alone/

It could be that, above anything else, it is the very sense of being lost in the poem that gives me the feeling that I'm inhabiting a real environment (and a massive one).

Moore's montage-work is also a *collage* of quotations, one that troubles ideas of authorship in a way that anticipates the concerns of today's ecopoets, asking questions such as: who is it that speaks? and what does it mean to represent, or to name, nature? The name Mount Rainier dates back to 1792, when George Vancouver, a captain in the British Navy, named the mountain in honor of rear admiral Peter Rainier. In all 193 lines of "An Octopus," however, Moore never refers to her subject as Mount Rainier. Instead, she privileges Native American connections to the mountain, calling it "Big Snow Mountain," or "Mount Tacoma." In fact, Native American tribes of the Pacific Northwest have many names for the mountain. The Lushootseed people refer to it as "Tahoma, Talol, Tacoba, or Tacoma," which translates to "the mother of all waters." I've also read that Tahoma means "higher than 'Kobah,'" with Kobah being a Salish word for neighboring Mount Baker. Currently, an alliance of tribal leaders is seeking to re-name it "Ti-Swaq," meaning "it touches the sky" or "sky swiper." Trusting Moore's prefatory note to *The Complete Poems* that "omissions are not accidents," I find her choice not to call the mountain Rainier consistent with the poem's implicit critique of a possessive, colonialist culture.[3]

---

[3] As Lesley Wheeler and Chris Galaver argue in "Imposters and Chameleons: Marianne Moore and the Carlisle Indian School" (Paideuma 33.2-3, December 2009), Moore's relationship to the Carlisle Indian School was complex. On the one hand, the authors provide persuasive evidence that Moore might have inspired her students in the business school to know and assert their rights. On the other hand, they emphasize that, during a Congressional investigation into "allegations of violence as well as corruption" at Carlisle in 1914, Moore "staked an isolated, neutral ground" (66). If she supported equal rights for indigenous Americans, Moore was decidedly silent at a crucial juncture.

In fact, throughout her work, Moore seems as much concerned with *how* we are looking as she is with *what* we are seeing. That is to say, the way we take in the view is not meaningless; there is an ethics to looking. The park in Leschi neighborhood is one example—the reason you can't see the mountain from every point along the downslope of Leschi Hill is because people built enormous houses there—something Moore might name, as she does in "A Grave": "Man looking into the sea, / taking the view from those who have as much right to it as you have to it yourself." Moore frequently calls attention to, and overturns, any notion that to see is to stake a claim, to see is to possess. In Moore's economy, possessiveness signals a lack of spiritual perspective, and in more than one poem, freedom from possessiveness is what marks a visionary.

————◆————

I've always known the seismic upheavals that created the stunning volcanoes and mountain ranges go hand in hand with earthquakes, eruptions, and tsunamis in the Pacific Northwest, but the level of destruction is hard to fathom. For the last century, like a giant screen, Mount Rainier hasn't seemed to change so much as register the changes happening around it—the weather, the pollution, the light, the season; the reflections signal passing time: the world is changing, you are changing. Still, I think the mountain astonishes onlookers mainly because, at any moment, it could erupt again. Since I am a poet, one way I come to terms with this inevitable fact is through the lens of my creative life, and my ambitions for poetry. Perhaps it is hard to identify, from the middle of this moment, the patterns evolving in poetic form right now, but I do think that there are key questions in the ether: To what extent is looking towards the future an imperative of the contemporary environmental poem? Can poems alter our awareness in such a way that will help us survive as a species? What does that look like? Or, rather, what kind of looking is that?

If the leap from Romanticism to Modernism has parallels in visual culture's expansion from panorama to cinema, how would we characterize our current relationship to visual culture? Today, since we are inundated with visual representations of places, it is not as necessary to stand on a pinnacle to see great distances—we can launch remote-control cameras, or travel via *Google Earth*.[4] If our view isn't limited by where we stand, then the place where we position ourselves in a poem becomes even more of an argument. Wouldn't today's great distance poet, taking the long view, write poems shaped by the knowledge of climate change, the fact of resource scarcity and war, and the unfathomable scale of human-induced destruction? I would argue that one way today's great distance poets assert vision is by calling us to take the long view not just across space, but also across *time*; we build a sense of colossal scale by taking historical events, and their repercussions, as our subject, and by finding forms that expose those consequences in new and innovative ways.

One poet who makes us look hard at our looking apparatus is Layli Long Soldier. Long Soldier's *WHEREAS* provides an essential counter narrative to American exceptionalism and the fraught history of manifest destiny. In her poem "38," she recounts the history of the Sioux Uprising in 1862, and the death by hanging of thirty-eight Dakota men. Her poem works against the annihilation of that history, and she performs this by adopting a tone of factual reporting, and a rejection of artifice, as she writes, "I do not regard this as a poem of great imagination or a work of fiction / Also, historical events will not be dramatized for an interesting read." Throughout the poem, she presents historical facts in unadorned sentences:

---

[4] For a thought-provoking discussion of visual culture in Anthropocene, see "Conditions of Visuality in the Anthropocene and Images of the Anthropocene to Come" by Irmgard Emmelhainz (*e-flux journal* #63, March 2015).

You may or may not have heard about the Dakota 38.

If this is the first time you've heard of it, you might wonder, "What is the Dakota 38?"

The Dakota 38 refers to thirty-eight Dakota men who were executed by hanging, under orders from President Abraham Lincoln.

To date, this is the largest "legal" mass execution in U.S. history.

The hanging took place on December 26th, 1862—the day after Christmas.

This was the *same week* that President Lincoln signed the Emancipation Proclamation.

In the preceding sentence, I italicize "same week" for emphasis.

Long Soldier, in her choice of tone, creates a radical relationship between poet and reader. Throughout the poem, she demonstrates a sympathetic awareness of her audience: she anticipates their questions, and she openly acknowledges the plurality of their experience ("You may or may not have heard about the Dakota 38"). In the context of perspective, I understand this as a profound shift from the solitary, sublime stance that is so entrenched in our understanding of the great distance poem. Here, Long Soldier calls us to understand that we do not look across the great distance as solitary viewers; instead, we look out, elbow-to-elbow, with others.

In "38," Long Soldier states: "Keep in mind, I am not a historian / So I will recount facts as best as I can, given limited resources and understanding." In this line, she makes clear that to create history requires resources. Can a poem be a history? Maybe the object of any work of art that tackles historical subjects is not to be objective—we go to art to engage with the artist's interpretation or argument. Long Soldier addresses this tension openly: "I want to tell you about The Sioux Uprising, but I don't know where to begin. / I may jump around and details will not unfold in chronological order." In these lines, Long Soldier both questions and preserves a distinction between the work of a historian and the work of a poet. While in today's age images are ubiquitous and disembodied from time and space, the work of the artist is to arrange images into context, and thereby create imagery. Since history is in many ways part of our collective experience, and since we are able to access historical facts through research, to choose a historical subject paradoxically frees the artist from the need for chronological organization. The non-chronological organization can foreground rhetorical argument, as well as the artist's sensibility and power of interpretation. I'd argue that it also opens possibilities for other modes of organization, including lyric forms that are governed by rhythm, musicality, and repetition.[5]

For Long Soldier, the fact that the recounting of history is often a non-linear process seems essential to what she's exploring:

> The U.S. treaties with the Dakota Nation were legal
> contracts that promised money.

> It could be said, this money was payment for the land
> the Dakota ceded; for living within assigned
> boundaries (a reservation); and for relinquishing
> rights to their vast hunting territory which, in

---

[5] For a great discussion on "continuity editing," see Bill Nichols, *Introduction to Documentary* (Second Edition, Bloomington: Indiana UP, 2010). Pages 28-30.

turn, made Dakota people dependent on other means to survive: money.

The previous sentence is circular, which is akin to so many aspects of history.

As you may have guessed by now, the money promised in the turbid treaties did not make it into the hands of Dakota people.

In addition, local government traders would not offer credit to "Indians" to purchase food or goods.

Without money, store credit, or rights to hunt beyond their 10-mile tract of land, Dakota people began to starve.

The Dakota people were starving.

The Dakota people starved.

In the preceding sentence, the word "starved" does not need italics for emphasis.

One should read, "The Dakota people starved," as a straightforward and plainly stated fact.

Long Soldier does recount historical facts, but the way that she breaks from a strictly chronological report shapes a clear argument about injustice, and how atrocities like genocide can recur. Her choice of diction, syntax, and repetition ensure that this history will not be archived, but will continue to be shared, performed, and kept alive.

While Long Soldier does not give ecstatic descriptions of panoramic vistas in this poem, nevertheless this poem is a portrait of the land, one that does not ignore the connected history of people, and the link between land and language. Harnessing the out-of-time powers of lyric, Long Soldier offers a conclusion that responds both to the body of history she's recounting, and to the body of the poem she's composing. Her speaker does what the hanged men cannot do, which is to call today's reader's attention to the inescapable fact of their death. She does not offer a solution, but an image of the body returning to the land:

> Things are circling back again.
>
> Sometimes, when in a circle, if I wish to exit, I must leap
>
> And let the body   swing
>
> From the platform
>   Out
>   to the grasses.

By refusing to adopt a historian's performance of a neutral stance, and asserting the techniques of the poet (storytelling, repetition, lyric fragmentation), Long Soldier shatters our perception for a new vision of what that event was like.

Long Soldier is a great example of how today's poets perform and re-think vision by taking the act of looking itself as the subject. Ultimately, I would argue that the great distance poem is important to us now for this very reason—because it is a poem *about* seeing. It asks us to think about *how* we see, and to question the limits of our seeing. Long Soldier's *WHEREAS* includes dozens of examples of poems whose forms jar readers out of a passive, absorptive space. I'm particularly interested in a poem from the chapter titled "Resolutions" where Long Soldier re-casts the sentences of the 2009 Congressional Resolution of Apology to Native Americans into a new format, highlighting a phrase, "this land," that gets repeated throughout the apology:

(2) Resolutions
(2)
I
commend   this land
and   this   land
honor   this   land
Native   this   land
Peoples   this land
for   this   land
the   this   land
thousands   this   land
of   this   land
years   this   land
that   this land
they   this   land
have   this   land
protected this land this land this land this land this land this land this
this

Along the left margin, Long Soldier distills the document to
a direct statement: "I commend and honor Native Peoples for
the thousands of years that they have protected this." The left
margin has a feeling of wholeness and order—this is, perhaps,
what makes the page into a place, but it also serves to heighten
the sense of dislocation and *displacement* that comes from reading
Long Soldier's repeated phrase "this land," scattered across the
page. In this poem, the space between language becomes a kind
of terrain encoded with the gaps and silences that mark the
consequences of trauma.

I'm also interested in how the text itself becomes the site
of intervention. Not only does Long Soldier highlight the
instability and changefulness of language (and all words evolve
across a nexus of political transactions), she also shows the way
that governmental texts, laws, resolutions, and treaties, can be
literally imposed on places, and how those texts in fact alter

the natural world, and the fate of those who live there. In fact, you could say Long Soldier develops scale both in the choice of subject (focusing on what the consequences of past actions have been and will be) and in form, because this form itself keeps a record of what existed, and how it has been altered, and it asks us to consider that evolution. Long Soldier's unfixing forms expose the seams of the sublime story, and let other stories surface.

———◆———

In the short time I lived near Lake Dell, Leschi, I saw the effects of a collective layering. When I first started going to the park, it was small. Half of what the park is now was the side-yard of a cliff-side house—I remember it as a huge, yellow house, with a turret room at street level. The house tilted eastwards towards the lake, and it was propped on the cliff by a crosshatch of beams. One time I walked by at night and saw a woman drinking coffee in the turret room, and I imagined how it would be to live there, on the side of the neighborhood that had the views. The house is totally gone now; workers dismantled it before it fell off the hill, and neighbors petitioned to expand the park.

What happened next seems like a symbol of community. Running by once, I saw a man sitting at a keyboard in violet sunlight; he played classical music under a magnolia tree while a work party planted the Madronas that are there now—seven or eight saplings spaced evenly on either side of the path. The trees took root in human music, in the baroque, and though Madronas are native to the area, these grow in a weirdly thriving garden of French hydrangeas and camellias that are remnants of the former owner's ideal landscape. Neighbors reshaped those ruins toward their dream of an open-access park, and what they created is itself a hybrid text. Over the next year, volunteers and city workers widened the path and covered it in wood chips. They added a split-rail fence around the lookout, and rolled in large boulders for sitting. The park is still small, and there seems to be an unwritten rule that if someone else is there, you leave to let them "be alone with nature." I've heard that some trees have grown so high they've partially blocked the view of Rainier, but you can still see it if you know where to stand.

How are we seeing? Shelley saw how seeing involves a dialogue between the world and the human mind. Moore understood that our seeing is a composite of looks, and how we only take in Shelley's *everlasting universe of things* through a chorus of quotations: *the cavalcade of calico competing / with the original American menagerie of styles.* But maybe the new question, the one poets like Long Soldier are leading us towards, is one that calls us to re-trace the circle, asking: What am I not seeing? Why can't I see?

Here's what happens when you shift the lens: houses on either side of the park are valued near a million dollars, and the roads that lead there are indirect. Even people who live a few blocks from it might not know the park is there—it's hidden on the curve of the road, and it's not on the way to anywhere else. When early pioneers built houses there, Lake Washington was already home to the Duwamish tribe. Although this history is preserved by the land, the people, and the place names, to see it requires a willingness to ask questions, and to fracture the manicured landscape with the long view. As Moore writes: *Completing a circle, you have been deceived into thinking that you have progressed.*

If we're to refashion our perception of the environment to something other than a commodity, maybe it begins by perceiving it in the stark light of elegy. Maybe it starts by pressing the name of the park like a hyperlink, and remembering one person for whom that park and the surrounding neighborhood are named: Leschi. His tragic story is emblematic of the conflicts between Native Americans and white settlers in Seattle. The first U.S. Governor of the Washington Territories, Isaac Stephenson, appointed Leschi and his brother (both respected members of the Nisqually tribe) to represent their people at the signing of the Medicine Creek Treaty in 1854, a treaty that ceded much of current-day Seattle and its surroundings to the United States, and restricted native peoples to reservations. Because United States law required that Isaac Stephenson negotiate with a tribal leader, he himself designated Leschi as chief, even though Leschi's Nisqually tribe was not organized into the power hierarchies that Stephenson understood. There is abundant evidence that Leschi sought peace, even after United States militias routed him from his home and his property. But Stephenson's view was myopic, as he forced the territory to conform to the military structures of the United States government.

Leschi protested the terms of the Medicine Creek Treaty as unjust, and he resisted white occupation of the land. Later, he was accused, convicted, and hanged for assisting the murderers of two white militiamen, though many people, Native Americans and white settlers alike, considered his actions justified in a time of war (many believed he wasn't actually involved in the first place), and his hanging unconscionable. No plaque or park sign at Leschi-Lake Dell explains this history. Most of the people I see at the park are white.

Why can't I see? What am I not seeing? Maybe the work of poet Arthur Tulee, whose poem "The Ascension" celebrated Mount Rainier's centennial as a national park, helps to reshape the frame:

> What's your approach to climbing Rainier? Longmire's?
> Or from the east?
>
> I do not have an approach, I have never had an approach.
> I do not climb mountains empirically, for ego, for
> western achievement, for claiming beauty.
>
> My appreciation of beauty involves distance and non-
> interference. I do not conquer anything by
> scrambling over it. [...]

> My boundaries are as much in thoughts and behaviors
> as in geography and geological features. My
> maps are drawn up by culture, custom, tribe,
> family, and myself.

In Tulee's poem, every line questions the history of the western, conquering mentality. Tulee aims for "non-interference," and the desire "to leave things as I have found them." He maps the long distance here by reconfiguring the topographic map as an interconnectedness of "culture, custom, tribe, family," and the self. As Tulee demonstrates, orienting towards non-interference takes an entirely different compass, an entirely different relationship to the environment, not as something to be exploited, but as something to respect and let be.

In my own poems, I've sought ways to represent my questions and wonderings about the earth and our relationship to it. I know I relate to Mount Rainier by way of Moore's poem, and how she animates the mountain as a creature and a home to creatures, and I also admire Tulee's call for respecting the mountain, for letting it be. When I look at the volcano, I perceive it not only as dynamic matter, but also as a kind of consciousness. As soon as I try to name what feels something like spirit, something like consciousness in the mountain, it coalesces as a voice. How does the lava itself speak? This is a question I've been wrestling with for the last four years, as I'm working on a manuscript titled "The Lava on Iceland." When I was searching for a form that would help me approach the voice of lava, I thought of the poetic form of erasure, a form that adds layers (of readings, of ink) over the existing text. During the process, the new poem emerges like a topography; the poem gains spatial depth. I've found that working in this form yields collisions of phrases and sound patterns beyond my go-to lexicon.

Erasure as a poetic form is highly controversial. In a series of blog essays, Andrew David King reads erasure as a political act; to some extent, he attributes the recent craze in erasure-making to the national climate post-9/11. His reading feels persuasive to me, and especially relevant today—as though erasure mimics the process of finding the truth inside political speech. Another central voice in this discussion is Solmaz Sharif. In "The Near Transitive Properties of the Political and Poetical: Erasure," Sharif argues that the poetic form of erasure is dangerously related to state tactics of the redaction and censorship of text, and of the disappearance and obliteration of bodies. Though Sharif finds the form highly problematic, she includes a list of "possible and political aesthetic objectives for poetic erasure." For example, Sharif cites M. NourbeSe Philip, who is herself aware of erasure as a mutilation of language and sees how this relates to the mutilation of slaves, as an example of an author who "expose[s her own] authority and, therefore [her] role as culpable participant." I think that in some ways, when the subject of the poem is obliteration, when the poet wants to call attention to annihilation or obliteration or mutilation, there can be value in using erasure as a process.[6]

When I think of the great distance view from Lake Dell, Leschi, I am aware that both to see it (the awesome scale of tectonic force), and to see how I'm seeing it (through the momentous forces of capitalism), are meditations on creation and destruction. In the way that erasure is a form of consuming text, it could be that it merely mirrors capitalism. Still, can tracking the process of consumption also point to what is lost? To me, the first thing erasure does is dismantle the idea of single-genius authorship by pointing back to the author of the source text. King argues that erasure is a kind of monument to reading: "the erasurist resembles the reader: there is something about any erasure [...] that mimics the sensory experience of encountering

---

[6] In an interview with Joanne Diaz for *Spoon River Poetry Review*, I have written more about erasure, and a longer response to Sharif's terrific argument: "The *SRPR* Interview: Katy Didden." Vol. 40.1, Summer 2015. Pages 40-51. http://srpr.org/files/40.1/interview-excerpt.pdf.

those source texts themselves." In this way, preserving the source text shines light on the basic mechanism of all writing by directly indexing the relationship between reading and writing. To create "The Lava on Iceland," I am erasing a series of source texts about Iceland (everything from geologic surveys, to interviews with Björk, to historical articles, to literary passages), to the voice of lava. I find the poems that emerge from this process can take any number of stances towards the source text—sometimes they engage with the subject of the source text (as a summary, or a response, or a talking back), and sometimes they riff on sound patterns and rhythms in the original. Erasure is a means of acknowledging how I appropriate source material.

Ultimately, I believe erasure is a form uniquely responsive to our current relationship to the environment. It registers our eco-conscious anxieties because it emphasizes both the instability of language and of place, particularly when the subject is the history of land. Take a work like Ronald Johnson's *Radi os*, and his undoing of Milton's Eden. Or look at Jen Bervin's *The Desert*, an erasure of John Van Dyke's 1901 book of the same name. I find erasure's ecopoetic possibilities to be true especially in the cases where erasure practitioners preserve the original layout of the source text—I'd name this particular technique not just "erasure" but "exposure." To what extent can this process expose the polyvocality already inherent in the poetic process? For "The Lava on Iceland," I am collaborating with graphic designer and illustrator Kevin Tseng, who figured out how to achieve the look of lava on the page by layering grayscale and highlighted text over photographs. Furthermore, we solicit photographs from fellow artists and writers who have traveled to Iceland. This has meant that every completed image-text is the result of a series of conversations and correspondences between myself, the texts, Kevin, our editors, and our friends who contribute photos. Somehow, the voice that emerges is a combined voice, its text is palimpsest, one that approximates a composite of visions.

I find erasure compelling in no small part because it shifts the spatial scale of the page. Where most erasure practitioners erase down to the words of texts, I work down to the letter, where the potential for finding lines (and rhyme) increases exponentially. In this encounter with language, words dissolve back to sound patterns, to graphemes and phonemes, and the yield is mystical. To what extent can this process expose our relationship to texts and lands and history? Erasure makes the page layered, more like a place. If the text is a field of potential collisions and separations, each word is a core sample.

———— ◆ ————

Earth's in motion; all rocks were molten flows. Why should the mind's-eyed image of a mountain make me still? It's a petrified wave. When tremors unseal the hot spot the mountain will triple its height as ash, flood the plains with boiling mud, and send us running. I've heard of poets who keep human skulls beside them as they write, to make every minute shine against death's shadow. Is that what staring at the mountain gives us? The certainty of knowing we're fleeting, an assurance of mortality that stays the impulse to flee? The more I see the mountain, even from thousands of miles away, the more I trust that nothing's mine, that to be is to belong to infinity. If this desire to perform distance requires moving and uprooting, can a poem, with its time-folding rhythms, be a home? Can an hour be? The more I move, the less certain I am of a fixed self, except as one who needs to share what I see: Moore's *white volcano with no weather side*. When it erupts, we will know the mountain was nowhere near what we imagined it was. It will alter its shape, slip the rigging of its names, and it will rename us.

Photo: Kara Lee Ruotolo, 2017.
Primary Source: Wickersham, James. "Is it Mount Tacoma, or Rainier?" *Proceedings of the Tacoma Academy of Science, Tacoma, Washington.* Second Edition. Tacoma: News Publishing Company, 1893. Retrieved on Google Books.
Layout and Graphic Design: Kevin Tseng.

'The White Volcano with No Weather Side': An Interview

Say how it is, to be named?

> *An honor if a metaphor, if a lien a fiction.*

What burst the healed seam and made you?

> *I rhyme air / ear / awe,*
> *leaking the name of eden.*

Was it preposterous? The idea of calling you home?

> *An agon by any other name, I darken the city.*

The way snow defines a gash, *Tahoma* shifts history.

> *The wounded see in detail, led by that name.*

You hold eerie bounties: pressure, winter, scale.

> *All called to Tahoma learn matter is a cloud.*
> *I recast shape.*

Draft of Terror, what rules you?

> *Planetary chords; ungainly rhythm.*

Anonym, who listens?

> *Any caged stone hums the name of the mountain.*

ONE CLUSTER, BRIGHT, ASTRINGENT

Shara Lessley

THE YEAR ELIZABETH BISHOP DIED I learned to read. 1979: *Voyager I* enters the Jovian system, streaming microscopic particles and dust. Approaching the planet's magnetic field, a robotic probe releases a greeting. Packaged with a message from President Carter, the gold-plated copper disk contains birdsong and whale song, salutations in fifty-five human languages, crashing waves of thunder and surf. After making its introduction the spacecraft continues its mission. In one of the more than 18,000 satellite-captured images, the planetary god almost seems to answer Earth's inquiry. Attended by its retinue of moons Jupiter hangs unmoving, its Great Red Spot mouthing the long *o* of *Callisto, Io, Europa*, its faint rings reverberating some untranslatable song across the orange-brown clouds, faint traces of white ice.

————◆————

Far from the banded atmosphere, I sit at a kitchen table in California moving my fingers across the coarse texture of letters raised on multicolored cards. Mother shuffles the deck, asks me to repeat the sounds I see. Vowels are yellow; double vowels, a limey green. Consonants are lavender; blended sounds like *dr, pl, sk*, a quirky shade of salmon. I love the soft *ah* housed in *box* and *wash*; the bristly *i* that so quickly turns from *fish* to *field*, *fire* to *bird*; *e*'s sudden silence.

The phonetic cards have pictures on their undersides. I flip one over after sounding out *s-e-a-g-u-l-l*, then run my finger the length of an outstretched wing. Mother encourages me to write those words I've mastered in a black-and-white ledger. (I've scrawled my name on its cover.) She litters the notebook's columns with metallic stars to encourage my unsteady, oversized print. Within weeks we're stringing phrases. Their sounds swell and turn degrees of purple and green and blue until my whole world becomes a prism of words. Soon, sentences animate not only the pages of my Little Golden Books, but the printed faces of cereal boxes and street signs, unopened bottles of shampoo.

———◆———

Nearly twenty years later, Bishop's work is teaching me to be a better reader. It's night in a Northwest corridor of Washington D.C. I'm in my third-floor bedroom at the Kirov Academy of Ballet, not studying exactly, but opening and closing books, searching for something I'll know when I find it:

> I have seen it over and over, the same sea, the same,
> slightly, indifferently swinging above the stones,
> icily free above the stones,
> above the stones and then the world [...]

With this, the Kirov's white-washed walls dissolve. Soon the entire building falls away taking the city with it. I'm pulled, as if by some electric current, into what Wallace Stevens calls "the planet on the table," this strange planet where, unlike what I've long been taught, repetition doesn't equal redundancy and things that are "cold dark deep" are also "absolutely clear."

I read Bishop's poem. I read it again and again. There are things about "At the Fishhouses" I recognize, things so intimate, immediate, they seem to spring from my own memory. The poem's parade of fir trees and evergreens, its oversized seaside tubs packed with herring carry me back to Northern California. Back, to where coastal waters are so cold "If you should dip your hand in / your wrist would ache immediately, / your bones would begin to ache and your hand would burn." As if my bones are sucking snow-ice, I feel a sudden chill. And in my head, a glacier whose song starts to coolly seethe and then to burn until all around me is liquid, all is rising and breaking in a series of dark gray waves...

But the poem's waters are not the Pacific's. Among California's "wild jagged rocks," there are no scattered "lobster pots." I've never known (or will ever know) any fisherman "friend of my grandfather" smoking Lucky Strikes while casually setting his nets. Whose waters are these? *What* waters are these? Water Bishop describes as "a transmutation of fire"? And what of the poem's all-too-human seal to whom the speaker sings several Baptist hymns? Why is the seal "interested in music"? What does Bishop mean by suggesting he is "like me a believer in total immersion"?

I put down the book. Re-enter the room. Taped to the wall: photos of me backstage. I think of the locked costume shop downstairs, its closets filled with dyed and embroidered fabric—beaded crystals stitched to tulle and chiffon, jewel-crusted asymmetrical seams and matching headpieces. Glass, paste, paper-thin metal strips. Faux flowers, plastic emeralds and garnets. Miles of uncut fabric waiting to be set to music. I think of Bluebird's silk bodice hanging unworn in the dark, and then once more of the poem's elderly fisherman with "sequins on his vest and on his thumb." I imagine the way he moves his body to rhythms of the tidal score, how Bishop stages language so precisely that this solitary figure can scrape and scrape again "the scales, the principal beauty, / from unnumbered fish with that black old knife, / the blade of which is almost worn away."

The white clapboard house off Highway 2 in Great Village, Nova Scotia, isn't what I expected, yet here is the childhood home of Elizabeth Bishop who believed the structure once served as an ill-reputed inn before her grandfather paid to have it moved. It's on this lot where the poet resided until October 1917 when the then-six-year-old was taken to Worcester, Massachusetts, to live with her paternal grandparents in a place "on a much larger scale, twice as large, with two windows for each of the Nova Scotia ones and a higher roof." I've studied enough photographs to recognize the building's face. Moving into the interior, however, is something else entirely—to take tea in the kitchen where Bishop's grandmother busied herself at "the Little Marvel Stove"; to occupy "the cold, cold parlor" where, peering into a coffin Bishop characterized as "a little frosted cake," she said goodbye to her "little cousin Arthur" awaiting burial, laid out "beneath the chromographs."

The steel grate bridge beside the house howls each time cars wheeze past—more like moans than howls. Along the curve of road: air swept then whipped uphill across the valley's meadows. Putting traffic's sporadic rumblings out of my mind, I imagine this space in another time: five-year-old Bishop scampering down the second level's ladder to take her porridge before the primer school's bell begins to ring. This is the year Gammie Bulmer teaches her to write her name (and her "family's names and the names of the dog and the two cats"). "Earlier," Bishop remembers, she'd "taught me my letters, and at first I could not get past the letter g, which for some time I felt was far enough to go. *My* alphabet made a satisfying short song, and I didn't want to spoil it."

In the strange planet called childhood, I am (once again) anticipating my turn on stage. Cast as an extra in a production of *Coppélia*, I stay with Mother in the balcony until my role is called to rehearse. While the butterflies, village children, and other walk-ons pass time in the aisles toying with jacks and cards, we watch Swanilda and her lover, Franz, enter the village square. By cue, the couple's attention turns to Coppélia—that beautiful life-sized doll—whom the pair confuses for a living woman. Franz blows her a kiss. Seemingly absorbed in a book, Coppélia takes no notice. *What is it*, the young man pantomimes, *about those pages that hold her attention?* He shakes his head. Tries again. The orchestra revs its machine. The conductor slings his notes. Swanilda scoffs; as the story dictates, she storms off. Although decades have passed I can still hear the woodwinds' murmurings and strings. But far from the theater I now see that in the world of ballet, women only pretend to read.

———•———

I cannot bring myself to choose "the large front bedroom with sloping walls on either side," the one where it's thought Bishop's mother had her final psychotic break. Nor do I choose the poet's room—so narrow it barely holds a bed, but deep (it is deep!)—with its slanted glass square cut into the old tin roof, the skylight's latch held shut by a pair of scissors. Instead, I sleep where Aunt Mary's bed might have been, but not before revisiting the lines of Bishop's "Cape Breton," which orchestrate "silken" water "weaving and weaving, / disappearing under the mist equally in all directions," the same mist

> among the valleys and gorges of the mainland
> like rotting snow-ice sucked away
> almost to spirit; the ghost of glaciers drift[ing]
> among those folds and folds of fir […]

Next morning, I wake to write but am distracted. Scattered throughout the house: artifacts from Bishop's history. I abandon a February 1918 issue of *National Geographic* for *Vassorium*— Bishop's velvet-covered 1934 college yearbook. Among its pages, secretarial schools' advertisements, instructions for swimming, the "perfect" design for constructing a smoking cap. Between photos of undergraduates Ann Billingsley and Elizabeth Blake, I find Bishop's senior portrait, an image I've seen but out of context. While almost all of the students confront the camera straight on, Bishop's decision to reveal only her profile seems telling. Toward what or whom is she gazing off in the distance? Exactly what does she seek out of frame?

Although there's a pair of Bishop's Norefjell skis (purchased, I'm told, near Harvard Square sometime during the poet's later years) propped in a hallway just off the mud room, it's a nook upstairs that captures my attention. Enclosed by beams and tucked beneath a gable, the space is dark and mostly wood but for the occasional wire and original "insulation" composed of turn-of-the-century newsprint turned the colors of deep amber and tan. This is the place, the house's caretaker explains, that young Elizabeth Bishop came to deposit those "bad thoughts" she couldn't bear.

Tacked to the walls are torn fragments of costume sketches, mechanical wheels, early models of cars. Page 18 tracks Canada's News in Brief; page 13, Books and Authors, as well as a column on Little Folks. "Secrets of the Sky" one headline proclaims to no great revelation. But among the ruin of printed sentences and illustrations, there is something to be discovered: an image of "Vesuvius in Eruption." The spewing peak leads me to question whether this space is, in fact, Bishop's earliest "waiting room"— the place she first "studied the photographs: / the inside of a volcano, / black, and full of ashes / [...] spilling over / in rivulets of fire." These, the papered walls the future poet used to distract herself when overwhelmed, evidence of a child's natural instinct of turning to the written word.

———◆———

The year I learn to read, my parents take me to the beach to celebrate my birthday. Even from our car's backseat, I can smell the first hint of salt-draped air as we round the rocky inlet overlooking the coast. Unlike Mother, who turns her face from the passenger window and hides her eyes to avoid confronting the drop-off, I like to be up high, to watch the waves curl and crash from above. My father points toward the ledge. Over the guardrail, as far as I can see: the cold dark Pacific whose breaking lines move toward us, wholly free.

———◆———

When I say Bishop taught me to be a better reader, I mean this: she taught me that readers of poetry should expect equal parts mystery and clarity, imagination and intellect. This practice requires attention, discipline, joy. To read deeply is to become more like "what we imagine knowledge to be: / dark, salt, clear, moving, utterly free." To read, in other words, is not only to see—to appreciate surface meaning—but also to perceive, both emotionally and physically. Poetry requires us to listen, to attune our ear to language's most subtle and emphatic arrangements. It demands courage of movement, a willingness to start in one place and arrive at the unknown. Poetry asks readers to investigate the universe and their place in it, to return and reenter images in order to rediscover them. Bishop's best work instructs us that a poem contains all its reader needs to know: leading details, moments of restraint. It is itself a "planet on the table," a body shaped by the magnetic pull of its own gravity.

———◆———

I am sitting on the back steps of the porch where Bishop's grandmother sent her to practice writing across her slate. July's night is clear, its sky abuzz with insects and stars. It's not Great Village's "inscrutable house" I'm thinking of, but of the distances between our lives, how some sixty-odd years after Bishop was here as a child summering near the world's highest tidal range at Mina's Basin, I passed my girlhood shuttling between dance studios and theaters more than 3,600 miles away.

"Think of the long trip home," Bishop proposes in "Questions of Travel," "Should we have stayed home and thought of here? / Where should we be today?" In fact, there is no place I'd rather be than near the sources of poems like "Sestina" ("hard tears / dance like mad on the hot black stove, / the way rain must dance on the house") and "The Filling Station," whose embroidered doily among "grease-impregnated wickerwork" reminds readers "Somebody loves us all." Beside the driveway I sketch the half-dying tree split into three large trunks, a birdhouse capping each, how its body rises up leaving one good branch to extend and arch over the property line toward what was once the blacksmith's shop. Surely, it would have been a pity

> not to have seen the trees along this road,
> really exaggerated in their beauty,
> not to have seen them gesturing
> like noble pantomimists, robed in pink.

Not to have seen them gesturing, exaggerated in their beauty... I imagine Bishop rehearsing these phrases, attending their music, reworking them again and again until any evidence of effort dissolves and what remains are just those *noble pantomimists, robed in pink* moving in purest form.

———•———

After the cake has been eaten and presents unwrapped, four half-melted candles tossed in the trash; after I've fallen asleep only to be nudged awake again, my father zips me into a sweatshirt and takes us to watch the grunion run. As he explains where we're going, I think the word is funny. *Grunion.* I say it again and again. Mother tells me they look like sardines. I've never heard of sardines.

But how quickly the beach fills with the little silver fish! Everywhere, their slick bodies arching and thrashing across the flattened sand. There must be thousands. Hundreds of thousands. Higher than anyone can count. I pick one up, hold it carefully in my hand and trace the bumpy blue-green stripes written across the fish's back. (What is it the slight stripes mean to say?)

My father's MagLite shines: dozens of scales ignite. Beneath starlight and his flashlight, they glimmer doubly.

"Where do grunion come from?" I ask.

My fish twists its body; its little head thrusts up.

"Do they swim from the moon?"

———— ◆ ————

The dancer's room is the studio; the poet's, the stanza. Each has the task of perfecting the line. Both value the integrity of movement, nuanced repetition. A sentence is said to be muscular. Its syllables point and flex. The musical phrase elongates, contracts. Meter, suspension, surprise—these are tools of the trade. Rippling currents. The rhythm of rich-toned idioms. A dancer trains herself to master classical and modern structures, as does the poet. To recharge and reinvent long-standing cadences and terms. To perfect the illusions of spontaneity and ease. To turn. Then counterturn. To stand.

———— ◆ ————

Just south of a town called Duck, July's humidity stalls in the air. The Atlantic's flat as a lake. Without the crest's white lip to ride, my husband floats on his back. Like an otter, he scuttles his feet. He can stay in the brine for hours.

A scattering of terns begins to groom, their belly-feathers skimmed by the sea. Sunscreen-slathered kids play by the surf, shaping starfish and castles with plastic molds, shoveling sand with sieves and trowels. I pick up a book, watch between pages as a fish hawk stalks minnows offshore. Yet, it's too hot to read, too hot to do much of anything but observe the small world orbiting my chair. Gulls mob washed-up debris. A toddler in pigtails squats in the tide, diaper swelling beneath her suit. She picks at the ground, searching for what? The ocean hisses, rolling up. The toddler claps her hands, applauds the rushing froth. A woman runs over, scoops the child up.

Three sanderlings dart toward the water's edge, investigate, retreat. A wave spills back to sea. The trio soon begins again: advance, repeat. *The beach hisses like fat*, I think, caught in the sudden surge of Bishop's phrase. What *is* that poem? I start a sentence, correct a mistake. Begin again—the bird *runs to the south, finical, awkward, / in a stated of controlled panic, a student of Blake.* I can't remember the rest, only that Bishop's bird is preoccupied, obsessed. It is *looking for something, something, something...*

My husband is back, still drenched from his swim. He shakes out a towel. Sand sticks to his ankles and feet. I adjust my glasses, rub my eyes, look down: *the millions of grains are black, white, tan, and gray / mixed with quartz grains, rose and amethyst.*

The photo's *grains are black, white, tan, and gray mixed with quartz grains, rose and amethyst.* 1999: the most intimate images of *Io* to date. Cliffs and rifts of lava take shape. Fissures slough from the moon's pocked crust. Through near-infrared, green, and violet filters we now can see mountains collapse into fumes, and the ground as it's fractured by tidal pressure, unleashing volcanic plumes. Each image, a study in precision. Resolution tuned to the highest degree. Sulfur dioxide spews from peaks the size of California. Their crests erupt and seethe, spilling over into frozen rivulets. Scientists are awed; skeptics, too. From some six and half million miles or more, the human eye perceives the mysterious clarity of Jupiter's storm-filled moon.

———◆———

February, 1975: I have no place in this scene, still a pinprick of light in my mother's womb. On a piece of lined paper she arranges letters, spelling words for daughters and sons. *Adam* and *Christopher*. *Maude* and *Jewell*. One night my name comes to her in sleep. Next morning she tucks it in her wallet till I am born late June.

But it is not June. It is February, 1975. Bishop paces the margins of the Lewis Wharf apartment where she'll collapse from a cerebral aneurysm in less than thirty-two months. For now she is unpacking, moving among mirrors and books, finding places for the crudely carved balsawood masks from Brazil, the *santos* she loves to display on glass stands.

It is late. She is tired. The room's high windows bait her nearer. Does she look out across Boston's lamp-lit warehouses, count the watery lanes? Does she record a passing ship in her journal? Does she think of other houses and studios? In Florida, Nova Scotia, Ouro Prêto? Is she tempted to return to that "Apartment in Leme," to the abandoned draft in which she describes Rio's coastal starlight as

> One cluster, bright, astringent as white currants
> hung from the Magellanic Clouds
> above you and the beach and its assorted
> lovers and worshippers, almost within their reach
> if they had noticed[...]?

All of this, of course, is impossible to know: about Bishop's living years only fragments of fact exist...

———◆———

Sally Streets' Sunday class begins in twenty minutes. I'm changing into tights and a long-sleeved navy leotard when a woman with blue eyes enters the dressing room. She says hello and drops her bag. This is my first visit to Berkeley Ballet Theater. Still, the woman's face looks familiar. I wonder whether we've met. Ten minutes into barre the studio's windows glisten with steam. We work the usual positions, doing our best to execute rigorous combinations. Exercises come and go. I want so badly to make a good impression, but am distracted. The woman from the dressing room is working double *ronde jambe en l'air* with perfect phrasing. She practices with purpose, accenting the circular movement of her extended leg as it passes at the height of the supporting knee. *En dehors, en dedans*—I watch in astonishment. Although she performs at a fever pitch, her pointe-work's mastery makes standing on one leg look effortless—even natural. I'm seventeen, have never seen such precise articulation, such instinctive musicality. Before we put the barre away and head center for *adage*, and *petite* and *grande allegro*, it comes to me: Kyra Nichols. I *do* know this woman—she's the New York City Ballet principal featured on a recent cover of my favorite periodical, *Dance Magazine*.

———◆———

In the collaborative arts—theater, film, music, ballet—performers speak the languages of rhythm and intent. Theirs is a shared preoccupation with pattern-making, discipline, technique. Like *currants hung from Magellanic Clouds*, they labor together. It's said, in contrast, that the poet's is a solitary act, one of self-immersion and isolation. But Bishop knew better. Throughout her working life, she had ongoing conversations with Marianne Moore and Robert Lowell, and apprenticed herself to bodies of work by George Herbert and Gerard Manley Hopkins. Her notebooks consider writings by W.H. Auden, Pascal, and Freud. She studied classical music and biology. She painted, translated. She fished. She'd take twenty years to finish a poem if that's what the poem called for, twenty years to line up its lovers and worshippers, to thread the line between an old tin washing tub and the shiny battered moon.

A Harvard student who once studied with Bishop said she'd admired the poet the way that dancers in the New York City Ballet looked up to George Balanchine, which makes me think of Ms. Nichols rehearsing Polyhymnia for the choreographer's neoclassical masterpiece, *Apollo*. She works to perfect the ballet's off-kilter *piqué attitudes* and iconic *arabesques*; Bishop tinkers with a sentence. Both artists, believers in "total immersion." Hanging in their studios' open air, that sense of space and of possibility as one phrase becomes two becomes the next; becomes, at last, one bright astringent cluster.

I HAD A PLACE

Spencer Reece

I have been an alien in a strange land.

Exodus 18:3

GEORGE HERBERT wrote one poetry book. We only have it because a friend named Nicholas Farrar decided to publish it after his death. Herbert handed the book over on his deathbed, dying of consumption at 40, much the way people had died of AIDS in my time, quick, the disease taking crowds of people rapaciously. Herbert said he desired to have it published only if his friend read it "and then, if he think it may turn to the advantage of any dejected poor soul, let it be made public." Three hundred years later that poor dejected soul was me.

I'd been waiting for him in the toolshed of the graveyard at Bowdoin hatching my suicide, when I felt I could no longer blunder on with the unzipped sex of myself I could never keep zipped. The poems like stained glass windows had lit my way out of the toolshed and up to the altar to my ordination, first to the deaconate and then to the priesthood, in Madrid.

And then, early one morning, I stripped and unbuckled and with a hurried throng through airport security, caught the plane from Madrid to London. I was going to visit the Archbishop of Canterbury at Lambeth Palace.

When I landed I hailed a taxi from Victoria Station. I could barely understand the taxi driver's Cockney accent, it was like trying to understand the Cubans in Madrid, half the words were missing. I ate a Cornish pasty in the cab which covered my black priest clothes in a snowstorm of pastry flakes. It was July. Hot for London. Along the embankments tourists advanced, sighing and wide-eyed, perhaps it might be their only trip to this place, wide and deep with history and the roots of my language. I saw children pointing at statues and buildings, and mothers with their noses in guide books. We were that once—Mom, Dad and me, the whole world in front of us, full of promise and excitement and wonder. Now much was behind us.

London, vast and ponderous and lonely and cheery—all the dwellings lined up the color of silverware, as the taxi moved towards the Archbishop of Canterbury, I queried the universe: *Could this really be happening to me?* Rows and rows of Georgian porticoes passed me by. All those people living their lives without concern for me—humbling to consider that and humble is good, Herbert stressed that.

Then I was there. Lambeth Palace, made of limestone and rag stone, timber and brick, impressed me immediately as Herbert's book had. A kind porter welcomed me. He called me "Father Spencer." I was staying the night at the invitation of His Grace, which is how we are to refer to the Archbishop in our church and he would call my Bishop "Your Lord." I felt decorum and convention comforting me as I stood before this palace. Startled, I felt for a moment I had a place somewhere in this world, and the peace of Herbert snuck up on me then and there, as if opening the paperback of Herbert's poetry in York thirty years prior was like a door through which I had passed that led now to this door—I'd gone in a wild circle. I had a place.

I thought about the Anglican Communion, half its members now Africans who would have the church crack open and break over the issue of homosexuality: 50 million members as opposed to the 26 million in Western Europe. My church may fall apart still. The Archbishop had tried mightily to hold it together. When the United States elected Gene Robinson, the first openly gay bishop, in 2003, our Humpty Dumpty church tittered on his ledge. Robinson later stepped down from death threats.

"Somebody loves us all!" Elizabeth Bishop writes in her poem, "The Filling Station," about a dirty little gas station that is somehow tended for and loved. Yes, indeed, somebody does. Loves me. As Bishop zeroes in her famous eye on the filling station in the poem, she sees a taboret (a small stool, a word I learned from this poem, and Bishop choosing such an elegant word rather than "stool" in a poem about a filling station always makes me chuckle):

> Why the taboret?
> Why, oh why, the doily?
> (Embroidered in daisy stitch
> with marguerites, I think,
> and heavy with gray crochet.)
>
> Somebody embroidered the doily.

Somebody or *something*, I felt, had loved my ragtag life all along, attended to it with tamborets and doilies and embroidered a path right up the Thames. I had a place. Gratitude filled me. I smiled thinking as I stood before the palace, how the surname of Elizabeth Bishop and my now constant use of the word "bishop" in my work life cleaved my long love of poetry to the church, and in a sense, right then and there, I cleaved. I had a place.

I stood before the palace gate, a Tudor door in a building called Morton's Tower from the 15th century, made of red brick with a crenellated roof like my freshman college dorm. Through the entrance I saw an old fig tree, raspberry-colored hydrangeas, green lawns, pebbled walks. A private, well-tended world where gardeners worked the bushes, coaxing the vines. The hint of night was scratching at the edges of the day, wanting to be uncaged. I had a place.

Tomorrow morning, I would meet His Grace, he who moved among crowns and kings and queens. I imagined I wouldn't be important to him (and I imagined right), he'd have much on his mind the following day: I was one small appointment—still I felt I'd come far. For, I had a place.

My bishop would fly in from Madrid later that night. Standing next to my bedroom window, I would hear him speak with his Spanish accent talking to the porter, he will sound nervous as one does when they enter a language that is not their native one, and then I will hear the bishop walk across the gravel walk to his room. My job will be to take notes at the meeting and help the bishop understand the subtleties of how the British speak. That will come tomorrow: that circle. I will serve in a quiet unnoticed way. I will guard my language.

But just for that moment, standing, I watched the moon come up and wander over Lambeth and her gardens like Florence Nightingale, touching and checking on the pond, the heron, the frogs, the roof, the beveled windows and *me*, my scalp. Listening to London trundle in the distance, I thought about this country, England, the land of my language, a language I'd come to love by being distanced from it, broad and deep, language that had helped me make sense of much, language that had connected me to faith. I felt the deep press of all the stacks and stacks of beautiful words to come from that island, so many leaves to leaf through in the books in all the libraries I'd known in my lucky life.

My devotions with their tumult of joy and sorrow, with words I'd found and known and sounded out in rooms across the world when place often eluded me, with their attempt to say something of love, they circle now in this hour as I stand before the door at Lambeth. My devotions, quietly, recalling Hopkins and Bishop and Plath and Herbert, each of them helping me stake some kind of place, accompanied me. I felt them near. I thought upon my compatriots coming to Madrid for our humble little author series, who with their art brought comfort to me when they sat beside me in my foreign land where at times I had been lonely, and likely would be again. I thought, as the porter smiled back at me, of my parents, their pride in me, their devotion.

Shakespeare wrote, "This blessed plot, this earth, this realm. This England." Wasn't Ariel alighting in the plane trees by the pond in the back of the palace, blessing the place? Plath's dew was everywhere. I felt the need to be obedient and respectful as the palace quieted for the night. How many dignitaries had walked these corridors? I felt my casual American ways, the way I talked, and thought, "So be it." I had a place. I had a place. I bowed my head down under the low door in the wall, in my hand was the key the kind porter gave me. The porter held the heavy door open, smoothed by the years of religious hands that had touched it. Once again, with decorum, he called me, "Father Spencer." He beckoned. I followed. I had a place. I had a place. I stepped through the little entrance.

FIVE ESSENTIAL POEMS OF PLACE: CONTRIBUTORS

FIVE ESSENTIAL POEMS OF PLACE: CONTRIBUTORS

KAZIM ALI

"Thorow" *by* SUSAN HOWE
"Pollen Fossil Record" *by* MYUNG MI KIM
"Shut Up Shut Down" *by* MARK NOWAK
"Whereas" *by* LAYLI LONG SOLDIER
"Sunday May 10 2015: Catalog in Seven"
    by KAMDEN ISHMAEL HILLIARD

NICKY BEER

"A Short Biography of the American People by City"
    by CATHERINE PIERCE
"Man on Extremely Small Island" *by* JASON KOO
"Multi-Use Area" *by* ELIZABETH BRADFIELD
"The Facts of the Art" *by* NATALIE DIAZ
"Tattoos and Theory" *by* ADA LIMÓN

ELIZABETH BRADFIELD

The Black Maria by ARACELIS GIRMAY
"Sam Kee, I Imagine" *by* SEAN HILL
"Southern History" *by* NATASHA TRETHEWEY
"Border Triptych" *by* EDUARDO C. CORRAL
"Iron" *by* MICHAEL MCGRIFF

ABIGAIL CHABITNOY

Flood Song by SHERWIN BITSUI
"American Coma" *by* JENNIFER ELISE FOERSTER
"The Straits" *by* JOAN NAVIYUK KANE
"Her/My Arctic: Corpse Whale" *by* DG NANOUK OKPIK
"*ginen* sounding lines [*Chamorro standard time: UTC + 10:00*"
    by CRAIG SANTOS PEREZ

HAYAN CHARARA

"Singapore" *by* MARY OLIVER
"Tu Do Street" *by* YUSEF KOMUNYAKAA
"Broadway" *by* MARK DOTY
"Sand Nigger" *by* LAWRENCE JOSEPH
"Pulse" *by* FADY JOUDAH

KATY DIDDEN

"38" *by* LAYLI LONG SOLDIER
"The Desert" *by* JEN BERVIN
"Cascadia" *by* BRENDA HILLMAN
"A Kind of Meadow" *by* CARL PHILLIPS
"Off the Santa Fe River Near MacClenny, Florida"
    by ELIZABETH ARNOLD

JEHANNE DUBROW

"Homo Will Not Inherit" *by* MARK DOTY
"The Colonel" *by* CAROLINE FORCHÉ
"Facing It" *by* YUSEF KOMUNYAKAA
"Elegy for the Native Guards" *by* NATASHA TRETHEWEY
"Between the Wars" *by* ROBERT HASS

KEITH EKISS

"Sonora for Sale" *by* RICHARD SHELTON
"Santa Fe" *by* JOY HARJO
"Coatscape and Mr. Begley" *by* SANDRA MCPHERSON
"Pilgrimage" *by* NATASHA THRETHEWEY
The Folding Cliffs by W.S. MERWIN

RIGOBERTO GONZÁLEZ

"At the Rainbow" *by* ROBERT VASQUEZ
"Aubade with Burning City" *by* OCEAN VUONG
"My Town" *by* ZENA HASHEM BECK
"Ayotnizapa" *by* JUAN FELIPE HERRERA
"W. 13th Street" *by* JEAN VALENTINE

JAMES ALLEN HALL

"Heart Condition" *by* JERICHO BROWN
"Broadway" *by* MARK DOTY
"The Enlightenment" *by* NATASHA THRETHEWEY
"Notes on the State of Virginia, II" *by* SAFIYA SINCLAIR
"Some Unsettling Connections" *by* KIMBERLY QUIOGUE ANDREWS

AMAUD JAMAUL JOHNSON

"At the Movies, Virginia, 1956" *by* ELLEN BRYANT VOIGT
"Venus's-flytraps" *by* YUSEF KOMUNYAKAA
"Driftless Elegy" *by* MARK WUNDERLICH
"First" *by* MAURICE MANNING
"Autumn Song" *by* SPENCER REECE

JANINE JOSEPH

"The Central Virginia Training Center" *by* MOLLY MCCULLY BROWN
"Split" *by* CATHY LINH CHE
"Facing It" *by* YUSEF KOMUNYAKAA
"Miscegenation" *by* NATASHA TRETHEWEY
"El Salvador" *by* JAVIER ZAMORA

JOAN NAVIYUK KANE

"History of the Discovery of the Aleutian Islands"
  by ABIGAIL CHABITNOY
"One Kind of Hunger" *by* LEHUA TAITANO
"Mangled, Letters, and the Target Girl" *by* SANDRA FRAZIER
"Still Life with Starlings and Man" *by* SEAN HILL
"Loving Horses" *by* JON DAVIS

CHRISTOPHER KEMPF

"Another Fourth" *by* W.S. DIPIERO
"Philadelphia, Negro" *by* GREGORY PARDLO
"At Pleasure Bay" *by* ROBERT PINSKY
"Inspiration Point, Berkeley" *by* SOLMAZ SHARIF
"Gilly's Bowl & Grille" *by* COREY VAN LANDINGHAM

NICK LANTZ

"A Detroit Hum Ending with Bones" *by* JAMAAL MAY
"With Ruins" *by* LI-YOUNG LEE
"Ode to the Midwest" *by* KEVIN YOUNG
New Jersey by BETSEY ANDREWS
"Urban Renewal" *by* MAJOR JACKSON

SANDRA LIM

Four Good Things by JAMES MCMICHAEL
"How I Got That Name" *by* MARILYN CHIN
The Public Gardens by LINDA NORTON
"Architecture" *by* CHASE TWICHELL
City Eclogue by ED ROBERSON

SABRINA ORAH MARK

"Imperialism" *by* JORIE GRAHAM
"My Mother's Nipples" *by* ROBERT HASS
"Facing It" *by* YUSEF KOMUNYAKAA
"The Only Yak in Batesville, Virginia" *by* ONI BUCHANAN
"Hey Allen Ginsberg Where Have You Gone and What Would
  You Think of My Drugs?" *by* RACHEL ZUCKER

SHANE MCCRAE

Ana Patova Crosses a Bridge by RENEE GLADMAN
"What the End is For" *by* JORIE GRAHAM
"Braid" *by* LAUREN LEVIN
"Lakeview Cemetery" *by* CHERYL PAGEL
"Comings and Goings" *by* PIMONE TRIPLETT

MOLLY MCCULLY BROWN

"Pilgrimage" *by* NATASHA TRETHEWEY
"Landscape, Dense with Trees" *by* ELLEN BRYANT VOIGT
"No One Was Born Here" *by* REBECCA GAYLE HOWELL
"Oxyana, West Virginia" *by* WILLIAM BREWER
"Nashville" *by* TIANA CLARK

PHILIP METRES

"Diaspo/Renga" *by* MARILYN HACKER AND DEEMA K. SHEHABI
"The Bob Hope Poem" *by* CAMPBELL MCGRATH
"Jerusalem" *by* NAOMI SHIHAB NYE
"Mimesis" *by* FADY JOUDAH
"Animals" *by* HAYAN CHARARA

WAYNE MILLER

"Reading Plato" *by* RICK BAROT
"Tour Daufuskie" *by* TERRANCE HAYES
"National Anthem" *by* KEVIN PRUFER
"Panopticon" *by* BRENDA SHAUGHNESSY
"Tentacled Motherfucker" *by* MIKE WHITE

CRAIG SANTOS PEREZ

"Waiting for the Sunrise at Heleakala"
　　by BRANDY NĀLANI MCDOUGALL
"Light in the Crevice Never Seen" *by* HAUNANI-KAY TRASK
"The Pacific Ocean" *by* BRENDA HILLMAN
"Down the Sidewalk in Waikiki" *by* WAYNE KAUMUALII WESTLAKE
"State of the Planet" *by* ROBERT HASS

EMILIA PHILLIPS

"Your Wild Domesticated Inner Life" *by* ARI BANIAS
"Dart" *by* ALICE OSWALD
"The Sun Got All Over Everything" *by* GABRIELLE CALVOCORESSI
"38" *by* LAYLI LONG SOLDIER
"Say It, Say It Any Way You Can" *by* VIEVEE FRANCIS

PETER STRECKFUS

"An Adventure" *by* LOUISE GLÜCK
"Cornell West makes the point that hope..." from *Don't Let Me Be
　　Lonely* by CLAUDIA RANKINE
"Prairie Style" *by* C.S. GISCOMBE
"Poland" *by* SABRINA ORAH MARK
"Blackacre" *by* MONICA YOUN

EDITORS' RECOMMENDATIONS: CONTEMPORARY POEMS OF PLACE

EDITORS' RECOMMENDATIONS

"Dear Gaza" *by* HALA ALYAN

from *The Mountain* ("I couldn't see my feet") *by* ELIZABETH ARNOLD

"The Feeling" *by* ARI BANIAS

"Snow Over Shavers Fork" *by* BRIAN BARKER

"On Gardens" *by* RICK BAROT

"Poem: External Scene" *by* DAN BEACHY-QUICK

"There, There, Grieving" *by* ZEINA HASHEM BECK

"Yom Kippur, Taos, New Mexico" *by* ROBIN BECKER

"The Reservoir" *by* MEI-MEI BERSSENBRUGGE

"Traveling by Train" *by* MALACHI BLACK

"Looking for the Gulf Motel" *by* RICHARD BLANCO

"Everywhere I Went that Spring, I Was Alone" *by* PAULA BOHINCE

"Oxyana, West Virginia" *by* WILLIAM BREWER

"At the Adult Drive-In" *by* GABRIELLE CALVOCORESSI

"Why Dad Doesn't Pay Attention to Iraq Anymore"
    by LAUREN CAMP

"Ars Amartoria: So You Want to Marry a Foreign National"
    by KARA CANDITO

"Field Guide Ending in a Deportation"
    by MARCELO HERNANDEZ CASTILLO

"Freeway 280" *by* LORNA DEE CERVANTES

"How to Live in an American Town" *by* JENNIFER CHANG

"I Once Was a Child" *by* VICTORIA CHANG

"Storm" *by* LEILA CHATTI

"Dear America" *by* CATHY LINH CHE

"America, I Sing You Back" *by* ALLISON HEDGE COKE

"Neptune.4" *by* C.A. CONRAD

"Sex in the Rain" *by* JAMES CREWS

"Sparks, Nevada" *by* CYNTHIA CRUZ

"In Defense of Small Towns" *by* OLIVER DE LA PAZ

"On the Uncertainty of Our Judgement"
    by DANIELLE CADENA DEULEN

SOURCES

SOURCES

KAZIM ALI: "WHAT'S AMERICAN ABOUT AMERICAN POETRY?"

America by JEAN BAUDRILLARD
BRIAN BEARHEART from *American Ghost: Poets on Life
    After Industry*, ed. LILLIEN WALLER
Flood Song by SHERWIN BITSUI
The Collected Poems of Lucille Clifton 1965–2010
The Adam of Two Edens by MAHMOUD DARWISH
When My Brother Was an Aztec by NATALIE DIAZ
"Poetics of Generosity" *by* JUDITH E. JOHNSON
Corpse Whale by DG NANOUK OKPIK
Another Attempt at Rescue by M.L. SMOKER
WHEREAS by LAYLI LONG SOLDIER
LETTERRS by ORLANDO WHITE

NICKY BEER: "TAPPING THE GLASS: ON POEMS, AQUARIUMS, & FORM"

The Ocean at Home: An Illustrated History of the Aquarium
    by BERND BRUNNER, trans. ASHLEY MARC SLAPP
Aquarium by DIANNE COOKE & LEN JENSHEL
Atlantis by MARK DOTY
My Feelings by NICK FLYNN
The Life of Philip Henry Gosse, by his son, Edmund Gosse
The Aquarium: an unveiling of the wonders of the deep Sea
    by PHILIP HENRY GOSSE
*Zoo and Aquarium History: Ancient Animal Collections to
    Zoological Gardens* by VERNON N. KISLIN
Men, Women and Ghosts by AMY LOWELL
The Price of Light by PIMONE TRIPLETT

ELIZABETH BRADFIELD: "FLUID STATES: OCEAN AS PLACE & POETIC"

Flight: New and Selected Poems by LINDA BIERDS
The Complete Poems: 1927–1979 by ELIZABETH BISHOP
Flood Song by SHERWIN BITSUI
Atlantic Studies by HESTER BLUM
The Complete Poems of Emily Dickinson
Poems Seven: New and Complete Poetry by ALAN DUGAN
The Selected Poetry of Robinson Jeffers
The Collected Poems by STANLEY KUNITZ
Collected Poems by ROBERT HAYDEN
How to Be Drawn by TERRANCE HAYES
"Feeling into Words" *by* SEAMUS HEANEY
The Folding Cliffs by W.S. MERWIN
Sleeping with the Dictionary by HARRYETTE MULLEN
Headwaters by ELLEN BRYAN VOIGT
Omeros by DEREK WALCOTT
The Complete Poems by WALT WHITMAN

ABIGAIL CHABITNOY: "A PLACE FOR GHOSTS"

"In Communion with the Nonbreathing" *by* ABIGAIL CHABITNOY
The Aleutians. Alaska Geographic 7.3. Lael Morgan, ed. The
    Alaska Geographic Society, 1980.

HAYAN CHARARA: "THINKING DETROIT"

The Alchemist's Diary by HAYAN CHARARA
The Sadness of Others by HAYAN CHARARA
Something Sinister by HAYAN CHARARA
The Triggering Town by RICHARD HUGO
Proofs & Theories by LOUISE GLÜCK

KATY DIDDEN: "A POETICS OF TECTONIC SCALE: THE GREAT DISTANCE POEM"

John Keats: Selected Poetry
"Politics, Erasure, and A Sometime Genuine Music"
  by ANDREW DAVID KING
"Touching with Eye, Seeing with the Hand: Erasure as Reading
  Experience" *by* ANDREW DAVID KING
Complete Poems of Marianne Moore
The Panorama: History of a Mass Medium by STEPHAN OETTERMANN
Selected Poetry and Prose by PERCY BYSSHE SHELLEY
WHEREAS by LAYLI LONG SOLDIER
The Collected Poems of Wallace Stevens
The Creative Habit: Learn It and Use It for Life by TWYLA THARP
"The Ascension" *by* ARTHUR TULEE
The Prelude by WILLIAM WORDSWORTH

JEHANNE DUBROW: "IN THE COUNTRY OF WAR"

Stateside by JEHANNE DUBROW
Clamor by ELYSE FENTON
War Is a Force that Gives Us Meaning by CHRIS HEDGES
When the Men Go Off to War: Poems by VICTORIA KELLY
Letter Composed During a Lull in the Fighting by KEVIN C. POWERS

KEITH EKISS: "FROM HERRICK TO HARJO: LOOKING FOR FOOD IN THE NATURE POEM"

Leaving Tulsa by JENNIFER FOERSTER
The Woman Who Fell from the Sky by JOY HARJO
The Complete Poetry of Robert Herrick
The Selected Levis by LARRY LEVIS, ed. DAVID ST. JOHN
At the Desert's Green Edge: An Ethnobotany of the Gila River Pima
  by AMADEO REA
The Pima Indians by FRANK RUSSELL
The Collected Poems of Theodore Roethke

RIGOBERTO GONZÁLEZ: "UNPEOPLED EDENS"

Borderlands / La Frontera by GLORIA ANZALDÚA

JAMES ALLEN HALL: "LOCATING SILENCE"

The Complete Poems of Emily Dickinson
Rapture by SUSAN MITCHELL

AMAUD JAMAUL JOHNSNON: "BROAD DAYLIGHT"

"Black Art" *by* AMIRI BARAKA
Hardheaded Weather: New and Selected Poems by CORNELIUS EADY
Collected Poems by ROBERT HAYDEN
Red Summer by AMAUD JAMAUL JOHNSON
"L.A. Police Chief Daryl Gates Dead at 83"
    by AMAUD JAMAUL JOHNSON
"Tar Baby" *by* AMAUD JAMAUL JOHNSON
Cane by JEAN TOOMER

JANINE JOSEPH: "RECOVERY"

"Ghazal: To Be Teased into DisUnity" *by* AGHA SHAHID ALI
    from *An Exaltation of Forms: Contemporary Poets Celebrate the
    Diversity of Their Art*, ed. by ANNIE FINCH and KATHRINE VARNES
The Complete Poems: 1927-1979 by ELIZABETH BISHOP
What Doesn't Kill Us: The New Psychology of Posttraumatic Growth
    by STEPHEN JOSEPH
Life on Mars by TRACY K. SMITH
The Half-Finished Heaven: Selected Poems by TOMAS TRANSTRÖMER,
    trans. ROBERT BLY
The Complete Poems by WALT WHITMAN

CHRISTOPHER KEMPF: "THE CLOUD, THE DESKTOP, & THE POETICS OF NO-PLACE"

Legitimate Dangers eds. MICHAEL DUMANIS & CATE MARVIN,
  "Preface" by MARK DOTY
The Medium Is the Message by MARSHALL MCLUHAN
Paradise Lost by JOHN MILTON
The Available World by ANDER MONSON
Coeur de Lion by ARIANA REINES
Selected Poetry and Prose by PERCY BYSSHE SHELLEY
Selected Poems by WILLIAM WORDSWORTH

NICK LANTZ: "GHOST TOWNS"

The Collected Poems of Lucille Clifton 1965-2010
Breach by NICOLE COOLEY
Brutal Imagination by CORNELIUS EADY
The Narrow Road to the Interior by KIMIKO HAHN
Sightseer by CYNTHIA MARIE HOFFMAN
Dog Angel by JESSE LEE KERCHEVAL
Warhorses: Poems by YUSEF KOMUNYAKAA
Things Are Disappearing by KATE NORTHROP
Cornucopia: New & Selected Poems by MOLLY PEACOCK

SHARA LESSLEY: "ONE CLUSTER, BRIGHT, ASTRINGENT"

The Collected Poems: 1927-1979 by ELIZABETH BISHOP
The Collected Prose by ELIZABETH BISHOP
Edgar Allan Poe & the Juke-Box by ELIZABETH BISHOP,
  ed. ALICE QUINN

SANDRA LIM: "MAKING SPACE: A NOTEBOOK"

Praise by ROBERT HASS
Diaries by FRANZ KAFKA
Paradise Lost by JOHN MILTON
Lunch Poems by FRANK O'HARA
The Notebooks of Malte Laurids Brigge by RAINER MARIA RILKE
"Eternity" *by* ARTHUR RIMBAUD from *The Anchor Anthology of French Poetry*
The Glass Menagerie by TENNESSEE WILLIAMS

PHILIP METRES: "HOMING IN: THE PLACE OF POETRY IN THE GLOBAL DIGITAL AGE"

The Le-Roi Jones/Amiri Baraka Reader
The Essential Rumi ed. by COLEMAN BANKS
Selected Poems of William Blake
On the Outskirts of Form: Practicing Social Poetics
    by MICHAEL DAVIDSON
Antonoio Gramsci: Life of a Revolutionary by GIUSEPPE FIORI
Postmodernism: Or, the Cultural Logic of Late Capitalism
    by FREDERIC JAMESON
New Seeds of Contemplation by THOMAS MERTON
Sand Opera by PHILIP METRES
Imperial Eyes: Travel Writing and Transculturation
    by MARIE LOUISE PRATT
The Spiritual Exercises of St. Ignatius ed. by LOUIS J. PUHL, S.J.
Cooling Time: An American Vigil by C.D. WRIGHT

WAYNE MILLER: "LYRIC CITY"

The Darker Fall by RICK BAROT
The Well-Wrought Urn by CLEANTH BROOKS
A Rhetoric of Motives by KENNETH BURKE
Colosseum by KATIE FORD
Search Party: Collected Poems by WILLIAM MATTHEWS
Interior with Sudden Joy by BRENDA SHAUGHNESSY
The Complete Poems by WALT WHITMAN
Selected Poems by WILLIAM CARLOS WILLIAMS

EMILIA PHILLIPS: "BONE WILL ADAPT TO LOADS OF PRESSURE: THE BODY & POETIC SPACE"

The Baron in the Trees by ITALO CALVINO
Poems and Prose by GERARD MANLEY HOPKINS
Stiff: The Curious Lives of Human Cadavers by MARY ROACH

SPENCER REECE: "I HAD A PLACE"

The Complete Poems: 1927-1979 by ELIZABETH BISHOP
Richard II by WILLIAM SHAKESPEARE

BRUCE SNIDER: "TROUBLE & CONSOLATION: WRITING THE GAY RURAL"

"The Woman, The Place, The Poet" by EAVAN BOLAND
Powerless: Selected Poems by TIM DLUGOS
Fire to Fire: New and Selected Poems by MARK DOTY
"The Gay Sublime" by LINDA GREGERSON
Spoon River Anthology by EDGAR LEE MASTERS
The Collected Poems of Frank O'Hara
Late Harvest: Rural American Writing by DAVID R. PICHASKE

A Wild Patience Has Taken Me This Far: Poems 1978-1981
    by ADRIENNE RICH
"Late Victorians" by RICHARD RODRIGUEZ
Imaginary Homelands by SALMAN RUSHDIE
Collected Poems by JAMES SCHUYLER
The Dirt Riddles by MICHAEL WALSH
The Salt Ecstasies: Poems by JAMES L. WHITE
The Complete Poems by WALT WHITMAN
Collected Poems by JAMES WRIGHT
The Anchorage by MARK WUNDERLICH

PETER STRECKFUS: "PLACE IN MIND"

"A Poem is a Horizon: Notes Toward an Ecopoetics"
    by MATTHEW COOPERMAN
If I Were Another: Poems by MAHMOUD DARWISH, trans. FADY JOUDAH
Faithful and Virtuous Night by LOUISE GLÜCK
Citizen: An American Lyric by CLAUDIA RANKINE
The Collected Poems of William Carlos Williams, Vol. 2: 1939-1962
    by WILLIAM CARLOS WILLIAMS

MARK WUNDERLICH: "FAMOUS MUSHROOM"

Collected Poems by ROBERT LOWELL

MONICA YOUN: "ON BLACKACRE"

The Complete Poems by JOHN MILTON

FOREWORD

EAVAN BOLAND is the author of more than a dozen volumes of poetry and nonfiction. A Professor and the Director of the Creative Writing Program at Stanford University, she is the winner of a Lannan Foundation Award. She lives in Stanford, California, and Dublin, Ireland.

THE EDITORS

SHARA LESSLEY is the author of *Two-Headed Nightingale* and *The Explosive Expert's Wife*. Her poems and essays have been recognized with numerous fellowships and awards. She lives in Oxford, England.

BRUCE SNIDER is the author of *The Year We Studied Women* and *Paradise, Indiana*, winners of the Felix Pollak and Lena-Miles Wever Todd prizes in poetry. He teaches at the University of San Francisco.

THE CONTRIBUTORS

KAZIM ALI's most recent books are a collection of poems, *Inquisition*, and *Silver Road: Essays, Maps, and Calligraphies*.

NICKY BEER is the author of *The Octopus Game* and *The Diminishing House*, both winners of the Colorado Book Award for Poetry. She is an Associate Professor at the University of Colorado—Denver, and a Poetry Editor for the journal *Copper Nickel*.

ELIZABETH BRADFIELD is the author of *Once Removed*, *Approaching Ice*, and *Interpretive Work*. She lives on Cape Cod, works as a naturalist locally as well as on expedition ships on high latitudes, is Editor-in-Chief of Broadsided Press, and co-directs the Creative Writing Program at Brandeis University.

ABIGAIL CHABITNOY earned her MFA in poetry at Colorado State University and was a Peripheral Poets Fellow. She is a Koniag descendent and member of the Tangirnaq Native Village in Kodiak, Alaska. Her poems have appeared in *Gulf Coast*, *Tin House*, *Red Ink*, *Nat Brut*, and *Pleiades*, among others.

HAYAN CHARARA is the author of three poetry books, *The Alchemist's Diary*, *The Sadness of Others*, and *Something Sinister*, and a children's book, *The Three Lucys*. He edited *Inclined to Speak*, an anthology of contemporary Arab American poetry, and with Fady Joudah he edits the Etel Adnan Poetry Prize.

KATY DIDDEN is the author of *The Glacier's Wake*. She holds a PhD from the University of Missouri, and her work has appeared in journals such as *The Kenyon Review*, *Ecotone*, *32 Poems*, and *Poetry*. She is an Assistant Professor at Ball State University.

JEHANNE DUBROW is the author of six poetry collections, including most recently *Dots & Dashes*, winner of the Crab Orchard Series in Poetry Open Competition Award. Her work has appeared in *Virginia Quarterly Review*, *Pleiades*, and *Southwest Review*. She is an Associate Professor at the University of North Texas.

KEITH EKISS is a Jones Lecturer in Creative Writing at Stanford University and a former Wallace Stegner Fellow in Poetry. He is the author of *Pima Road Notebook* and translator of Eunice Odio's *The Fire's Journey* and *Territory of Dawn: The Selected Poems of Eunice Odio*.

RIGOBERTO GONZÁLEZ is the author of eighteen books of poetry and prose. His awards include a Guggenheim, an NEA grant, the USA Rolón fellowship, the Lenore Marshall Prize, a Lambda Literary Prize, and the American Book Award. He is currently Professor of English at Rutgers-Newark.

JAMES ALLEN HALL is the author of two books: *I Liked You Before I Knew You So Well* (essays) and *Now You're the Enemy* (poems), which won awards from the Lambda Literary Foundation, the Texas Institute of Letters, and the Fellowship of Southern Writers. He teaches at Washington College.

AMAUD JAMAUL JOHNSON is the author of *Darktown Follies* and *Red Summer*. A former Stegner Fellow in Poetry at Stanford, Robert Frost Fellow at the Bread Loaf Writers' Conference, and Cave Canem Fellow, his honors include a Pushcart Prize, the Hurston/Wright Legacy Award, the Edna Mcudt Book Award, and the Dorset Prize. He teaches at the University of Wisconsin—Madison.

JANINE JOSEPH was born and raised in the Philippines and Southern California. She is the author of *Driving Without a License*, winner of the Kundiman Poetry Prize. She is an Assistant Professor of Creative Writing at Oklahoma State University. Learn more at www.janinejoseph.com.

JOAN NAVIYUK KANE has authored several books, most recently *Milk Black Carbon*. She has received a Whiting Award, the Donald Hall Prize, and the American Book Award. She raises her sons in Alaska and teaches in the low-residency program at the Institute of American Indian Arts.

CHRISTOPHER KEMPF is the author of *Late in the Empire of Men*, winner of the Levis Prize in Poetry from Four Way Books. Recipient of an NEA, as well as a Wallace Stegner Fellowship in Poetry from Stanford University, he is currently a PhD candidate in English Literature at the University of Chicago.

NICK LANTZ is the author of four poetry collections, most recently *You, Beast*. He teaches in the MFA program at Sam Houston State University, where he is also the Editor of *Texas Review*.

SANDRA LIM is the author of *Loveliest Grotesque* and *The Wilderness*, selected by Louise Glück for the Barnard Women Poets Prize. A recipient of fellowships from the MacDowell Colony, the Vermont Studio Center, and the Getty Research Institute, she is an Associate Professor of English at the University of Massachusetts—Lowell.

SABRINA ORAH MARK is the author of the *The Babies* and *Tsim Tsum*. Mark's awards include a National Endowment for the Arts Fellowship, a fellowship from the Fine Arts Work Center in Provincetown, and a Sustainable Arts Foundation Award. Her website is www.sabrinaorahmark.com.

SHANE MCCRAE teaches at Columbia University and Spalding University's low-residency MFA in Writing Program. His most recent books are *In the Language of My Captor* and *The Animal Too Big to Kill*. He has received a Whiting Award, a fellowship from the NEA, and a Pushcart Prize.

MOLLY MCCULLY BROWN is the author of *The Virginia State Colony for Epileptics and Feebleminded* which won the 2016 Lexi Rudnitsky First Book Prize. She is the 2017-2018 Jeff Baskin Writers Fellow at *The Oxford American*, and is at work on a collection of essays.

PHILIP METRES is the author of *Pictures at an Exhibition*, *Sand Opera*, *A Concordance of Leaves*, and *To See the Earth*. A recipient of the Lannan, two NEAs and two Arab American Book Awards, he is Professor of English at John Carroll University.

WAYNE MILLER is the author of *Post-*, *The City, Our City*, *The Book of Props*, and *Only the Senses Sleep*. The recipient of the UNT Rilke Prize, George Bogin Award, Lucille Medwick Award, Ruth Lilly Fellowship, Bess Hokin Prize, and a Fulbright, Miller teaches at the University of Colorado—Denver.

CRAIG SANTOS PEREZ is a native Chamorro from the Pacific Island of Guam. He is the author of three collections of poetry, most recently *from unincorporated territory [guma']*, which received the American Book Award in 2015.

EMILIA PHILLIPS is the author of three collections from the University of Akron Press, most recently *Empty Clip*. She is an Assistant Professor of Creative Writing at the University of North Carolina—Greensboro.

SPENCER REECE is the author of *The Clerk's Tale* and *The Road to Emmaus*, and the Editor of *Counting Time Like People Count Stars: Poems by the Girls of Our Little Roses, San Pedro Sula, Honduras*. He is the national secretary for the Spanish Episcopal Church, Iglesia Española Reformada Episcopal, and lives in Madrid, Spain.

PETER STRECKFUS is the author of *Errings*, winner of Fordham University Press' POL Editor's Prize, and *The Cuckoo*, which won the Yale Series of Younger Poets competition. He lives in the Washington D.C. area with his wife, poet and translator Heather Green, and is on the faculty of the Creative Writing Program at George Mason University.

MARK WUNDERLICH is the author of *The Earth Avails*, *Voluntary Servitude*, and *The Anchorage*. Director of the Bennington Writing Seminars, his poems, interviews, reviews, and translations have appeared in journals such as *Slate*, *The Paris Review*, *Tin House*, *Poetry*, and in more than thirty anthologies.

MONICA YOUN is the author of *Blackacre*, *Barter*, and *Ignatz*. Her poems have appeared in the *New Yorker*, *Paris Review*, and the *New York Times Magazine*, and she has been awarded fellowships from the Library of Congress and Stanford University, among other awards. A former attorney, she teaches poetry at Princeton University.